NEVADA'S GREAT RECESSION

NEVADA'S GREAT RECESSION

Looking Back, Moving Forward

Elliott Parker, with Kate Marshall

Foreword by Senator Harry Reid

UNIVERSITY OF NEVADA PRESS *Reno & Las Vegas*

University of Nevada Press | Reno, Nevada 89557 USA
www.unpress.nevada.edu
Copyright © 2017 by University of Nevada Press
Cover photograph © Arthur Eugene Preston / shutterstock.com

LIBRARY OF CONGRESS CATALOGING-IN-PUBLICATION DATA
Names: Parker, Elliott, 1960- author.
Title: Nevada's great recession : looking back, moving forward / Elliott Parker ;
    contributions by Katherine Marshall.
Description: Reno & Las Vegas : University of Nevada Press, 2017. | Includes
    index.
Identifiers: LCCN 2017005435 (print) | LCCN 2017025446 (e-book) |
    ISBN 978-1-943859-41-2 (paperback) | ISBN 978-0-87417-597-4 (e-book)
Subjects: LCSH: Recessions—Nevada. | Financial crises—Nevada. | Nevada—
    Economic conditions—21st century. | BISAC: BUSINESS & ECONOMICS /
    Economic History. | HISTORY / United States / State & Local / West (AK,
    CA, CO, HI, ID, MT, NV, UT, WY). | POLITICAL SCIENCE / Public Policy /
    Economic Policy.
Classification: LCC HB3753.N3 (e-book) | LCC HB3753.N3 P37 2017 (print) |
    DDC 330.9793/034—dc23
LC record available at https://lccn.loc.gov/2017005435

The paper used in this book meets the requirements of American National
Standard for Information Sciences—Permanence of Paper for Printed Library
Materials, ANSI/NISO z39.48-1992 (R2002).

FIRST PRINTING

Manufactured in the United States of America

Contents

Illustrations

Figures

Tables

Foreword

by Senator Harry Reid

The Great Recession ravaged Nevada families. We were, without question, the hardest-hit state in the nation. Thousands upon thousands across Nevada were forced to surrender to financial ruin and watch as the American Dream slipped through their fingers.

To fully appreciate the enormity of the Great Recession and the accompanying housing collapse, we must do more than acknowledge the statistics—we must also recognize the underlying causes of the financial crisis. Only then will we comprehend the brutal toll it exacted on the people of Nevada.

That is precisely what Elliott Parker, PhD, and Kate Marshall have achieved with their in-depth analysis, *Nevada's Great Recession: Looking Back, Moving Forward.* Parker and Marshall account for a wide range of factors: from Nevada budget shortfalls and failed state economic development plans, to repeal of the Glass-Steagall Banking Act of 1933 and the collapse of mortgage-backed securities.

A professor of economics at the University of Nevada, Reno (UNR), and later chair of that department, Elliott Parker analyzed the recession and its fallout in Nevada. *Nevada's Great Recession* benefits from Parker's expertise and his many decades studying economic trends in Nevada. Of particular benefit to the reader is Parker's ability to condense intricate concepts into digestible ideas. He makes the economic lessons in the book accessible to the reader.

I have known Elliott Parker's wife and coauthor, Kate Marshall, for many years. As Nevada state treasurer for two terms, from January 2007 to January 2015, Kate Marshall was on the front lines of the crash. She was responsible for the state's investment portfolio at a time when world markets were plunging. She also issued and managed the debt approved by the state legislature during a time of massive budget shortfalls—an unenviable job, but she did it well.

I witnessed Kate's resolve firsthand as we partnered on different undertakings to help Nevada homeowners and businesses. Kate worked with my senate office in offering free foreclosure workshops to Nevadans who were underwater on their mortgages. Had Kate Marshall not been at the helm of the State Treasury, Nevada might not have rebounded from the recession as soon as it did.

In *Nevada's Great Recession*, Kate shares insights born of her experience. The vignettes she offers are sometimes funny, sometimes stunning, but always astute and penetrating. Because of her brief anecdotes, the reader is able to gain a situational awareness of the economic crisis.

The Great Recession left our state and nation with many lessons to be learned. Now, it is incumbent on us to face the reality of what caused the greatest financial collapse in nearly a century. We must resolve to address the broken system that wreaked havoc on millions of people. But we cannot fix what we fail to acknowledge. That is why *Nevada's Great Recession: Looking Back, Moving Forward* is a must-read.

Acknowledgments

Kate and I try to go through our day being grateful. We are grateful we have found each other, and we are grateful for our families, our friends, and our supporters. We are grateful for the chance to contribute, however meagerly, to our community. We are grateful to live in a place we love.

I acknowledge the chance given to me by Tom Gorman and Mike Campbell of the *Las Vegas Sun,* as well as by Adam Trumble, Matt Hufman, and Dennis Noone of the *Nevada Appeal,* to allow me to write a regular column for them. Kate and I are deeply appreciative of Justin Race of the University of Nevada Press for his enthusiasm for this book, as well as to two reviewers who made very helpful suggestions for improvement.

Kate and I both thank Frankie Sue for originally bringing Kate to Nevada and encouraging her to run, and we thank the voters of Nevada for giving Kate the chance to serve them. I am indebted to the faculty and administration of the University of Nevada, Reno, for the trust they have given me, and for the freedom to write about issues important to me. Finally, we both thank "The Senator," Harry Reid of Nevada, for writing a foreword to this book and for all he did for us and for the state.

NEVADA'S GREAT RECESSION

CHAPTER 1

Introduction to Nevada's Great Recession

The only way in which a human being can make some approach to knowing the whole of a subject, is by hearing what can be said about it by persons of every variety of opinion, and studying all modes in which it can be looked at by every character of mind. No wise man ever acquired his wisdom in any mode but this; nor is it in the nature of human intellect to become wise in any other manner.

— JOHN STUART MILL[1]

Introduction

Of all economic recessions experienced by the United States in the postwar period, the Great Recession that began in 2008 was the deepest, longest, and most destructive. Of all states in the union, Nevada was the hardest hit. Nevada has long had a history of being low on the lists you want to be high on and high on the lists you want to be low on, but it became a state of superlatives: it had the highest unemployment rate, the largest fall in average income, the greatest share of population entering poverty, the biggest drop in housing prices, the highest foreclosure rate, and the greatest percentage of mortgages underwater.[2] It also experienced a severe government fiscal crisis that lacked superlatives only because it had one of the smallest state governments in the country.

The two of us were well placed to watch this train wreck as it occurred. Kate Marshall served two terms as Nevada's elected state treasurer, from 2007 to 2014, and it was her job to manage the state's investments and make sure that the state had the cash flow to pay the bills the state legislature had budgeted for. This became extremely challenging as the recession developed into a depression. As for me, Elliott Parker, I was (and remain) professor of economics at the University of Nevada, Reno (UNR).[3] Elected to serve as chair of the university's faculty senate, I was near the center of the university's efforts to cope with the crisis. Immediately afterward, I became chair of the Department of Economics, where I tried to encourage my colleagues to do a better job bringing their expertise to the people of Nevada.

I had come to my interest in Nevada's economy by a circuitous route. My doctorate, my teaching experience, and my published research were all focused on comparative international economics, and I dreamed of making my university a center of international studies. I had grown to love Nevada, but when Professor Bill Eadington, my late colleague, asked me to apply my economic studies to Nevada's economy, I did not take him very seriously. Even my own mother told me I should pay more attention to understanding those economies closer to home.

For more than a decade, however, I had been doing research on the effects of financial crises in East Asia, and this had led me to try to better understand how some recessions were distinctly different from others. Price deflation could deepen a recession and even become a self-fulfilling prophecy. In the wrong circumstances, financial crises could cause deep and long depressions. And then, in 2008, everything I had learned about other countries suddenly came home, and Nevada was at the epicenter. I knew that we were in the middle of something distinctly different, and that our normal ways of coping would not be enough.

Like most of my colleagues, I had preferred to keep my head down and focus on my students and my research, though in 2006 I had been lucky enough to be invited by Senator Harry Reid of Nevada to visit the U.S. Capitol building and present a short paper to the Senate Democratic leadership. A couple of years later, when Regent Bill Cobb visited the faculty senate to encourage faculty to get more involved in the greater community, I decided I needed to speak out to try to provide balance in light of the nonsense that some politicians were saying about the recession. Perhaps because I was recently divorced and hated coming home to an empty house, I made myself busy. I began to give talks and submit columns to newspapers across the state, to help other Nevadans better understand our situation.

In the middle of the crisis Kate and I would meet occasionally for coffee. Kate wanted my advice, as she looked for advice from many others, because she wanted to make the best possible decisions about the state's finances. I wanted to help, of course, but I also wanted reassurance that at least some people in state government knew what they were doing, and understood how bad the crisis could become.

Kate would later run for Congress, in a district that has never been won by a Democrat. After her almost-inevitable loss, our professional relationship turned romantic. The two of us began dating in the fall of 2011, and we were married in the spring of 2014, each bringing two teenage children from a previous marriage.

This book contains new material, particularly Kate's vignettes, plus a lot of material that was previously published as op-ed columns in newspapers such as the *Las Vegas Sun,* the *Nevada Appeal,* and the *Reno Gazette Journal.* These columns relied on the most current data available at the time. Because these data are often updated or revised, the numbers cited are not always precisely consistent from column to column, but the story that the data tell is always consistent.

In this first section, I provide an introduction to Nevada's great crisis. I review Nevada's peculiar history, and trace out themes such as education and fiscal policy that permeate the entire book. I then give a broader economic context for the problems Nevada faced, since these are problems shared with many small states during big crises.

Chapter 2 focuses on Nevada's fiscal issues, and contains seven columns published between 2009 and 2011. Chapter 3 includes seven more columns published from 2008 to 2011, and discusses the proposals by Governor Jim Gibbons (2007–11) and Governor Brian Sandoval (2011 to present) to cope with collapsing revenues by shrinking the state's government. Chapter 4 contains eight more columns on budget cuts particular to higher education, specifically my own UNR.

The next two chapters look to the national context for Nevada's crisis. Chapter 5 includes eight columns written about the U.S. economy between 2011 and 2014, and starts with observations written a decade after the terrorist attacks of September 11, 2001. In Chapter 6, we include seven columns on taxes, the federal budget deficit, and the so-called fiscal cliff crisis of 2012.

Chapter 7 comes back to Nevada with five columns written from 2013 to 2015 on Nevada's slow recovery. Chapter 8 then adds nine columns we coauthored in 2015 that reflect on some of the problems that economic recovery has left exposed. These are issues that need to be faced as the state tries to create itself anew. We end with a short conclusion in chapter 9 to wrap up some of the lessons learned.

1. Causes of the Crash

The crash of 2008 was more than a decade in building. The Roman historian Tacitus once wrote that success has many parents, while failure is an orphan.[4] But the economic failure of the Great Recession had many causes.

In the first place, crashes are initiated by booms, and the 1990s were a good decade for the U.S. economy. Growth rates were relatively high, price inflation was low, poverty was declining, the federal government budget was on its way from deficit to surplus, and interest rates were low. Table 1.1 shows the average annual growth rates for the United States after 1952, by presidential administration. Both gross domestic product (GDP) and after-tax disposable personal income are adjusted for both inflation and population growth. Two measures of inflation are shown, the official GDP deflator and the consumer price index (CPI). It is clear from this table that the Clinton years were topped only by the economic boom of the Kennedy and Johnson administrations. This was especially true for the stock market; adjusting for inflation, the Dow-Jones index grew by an average rate of 9.7 percent per year, and the Standard & Poor (S&P) 500 grew by 8.6 percent, a record that only the Obama administration came close to matching.

Rising incomes in the 1990s led more people to purchase homes. Between 1994 and 2004 the United States had 15 million new owner-occupied homes, 6 million more than can be explained by population growth alone. Both California and Nevada, states that had relatively more renters than the rest of the nation, began to catch up.

Second, changes in the regulatory environment made it easier for many people to get mortgages. The Gramm-Leach-Bliley Act of

TABLE 1.1. Postwar U.S. Growth Rates (Annualized), by Administration

	REAL GDP	POP.	REAL GDP PER CAPITA	REAL DPI PER CAPITA	GDP DEFLATOR	CPI
Eisenhower: 1953–60	2.5	1.8	0.7	1.4	1.9	1.4
Kennedy/Johnson: 1961–68	5.2	1.3	3.9	3.7	2.3	2.2
Nixon/Ford: 1969–76	2.7	1.0	1.7	2.4	6.1	6.4
Carter: 1977–80	3.2	1.1	2.1	1.7	8.0	10.3
Reagan: 1981–88	3.6	0.9	2.6	2.6	4.0	4.3
G. Bush: 1989–92	2.2	1.2	1.0	1.1	3.2	4.2
Clinton: 1993–2000	3.8	1.2	2.6	2.4	1.9	2.6
G. W. Bush: 2001–8	1.8	0.9	0.8	1.5	2.4	2.4
Obama: 2009–16	1.7	0.8	0.9	1.1	1.5	1.7
Average: 1953–2016	3.0	1.1	1.8	2.1	3.2	3.5
Republican Administrations	2.6	1.2	1.4	1.9	2.6	3.7
Democratic Administrations	3.8	1.2	2.6	2.4	2.7	3.3

Source: http://www.bea.gov, author's calculations.

1999, passed by a Republican Congress and signed by President Clinton, removed many restrictions on how banks did business. Most famously, it repealed the Glass-Steagall Banking Act of 1933 that kept commercial banks out of more-risky securities markets, but it also removed regulatory oversight of investment bank holding companies, and retroactively legalized a wave of mergers and financial consolidation.

One of the effects of this deregulation was a rapid expansion in the derivatives market. A derivative is a financial asset derived from other assets, like a stock option or a future price guarantee. When these markets work well, they allow investors to purchase a financial insurance policy, to hedge against the unexpected, in the same way that a homeowner might buy insurance against the chance of flood or fire. But normal insurance markets are regulated. Among other things, homeowners cannot buy insurance on somebody else's home, insurers must maintain adequate capital reserves to make sure they can pay off when disaster strikes, and both the buyer and the seller understand the risks and payouts. Derivatives markets became much more complex, however, and lacked the clarity of normal insurance markets. New types of assets, like credit default swaps and collateralized debt obligations, brought risks that neither buyer nor seller really understood.

A third factor was human nature, especially since it was about money. Yogi Berra is supposed to have said that it is tough to make predictions, especially about the future.[5] Financial markets are inherently risky because they involve forecasting the unknowable. Investors often look to price behavior for signs of what other people think; this herding behavior can lead to what economists sometimes call the Biggest Fool Theory. That is, an investor who buys an asset based on its recent price behavior is a fool, but if he is a lucky fool he can find a bigger fool to sell it to. Eventually, however, the biggest fool enters the market, buyers evaporate, and the speculative bubble bursts.

In the late 1990s the United States saw a bubble in technology stocks, a bubble exacerbated by the so-called Y2K problem. Due to memory limitations, most computer programs written before the 1990s used only two-digit fields for dates; the danger that the year 2000 posed for a computer network collapse led to high spending on new software, new equipment, and programmers to fix existing software. Once the emergency passed, spending slowed. The NASDAQ, the second-largest stock market in the United States, had quickly tripled and then just as rapidly returned to earth. The result was an economic slowdown that turned into a recession after the events of September 11, 2001. The Federal Reserve Bank took monetary action that dropped interest rates, and the federal government implemented a ten-year tax cut that turned federal budget surpluses back into deficits.

As the economy began to recover from the 2001 recession, investors began looking for the next big thing, and a worldwide glut of savings began finding its way into the U.S. market. These foreign savings inflows not only led to rising trade deficits, since every dollar a foreigner spends buying U.S. assets is a dollar not spent on U.S. exports, they also helped to finance growing federal budget deficits and left financial markets awash with cash looking for a higher rate of return.

For five years, the result was a financial free-for-all. Housing prices began to rise at unprecedented rates, especially on the coasts. With low interest rates and the assumption that housing was a safe bet, Americans began borrowing more to buy bigger houses, and using their home equity to finance not only home remodeling but also college costs, vacations, and even gambling in Las Vegas. People with limited means bought several houses at a time, intending to flip them for a quick profit. A colleague of mine once said there is no pain so great as watching your neighbor get rich from doing dumb things.

Subprime markets with higher default rates grew to almost 10 percent of the mortgage market. Mortgage brokers could earn their commissions without taking responsibility for the credit-worthiness of their customers, and so-called liar loans made it possible for people to take on mortgages they could not afford. Ratings agencies earned higher commissions for better ratings on securitized mortgage assets, and even the government-sponsored enterprises Fannie Mae (Federal National Mortgage Association) and Freddie Mac (Federal Home Loan Mortgage Corporation) began to reduce the quality of the loans they resold as investment-grade securities in order to protect their market share from the growing competition from investment banks.

Many Nevadans saw the housing boom as the next great bonanza. The state had the nation's fastest-growing population for decades, but now the state began building homes at a run. Californians moved to Nevada looking for more-affordable homes, as well as lower taxes, and other people came to Nevada to build those homes. Nevada soon was building homes for construction workers who were moving to Nevada to build homes for other construction workers. In fact, Nevada had twice the proportion of construction workers in the workforce as the rest of the nation, and the highest rate of any state. Nevada also had the highest proportion of new homes, along with the highest proportion of new mortgages.

Housing prices finally peaked in 2006, and soon sellers could not find buyers. Once home prices began to decline, housing starts plummeted, and contractors began to lay off their construction workers. By the end of 2007 it was clear that the economy was entering a recession. The Bush administration, which had used tax cuts in 2001–2 to stimulate spending, once again proposed tax cuts to address the economic slowdown. The Economic Stimulus

Act of February 2008 included a recovery rebate of up to $300 per taxpayer plus tax incentives for business investment, but the increase in consumption spending was almost precisely offset by increased imports. As one wag put it, we borrowed from China to pay for tax cuts that were spent on goods from China, and were puzzled why it didn't seem to help our economy.

As home prices continued to fall, defaults began to increase and many assets once considered safe now looked increasingly precarious. Losses rose, and big investment banks began to sell off their holdings before the bottom dropped out. In March 2008 the investment firm of Bear Stearns failed and was bought up by JPMorgan Chase at 7 percent of its previous value. In September 2008 Lehman Brothers closed; its bankruptcy filing was the largest in U.S. history. The resulting panic led the Bush administration to propose an unprecedented bailout of the financial sector through the Emergency Economic Stabilization Act of October 2008, which provided $700 billion to purchase troubled assets and keep financial markets from collapsing.

In the last quarter of 2008 and the first quarter of 2009, almost 4.3 million jobs were lost. By the end of 2009 the U.S. economy employed 8.6 million fewer people than it had two years before. The American Recovery and Reinvestment Act, which passed within a month of President Obama taking office, reduced the depth of the recession, but the damage was done and a full recovery would take many years.

>> Treasurer's Vignette: Money Is Boring

The day Lehman Brothers went bankrupt I was scheduled to be interviewed by Melissa Block of NPR, who had come out to Nevada to do a story on the bellwether county in the swing state of Nevada and how Sarah Palin was shaking things up. No amount of pleading or excuses could get me out of the interview, and I was instructed by the Obama campaign to talk about how unfit Sarah Palin was to be a "heartbeat away from the presidency."

"Five minutes," they told me. "It'll take five minutes. Ten minutes, tops."

But I was preoccupied and Ms. Block, as superb as she was, could not find a message in my inartful answers, and so, coming up on an hour, there we still sat, both eager to finish the interview.

"Do you think Sarah Palin talks to Democratic women?" she asks.

"No, she can't handle the budget."

"Well, how do you think Democratic women respond to her?"

"She has no experience with the kind of financial issues she would face. That's why she can't be elected."

My chief investment officer had called me early that morning to give me the news that Lehman Brothers had gone bankrupt and $50 million in the form of two senior notes was now worth pennies. She then promptly offered her resignation, to which I responded, "No way. We're in this together to the bitter end."

Ms. Block was patient, but all I could think of in answer to any question was, "Palin doesn't know finances," and I was getting frustrated.

"Well, how are you getting Hillary supporters excited about Obama?"

"I used to do that," I interrupted. "I don't have to do that anymore: Sarah Palin does it for me."

And that was it. Ms. Block stood up. The camera people started to fold up their gear. I wasn't sure if I had blown the interview, and could only sit there trying to think through the ramifications on everyone of the financial tsunami that I believed Lehman's bankruptcy had created.

"We're done," Ms. Block said.

I stood up. "You have no idea. The whole world has changed."

"Oh, really? How so?" Ms. Block asked.

"Just check the markets," I said. "Just check the markets."

2. Nevada's Economy after the Crash (2011)[6]

Nevada is in the midst of what is, essentially, an existential crisis. Creating a viable economy in a state with few resources has always been a challenge. It will be difficult to recover from the crash of the gaming/construction model. A key issue for Nevada's decision-makers to grapple with is the role of the state's government itself, because many Nevadans misunderstand the role government has played, and must play, in the state's economic development.

But this is not the first time the state is being forced to re-create itself. A brief review of Nevada's economic history shows that more than a century ago Nevada saw the effects of its major industry on the wane, in a state with few other productive resources. At that time, Nevada struggled for decades until it found a viable model in gaming. Now that gaming is in decline, time will tell whether Nevada is able to create a new productive resource, or if it will once again enter a time of decline.

The Rise and Fall, and Rise and Fall, of Nevada's Economy

Nevada was created, both politically and economically, in the backflow from the rush to California. With the discovery of the Comstock silver lode in the late 1850s, its bank-financed expansion in the 1860s, and its connection to the rest of the country with the Central Pacific, Nevada entered its first big boom, and Virginia City came to think of itself as one of the richest cities in the world, at least in per capita terms.

The boom was relatively short-lived. By the late 1870s silver had been effectively demonetized by the Fourth Coinage Act of 1873, though the negative impact on silver prices was softened somewhat with the short-lived production of silver dollars by the Carson City mint. Soon after the completion of the Sutro Tunnel, the silver mines were exhausted. Though the search for minerals continued elsewhere in the state, Nevada entered a period of long-term decline. By the turn of the century, the state would lose half of its population as miners left for Bodie, Tombstone, and other boomtowns. Thereafter, population in Nevada fluctuated for a couple of decades, with only a few new mineral finds in Goldfield, Tonopah, and elsewhere.[7]

The effort to create a viable economy in Nevada did not end with mining.[8] The railroad town of Reno became the center of a divorce-driven tourist industry as Nevada tried to take advantage of the fact that, until 1969, other states required lengthy residency periods and were stringent about the grounds for divorce. Ranching and farming provided some economic stability as a few small communities became dependent on the federally funded diversion of water once flowing to Pyramid and Walker Lakes. Federal construction of the Hawthorne Naval Ammunition Depot in the 1920s helped the state economy, and the small town of Las Vegas

became host to the Depression-era federal workforce constructing Hoover Dam.

But the legalization of gambling in 1931 provided a means
to help fend off the worst effects of the Great Depression, and
Nevada also promoted its lack of taxes to encourage millionaires
to relocate.[9] Nevada's effective monopoly over gaming was the primary cause of its postwar growth, though it attracted more than
its fair share of unsavory characters. The proximity of Las Vegas to
Southern California, which grew rapidly due in part to the effects
of a great influx of federal defense spending, started the economic
shift from north to south. Federally funded interstate highways
brought trucking, warehousing, and tourists to both northern and
southern Nevada. After the mid-1980s, once the reputation of
Nevada's gambling industry was cleaned up, Nevada became the
fastest-growing economy in the country, with the fastest-growing
population and a mean per capita income significantly above the
national average.

But Nevada's success sowed the seeds of its own downfall.
Other states and countries learned from it, legislating their own
casinos as new sources of tax revenue. In California, new casinos
on small Indian reservations intercepted the flow of gaming
tourists headed over the mountains, eventually cutting gaming
revenues in Reno and Tahoe by two thirds. Las Vegas was able
to keep the tourists coming, at least for a while, by continuously
upping the ante, creating new and bigger properties as they de-
stroyed the old ones. Even so, gaming declined from 17 percent of
gross state product (GSP) in the 1980s to 10 percent in 2007, and
then to 8 percent by 2009, during the Great Recession. This created serious revenue problems in a state that depended significantly on gaming and tourism to finance its government.

As gaming slowed, construction, instead of a more general
economic diversification, took up much of the slack. Once again
the backflow from California brought a boom to Nevada. The construction of new casinos was augmented by the construction of
new homes for the casino and construction workers moving here;
when another housing bubble began in California, Nevada's construction sector became the largest in the nation as a share of the
economy, and twice as big as the national average.

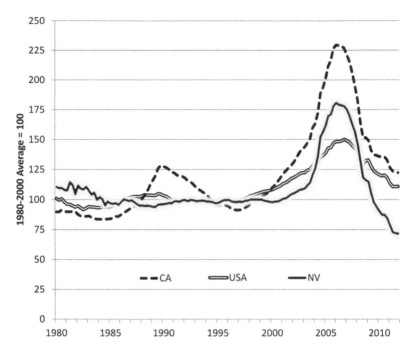

FIGURE 1.1. Housing Prices Adjusted for Inflation. *Source:* Author's calculations from the Federal Housing Finance Agency; and Bureau of Labor Statistics, U.S. Department of Labor.

Housing prices in Nevada roughly kept pace with inflation until 2000, several years after prices in California started rising rapidly (see figure 1.1). Many in California were able to sell their homes and relocate to Nevada, especially once they retired and lower taxes and home prices mattered more than their jobs.

When the bubble finally burst, Nevada went from the fastest-growing state in the nation to the fastest-declining state. GDP per capita in Nevada fell substantially relative to the nation as a whole, and the postrecession recovery was flat (see figure 1.2). Real per capita personal income declined by 11.9 percent in Nevada, compared to a 4.2 percent average decline for the nation as a whole. Homeowners lost half the market value of their homes, and inflation-adjusted housing prices fell to their lowest levels in several decades. Two thirds of mortgages in Nevada exceeded the home's value, and Nevada had five times the national foreclosure

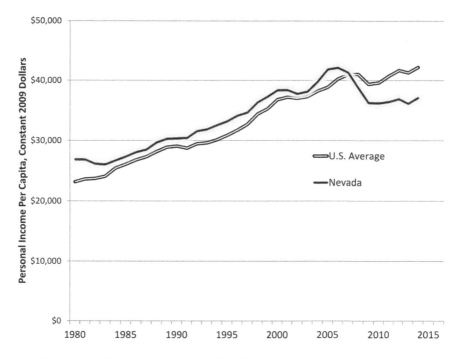

FIGURE 1.2. Personal Income per Capita. *Source:* Courtesy of the U.S. Bureau of Economic Analysis.

rate. The loss of casino and construction jobs increased Nevada's unemployment rate to the highest in the country. By 2010, the rate had held steady only because Nevada was losing people from the workforce as fast as it lost jobs.[10]

The Economic Pros and Cons of Government

In an interdependent and technologically driven economy, with external economies of scale, the unassisted free market offers little hope for Nevada's return to the good old days before the crash. While Nevada in 2008 was very different from Nevada in 1878, nonetheless Nevada remains relatively short of productive resources once the particular advantages of its geographic proximity and its gaming monopoly have ended.

Private investment, like water, tends to flow downhill. Firms tend to put their money where other firms are already investing, productive people prefer to live with other productive people, and firms follow suit to have access to the labor pool, the ready availability of suppliers, and the infrastructure that helps them all become more productive.[11] This is, essentially, why many firms in the computer industry are willing to pay higher rents and wages to locate in California's Silicon Valley.

Nevadans, however, have long had a mixed relationship with taxes and government. The first push for statehood in 1863 failed largely due to fears over taxes, but within a year a depression hit Nevada and voters changed their minds.[12] Once mining collapsed, Nevada's efforts to create a viable economy in the high desert depended largely on federal spending projects and the excessive regulation (e.g., divorce laws) of the other states.

During the Depression, Nevada's "one sound state" campaign tried to take advantage of the fiscal crisis other states were experiencing. Other states were implementing sales taxes and income taxes to replace their severely declining property taxes, while Nevada tried to rely primarily on the gaming tax—though after the war Nevada found this to be insufficient and implemented a sales tax anyway.[13] Nonetheless, Nevada continued to rely on its reputation as a no-tax state and thus a good home for the wealthy, and it attracted many people who preferred it that way.

In theory, the relationship between the size of government and economic growth is a complicated one. Free and private markets are efficient under certain conditions, but those conditions—perfect information, perfect competition, and complete markets in which sellers pay all the production costs and buyers receive all the benefits—are often not met. When they aren't met, governments might be able to address some of these market failures. In particular, government can provide or subsidize public goods, which are called that because they are things that benefit society but that can't or won't be adequately provided by the private sector. Police and fire protection, a justice system, national defense, financial regulation, highways, pollution control, sanitation, public health, and education are all good examples of public goods.

The taxes that pay for these public goods can distort incentives, however, because if we raise the cost of doing something, people will do less of it. Of course, there are times when we want people to do less of something, which is why so-called sin taxes are popular, but in most cases economists think higher tax rates are inefficient. Taxes are less likely to distort incentives when rates are relatively low and are collected from a wide range of activities, so that the relative prices of different goods are unaffected. And when taxes cannot be applied equally, taxes will have a higher ratio of revenue to inefficiency when we tax goods for which buyers or sellers are not very price sensitive.

There are also other potential inefficiencies in government intervention that can sometimes lead to making things worse. Governments, like private firms, are made up of human beings, and they share the same pitfalls. Because the state usually produces goods that the private sector does not, and monopolies tend to become inefficient whether they are public or private, the public sector has a particular disadvantage in being efficient. All organizations require good management so that the actions of individuals are made consistent with the interests of society. When state agencies lack information or proper incentives; when they lack competition, especially in light of government's potential for coercive power; or when their political leaders make spending decisions based on what is good for their own reelection and fund-raising prospects, then government intervention can make markets even more inefficient.

Jacques Poot, professor of economics at the National Institute of Demographic and Economic Analysis in New Zealand, argued that there are at least seven separate effects of government spending on growth, including the provision of public and quasi-public goods, the comparative inefficiency of government control over resources and production relative to the private sector it replaces, and the distortionary effect of taxes on resource allocation.[14] In considering the trade-offs, Robert Barro, professor of economics at Harvard University, argues that the relationship between economic growth and the size of government is shaped like an inverted U, so that there is potentially an optimal size.[15] Too little government, like too much, leads to slower growth.

There are also short-term effects that have little to do with the incentive problems of taxes or the relative value of public goods for the economy. These effects have to do with the aggregate level of spending in the economy. When the economy is near full employment, the public sector competes with the private sector for resources, and increases in public spending are likely to crowd out the private sector by increasing prices, wages, interest rates, or—for the federal government at least—the value of the dollar. In a recession, however, high unemployment of workers combined with little investment demand leads to a potential stabilizing role for the state.

In a severe downturn, states would be better off if their governments could cut taxes and increase spending, rather than the opposite. Even the Hoover administration presided over a net increase in government expenditures and a reduction in tax revenues during the Great Depression, but most of this was a natural outcome and not the result of intentional policy. As GDP fell by 43 percent from 1929 to 1932, government expenditures rose a little overall due to an increase in social benefits to the unemployed, while tax revenues declined as the economy collapsed. As a share of GDP, however, total tax revenues actually rose by a third. The Revenue Act of 1932 reflected President Hoover's primary concern with returning to a balanced budget, and it raised tax rates significantly even as the economy continued to slide.

While the federal government has apparently learned its lesson too well, and often runs deficits even during good times, state governments are usually bound by balanced-budget rules that lead them to become "fifty Herbert Hoovers," in the phrase of Paul Krugman.[16] They are prohibited from saving adequately, and find it difficult to borrow. After booms they have an incentive to spend too much, whereas during recessions they are forced to cut spending or raise taxes, albeit with a lag. Since state and local governments together purchase more goods than the federal government and employ far more people, cutbacks by states during a recession can overwhelm the efforts of the federal government to stave off a deeper recession.

I examined the relationship between GSP and state and local government production for all fifty states plus the District of Columbia, for all years from 1963 to 2009.[17] After adjusting for inflation, a larger relative size of state and local government is found to have a positive, but statistically insignificant, correlation with the growth of the overall state economy in the following year. However, changes in state and local government production have a very significant effect on economic growth, depending on how close the economy is to full employment. On average, a dollar cut from state and local spending reduces the total economy by two dollars in the following year, and the deeper the recession, the more significant the effect. When the state economy is producing significantly above the average trend, however, the net effect goes to zero.

But economic reasons are not the only basis for political decisions about taxes and the role of government. For many people, taxes and spending are normative moral issues. Taxing one person to provide benefits to another raises issues of fairness and justice that are very subjective, and government taxation is by its very nature coercive. Should government provide a social safety net for those who become unemployed, or should government expect them to have saved for this unfortunate event themselves? If the economy as a whole is suffering, shouldn't state and local employees have to share the pain? Should the rich pay a greater share of their income to the state than the poor pay, instead of the opposite? Should people who benefit from higher education have to pay for the full cost of that education themselves, instead of having it subsidized by taxpayers?

State and Local Government in Nevada

In deciding what should be done to recover from the crash, Nevadans will debate both the size and the growth of their government. By most measures, Nevada has one of the smallest governments in the country. Whether measured by the average tax burden or the size of the general fund relative to the overall state economy, Nevada's state government is the smallest in the nation, even though the general fund includes spending on items that other states assign to local governments.

Budgeted general fund expenditures grew faster than the overall state economy in the decade before the crash. The total budget was a larger share (2.9 percent) of GSP in the peak of fiscal year 2008, compared to 2000 (2.1 percent) or even 1994 (2.4 percent). Still, even the 2008 peak was less than the 1979 share

(3.3 percent), and even then our general fund share remained among the smallest in the nation.

But there are many ways to measure government size. Should we include the highway fund that finances construction largely through a fixed gasoline excise tax, and should we include other funds that come from federal grants and subsidies? Since states are not entirely consistent about the division of budgeted revenues and expenditures with local governments, shouldn't we consider the aggregate? One approach is to consider what government actually produces and what it actually pays to those who work for it, rather than the sum total of its budget.

Nevada's state and local government production, as a share of GSP, is substantially lower than the mean for other states.[18] The mean is weighted by size, so as not to weigh Wyoming the same as California. Smaller states tend to have larger shares on average, and Nevada is an outlier.

While this measure of government size has not shown much directional trend on average, Nevada has trended downward relative to other states. Nevada's ratio ranked thirty-first out of fifty states for the first decade of the sample, but forty-sixth out of fifty over the past ten years in spite of its smaller population and larger geographic size. In spite of concerns from some quarters about unsustainable government spending, Nevada had a lower average share from 2003 to 2008 than it did from 1963 to 1972, even though there was a significant devolution of responsibility from the federal government to the states in the 1970s and 1980s.

An even better measure to consider, however, is the total number of government workers. According to the Census Bureau, Nevada has the lowest number of state and local employees in the nation as a share of population.[19] Yet in per capita terms, state and local expenditures were only average, not the lowest in the nation. The only way to explain this inconsistency is that Nevada spent more on its average worker.

The Census Bureau also reported that the average wage for Nevada's state employees was about 7 percent higher than the national average in 2008, while city and county employees earned 20 percent more. However, Nevada's cost of living was about 10 percent higher than the national average, at least before the crash. These figures are further muddled by the fact that private-sector workers have seen their benefits decline over time, by the fact that public employees tend to be much better educated than the workforce as a whole, and by what appears to be a much narrower wage gap between blue-collar and white-collar workers in the public sector: lower-paid workers earn more in the public sector while higher-paid workers earn less.

Averages disguise significant variation. State corrections officers made about 30 percent more in Nevada than they would have elsewhere, while local firefighters, especially in Las Vegas, made pretty high incomes compared to firefighters elsewhere. Salaries for K–12 teachers, however, were close to the national average. And before the crash, college professors were paid about the same average salary they would have earned at similar universities in other states.

Similarly, aggregates also disguise variation. While the overall state budget might have grown faster than the economy in the decade before the crash, some parts grew faster than others. In the general fund the largest two components were K–12 education, which grew from 35 percent of the 2000–1 budget to 40 percent of the 2010–11 budget, and human services, which grew from 25 percent to 31 percent. The remainder of the budget, including public safety, higher education, and everything else, fell from 40 percent of the budget to 29 percent.

Higher Education in Nevada

In the effort to generate resources that attract or create businesses and promote economic development, access to a good system of higher education is considered key. As a share of national income, higher education spending in the United States tripled between 1960 and 2005, rising to 2.9 percent of our total national income. Higher educational enrollments rose almost as fast. The number of degrees conferred grew almost fourfold, relative to population, and the share of graduate degrees doubled. This accumulation of human capital is one of the reasons our national economy has done so well over the long run.

Most states have a large number of private universities, which on average pay their faculty roughly 20 percent more than public ones and spend significantly more per student. Even so, most other states make a significant investment in their public universities.

With two public universities and no comparable private ones, Nevada still has the smallest higher education system in the nation. Nevada ranked forty-ninth in the country in the number of public higher education employees per person in 1999, with four employees per thousand people, ahead of only Massachusetts, which has a substantial number of large private universities. This was a third fewer employees per capita than the national average, and the gap between Nevada and the rest of the country has only widened over the past two decades.

Nevada had the lowest proportion of college students in the nation, and with an open admissions policy and a significant number of part-time working students, graduation rates were relatively low. While this proportion was affected by the small size of the higher education system in Nevada, it was also affected by the numbers of high school graduates ready for college. Graduation rates in public K–12 schools were among the lowest in the nation, and K–12 schools had 25 percent fewer employees than the national average, relative to population. But there was also a demand side to the problem, since before the crash many young people without a diploma or college degree could earn above-average wages working in casinos or construction, at least for a while. Many of those who chose to get a college degree went out of state and never returned.

With Governor Guinn's Millennium Scholarship program, a growing economy, and legislative support, an effort was made to turn this around. Nevada System of Higher Education's (NSHE's) operating budget increased by 8.5 percent per year from fiscal year 1999 to fiscal year 2009, growing almost a full percentage point faster than our overall economy. By 2008, the number of NSHE employment had grown to 4.1 per thousand persons, leaving the state in forty-ninth place nationwide. The total NSHE operating budget rose to a peak of 0.65 percent of GSP, still one of the lowest shares in the country.

The actual budget cuts under Governor Gibbons brought university funding nominally back to its fiscal year 2007 level, but actually back to fiscal year 1995 levels in real spending per student, even though faculty salaries nationwide grew significantly faster than overall inflation. Therefore, in real terms, additional cuts to the state budget would in fact reduce the operating budget to levels not seen in several decades.

Conclusion

Now that the state has lost its gambling monopoly and the California-driven housing bubble has burst, Nevada must find a way to begin the accumulation of productive resources if it is to return to growth. Free markets can do many things, but relying on the magic of the free market alone will not bring Nevada back to a path of economic growth. Low taxes notwithstanding, in a state with few resources, in the high and dry desert of the Great Basin, productive investments and productive people are likely to flow out of the state, not in.

But the budget crisis that the crash created is leading Nevada to do the wrong thing. In an economy in which productive people are the primary resource, Nevada is on the verge of significant cuts to education that could lead to a brain drain and an economic downward spiral. The proposed cuts to higher education are only likely to worsen the crisis, leading to a decline in the attractiveness of an in-state college education for Nevadans, and pushing firms out instead of pulling them in. If we don't rethink our approach, Nevada's economic path of the future could be uncomfortably similar to the one it followed the last time its main industry withered, with a decade or more of depopulation ahead.

>> Treasurer's Vignette: No Faith-based Financing

Within a few weeks of the Lehman bankruptcy, the Reserve Primary Fund, a money market fund of some $60 billion, "broke the buck" when its shareholders, realizing it had held $785 million in Lehman debt, began a run on the fund to redeem their shares, forcing the price below $1.00.

The ensuing panic created a domino effect, and in one week investors withdrew approximately $300 billion from money market funds across the country and the market for short-term debt froze up. Cities, municipalities, and public institutions everywhere that relied on short-term notes for routine financing suddenly had their cash stuck in funds they could not redeem, with nowhere to go.

And so on the very morning that the U.S. House of Representatives voted down the first bailout package, my office received a call from the staff of just such an institution in Nevada, telling us it could not make payroll.

The call came in around 9 AM, asking to borrow $45 million. My staff rang off, and we gathered in my office to figure out what to do. Most of the state's money that is not needed on any given day is invested by 9 AM so we didn't have $45 million just lying around. The legislature was not in session. The governor at the time was, to be blunt, not considered a person of good judgment.

A question that was out of our hands was, When would the markets unfreeze? After running through our options, I called the institution back and asked if it was possible to make do with $15 million today and $15 million tomorrow. We waited while they ran through their options. A half hour later we received a call back that they could make it.

"Now," I said, "when can you pay me back?"

"We *hope* to have access to our funds by the end of next month."

I paused. "I don't do faith-based financing, guys. I won't be able to lend you money next month, so if you don't have it by then we will have to go through a more formal process. This could only be a one-time situation."

My staff left to work out the transfer and I decided I had to make a couple of calls. My first call was to a member of our House delegation and I got hold of the chief of staff.

"Why," I asked, "have they voted 'no' on the bailout?"

The staffer, obviously surprised, responded, "Give me one good reason why anyone would vote for that!"

"I have no good reasons," I said, "except the alternative."

"That doesn't sell," he responded sharply, and the call ended soon thereafter.

At this point, I could think of only one person in the entire state of Nevada that might be able to help. I called Senator Reid, or just "The Senator" as everyone called him, and requested to speak to him directly. When he called back, I asked him politely if it were possible to get the bailout passed.

"You're the only person who has called me in favor of the bailout," he said.

I poured out the details of what was happening. "We are dead in the water," I said. "Someone, something has to get the markets to move again or the country's entire economy will screech to a halt!"

I know I sounded panicky. I felt panicky. We, as states, as cities, as municipalities, had no control and few options if the situation continued.

"I'll see what I can do," he said, and hung up.

3. The Economics of Small States in Big Crises (2014)[20]

Small market economies need to integrate with larger economies in order to grow, and in order to gain access to outside trade and investment, but these benefits come with a price. The small economy needs some advantage in what it offers, whether tourist services or exports, and the demand for these offerings is affected by relative prices and exchange rates. The small economy is cushioned from its own recessions by external demand, but is unable to prevent external events from affecting domestic demand. Small economies can get access to outside investment, but when financial markets are unregulated these inflows can lead to asset bubbles and—unless states share a currency—currency instability. Small states are more likely to use a currency managed by larger economies, and this implies that monetary and exchange policies are unlikely to be in the small economy's interest.

In addition to the many factors that contribute to economic growth and the ability to find export markets, such as public investment in education and infrastructure, some factors play a major part in how a small market economy responds to an economic crisis. One key is the economy's tax structure—not only to finance investment in education and infrastructure that supports market-driven growth, but also to provide a stable stream of government revenue during downturns. Small states with unstable revenues need access to capital markets to prevent untimely austerity. With common currency areas that do not easily allow for secular readjustment through higher inflation rates or currency depreciation, participation in a federal system helps to spread the cost of adjustment.

Economic activity can slow for many reasons. However, most shocks to aggregate demand or supply tend to be relatively short-lived, and in the postwar period most developed-economy recessions have lasted a year or less. Growth during the following recovery is typically faster than usual, since potential GDP is not much affected, and economic growth soon catches back up to its prior path. In normal recessions, what matters more is the long-term structure of the economy.

Balance Sheet Recessions

Financial markets are fundamental to economic development in a market economy, but they are particularly prone to market failure. Financial markets are inherently risky, of course, because they are pricing future uncertainties, with information that is often asymmetric and investors who are often unaware of actual risks and returns. The tendency for things to spread—what economists call the externalities of contagion—can be severe in countries with an inadequate regulatory structure. However, with regulation comes implicit guarantees, and insurance—whether explicit and private or implicit and public—often creates incentives that lead to excessive risk-taking, a phenomenon economists call "moral hazard." When investments pay off, the returns remain private, but when risky investments go bad, many of the costs are borne by the rest of the economy.

When financial crises occur, they can lead to a much deeper and longer recession, which the late Hyman Minsky, professor of economics at Washington University in St. Louis, Missouri, defined as a depression.[21] Richard Koo, chief economist at the Nomura Research Institute, calls this a "balance sheet recession," since a financial crisis that significantly reduces asset values for firms and consumers can lead to a long period of deleveraging.[22] Earnings and savings that might have been available for spending are instead used to reduce liabilities, and net wealth declines for a significant portion of the population. One person's spending is another person's income, and the effect is a long-lived recession. The longer people remain unemployed as a result, the less likely they will ever reenter the workforce and regain their prior productivity. The recovery tends to be slower, and because potential GDP is adversely affected by long periods of high unemployment and low investment, the economy never regains its former growth path.

Since the Panic of 1792 following Secretary of the Treasury Alexander Hamilton's establishment of the Bank of the United States, depressions set off by financial panics were common in the United States until the Great Depression of 1929–33, and they have been common in other more-developed economies as well. On average, the decline in aggregate economic output during balance sheet recessions tends to be twice as deep and twice as long as that of other recessions. Following balance sheet recessions, GDP remains roughly 10 percent below its prior path even seven years after the event.[23] In the postwar period, the two best examples of this type of recession are the lost decade following the collapse of Japan's bubble economy, and the Great Recession of 2007–9.

The normal mechanisms of monetary policy, such as reducing short-term interest rates, do not work in such an economy, especially if price inflation is already low. Financial institutions seek safer assets like government bonds to reduce the overall risk of a portfolio of nonperforming loans, and both consumers and firms move their financial assets into cash. This move out of traditional lending puts downward pressure on the money supply even as money demand rises, and this can push an economy with already weak demand for goods and services into price deflation.[24] Real interest rates rise with expected price deflation even with a low nominal rate of interest on interbank loans, and spending is delayed. On average, price deflation slows subsequent growth.[25] As both Japan and the United States have shown, even a policy of quantitative easing has difficulty reversing the problem.

Of course, the economic damage done by a financial crisis depends on the severity of the crisis, which is determined in part by the government regulatory structure, and the size of the financial sector relative to the overall economy. Real estate bubbles affect consumer wealth for a large share of the population with credit constraints, whereas stock market bubbles tend to affect the wealth of those who have other savings, so they aren't forced to reduce their consumption spending as much.

Fiscal Intervention and Austerity

One option for a small state in crisis is for it to allow its currency to depreciate. This would make its goods cheaper, and rising exports to other states would assist in its recovery. As one of the United States, however, Nevada shares a common currency with the rest of the union. A common currency has many benefits, in that it allows a state to trade with other states without exchange risk and without the transactions cost of currency conversion, and thus it eases both trade and investment across borders. With a common currency, states with markets that overheat during booms are unable to easily adjust their real relative prices downward through currency depreciation. Unless other states in the union are in an identical crisis, the Federal Reserve is unlikely to allow the dollar to depreciate.

In a typical recession, government fiscal intervention beyond automatic stabilizers such as taxes (which decline during recessions) and social spending (which rises during recessions) is often ineffective and poorly timed, and the crowding-out effects on private spending or the increase in public debt can be counterproductive. Monetary intervention by the central bank is usually more effective in restoring spending, though it might be destabilizing and inflationary if used excessively.

In a balance sheet recession, public spending and private spending are more likely to be complements than substitutes, and large developed nation-states with access to capital markets have the option of fiscal intervention. Tax cuts for those with credit constraints not affecting consumption are not likely to be effective, since the resulting savings go primarily toward paying down debt. Public spending can raise private incomes, and if spending focuses on the development of productive infrastructure, the result can be increases in the nation's potential output. Although the central bank often acts as the lender of last resort, the government in effect becomes a borrower of last resort in an economy wary of other financial assets.

For a small state, however, significant public borrowing is often not an option. During a typical recession, these states usually have financial reserves sufficient to weather the likely declines in revenue. In a balance sheet recession, however, these financial reserves can be quickly used up. In such a situation, the fiscal policy of a small state becomes an automatic destabilizer. States are forced to engage in austerity by raising taxes, cutting public spending, or both, and this further reduces private incomes and makes the recession deeper or the recovery slower.

Unlike small states sharing a common currency in the Euro zone, Nevada is not a sovereign country. While this comes with costs, it also comes with many benefits. One of those benefits is that much of its public spending comes directly or indirectly from the federal government. Shortfalls in state tax revenues might affect the state's general fund, but they do not affect all of its funds. Similarly, when a recession leads the state to contribute fewer taxes to the federal government, this does not automatically lead to cuts in federal spending in the state. These implicit inter-state transfers provide a cushion to Nevada that is not available to small states in the Euro zone.

Nonetheless, in the Great Recession state and local governments were forced by effective credit limits and reduced tax revenues to cut spending significantly, particularly on education and infrastructure investments that have positive long-run effects. Because state and local governments cumulatively make the vast majority of public purchases, Paul Krugman predicted this would serve as "fifty Herbert Hoovers" in depressing overall demand, unless the federal government could overcompensate with fiscal policy.[26] This stimulus occurred in 2009–10 as a result of the American Reinvestment and Recovery Act, but by 2011 public austerity had become the net effect.

» Treasurer's Vignette: It Is Flat

As state treasurer I tried to get out to the eastern edge of Nevada at least once a year.

So it was that in midsummer I drove a broad loop from Vegas over to Caliente and Pioche, up to Baker and Ely, and back along the loneliest highway passing through Eureka, Austin, Fallon, and Fernley until finally reaching Reno. In each place I would stop and chat and listen.

In Caliente, local officials worried about arsenic in the water, and in Pioche I was ribbed and chided about whether I would eat Rocky Mountain oysters, but it was in Baker that I got a clear picture about what small business owners were facing as the financial crisis lingered.

It was evening and the residents of Baker were having a potluck at a house partway up the mountain. The sky was clear, and without any city lights one could see quite a ways off. Standing out on the porch, I asked the owner of the Border Inn whether business was picking up.

In response, she pointed to the road stretching out across the valley and into Utah. "See those headlights?" she asked, pointing to two clear orbs dipping and surfacing and dipping again as they made their way into Nevada. "Used to be I would see three or four cars like that coming down the road and I would get down to the inn just in time to check them in as they came over the border. But now you see I get only one. Business is flat," she said.

We stared out at those headlights for a moment, watching them disappear and then catch on the road ahead as they got closer to the state line. "Can you do flat?" I asked. "Can you do flat for another year?"

She pulled on her jacket, ready to head down to the inn. "One more year," she said as she turned to look at the two tiny beams of light. "I can do flat for one more year."

Notes

1. J.S. Mill, *On Liberty* (London: Longman, Roberts & Green, 1869).

2. Jeremy Aguero of Applied Analysis once remarked that Las Vegas named its professional baseball team the 51s because Nevada was fifty-first on so many lists (if you include the District of Columbia). I suggested that Reno named its team the Aces for being first on so many others.

3. The use of first person refers to Elliott Parker, unless otherwise noted.

4. A more precise translation from Tacitus, *Agricola*, Book 1, Section 27, is, "It is the singularly unfair peculiarity of war that the credit of success is

claimed by all, while a disaster is attributed to one alone." http://www.sacred -texts.com/cla/tac/ago1020.htm

5. As was frequently the case with Yogi Berra, he didn't always say what people said he said. This quote apparently originated with the Danish politician Karl Kristian Steincke.

6. This is revised from E. Parker, "Will History Repeat Itself? Nevada's Economy After the Crash," *Nevada Review* 3, no. 1 (2011): 4–17.

7. *Nevada History,* http://nevada-history.org/charts.html

8. M. Mack, *Nevada: A History of the State from the Earliest Times Through the Civil War* (Glendale, CA: Arthur H. Clark, 1936).

9. R. DePolo and M. Pingle, "Nevada Gaming: Revenues and Taxes (1945–95)," *Journal of Gambling Studies* 13, no. 1 (1997): 49–67.

10. Bureau of Labor Statistics, U.S. Department of Labor, http://www.bls .gov/lau

11. The literature on this is large, but for a start consider M. Fleming, "External Economies and the Doctrine of Balanced Growth," *Economic Journal* 65, no. 258 (1955): 241–56; and P. Krugman, "Increasing Returns and Economic Geography," *Journal of Political Economy* 99, no. 3 (1991): 483–99.

12. D. Bartholet, "Historical Overview of Nevada's Economy and Fiscal Policy: Statehood to 2010," http://unrbusinessresearch.org/wp-content /uploads/2012/02/Historical-Overview-of-Nevada-Economy-and-Fiscal-Policy .pdf (2010).

13. G. Rocha, "Myth 144: One Unsound State," nsla.nv.gov/Archives/Myths/ One_Unsound_State

14. J. Poot, "A Synthesis of Empirical Research on the Impact of Government on Long-Run Growth," *Growth and Change* 31, no. 4 (2000): 516–46.

15. R.J. Barro, "Government Spending in a Simple Model of Endogenous Growth," *Journal of Political Economy* 98, no. 5 (1990): S103–S125.

16. P.R. Krugman, "Fifty Herbert Hoovers," *New York Times,* December 28, 2008.

17. E. Parker, "Fifty Herbert Hoovers and the Effect of State and Local Government on Gross State Product," http://www.business.unr.edu/faculty /parker/FiftyHerbertHoovers.pdf (2011).

18. Bureau of Economic Analysis, U.S. Department of Commerce, http:// www.bea.gov/regional

19. Census Bureau, U.S. Department of Commerce, Statistical Abstract of the United States, http://www.census.gov/library/publications/time-series /statistical_abstracts.html.

20. This is a revised excerpt from E. Parker, "Small States in a Time of Big Crises: Nevada, Ireland, and the Basque Autonomous Community during the Great Recession," in *A Comparative View of the Resilience of Public Finances and Self-Government in the Basque Country, Catalonia, and Nevada,* edited by X. Irujo and J. Agirreazkuenaga (Reno: Center for Basque Studies' Conference Series, 2017).

21. H. P. Minsky, *Stabilizing an Unstable Economy* (New York: McGraw-Hill, 1986).

22. R. C. Koo, *The Holy Grail of Macroeconomics: Lessons from Japan's Great Recession* (Hoboken, NJ: Wiley Press, 2009).

23. C. M. Reinhart and K. S. Rogoff, *This Time Is Different: Eight Centuries of Financial Folly* (Princeton, NJ: Princeton University Press, 2009).

24. T. F. Cargill and E. Parker, "Why Deflation Is Different," *Central Banking* 14, no. 1 (2003): 35–42.

25. F. Guerrero and E. Parker, "Deflation and Recession: Finding the Empirical Link," *Economics Letters* 93, no. 1 (2006): 12–17.

26. Krugman, "Fifty Herbert Hoovers."

CHAPTER 2

Understanding the State Budget

The budget is not just a collection of numbers, but an expression of our values and aspirations.

— Secretary of the Treasury Jacob Lew[1]

Introduction

The state budget is decided in the legislature, but it is not a smooth process. With only sixty-three members in the assembly and senate combined, Nevada has one of the smallest legislatures in the nation. Nevada is one of four states in the nation with a biennial legislature meeting in odd-numbered years. The legislative session is also brief, beginning the first Monday in February and running for 120 consecutive days. With term limits for a citizen legislature and less than three months between election day and the governor's State of the State speech, we find there is not much time for legislators to negotiate good outcomes or even really understand the complexities of the budget.

The primary budget that state legislators control is the general fund. Figure 2.1 shows the budgeted expenditures for the legislatively approved general fund budget in the 2007–9 biennium. Most of the budget went to support K–12 education (the state's contribution to the distributive school account used by county school districts) and human services, while NSHE and public safety accounted for most of the remainder. Everything else, including the budgets for state officers, finance and administration, commerce and industry, and infrastructure, accounted for 8 percent of the total. As one of its budgeted expenditures, the state usually tries to maintain a small rainy-day fund to cover budget shortfalls, but these savings were completely inadequate to the needs of the Great Recession.

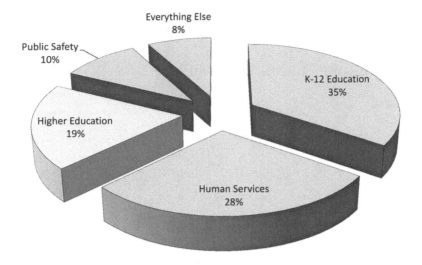

FIGURE 2.1. Nevada General Fund Spending in 2007–9 Budget.
Source: Courtesy of *Revenue Reference Manual,* Fiscal Analysis Division, Nevada.

It is the state treasurer's job to manage the cash flow that makes all this spending possible, investing the balance wisely to ensure the greatest possible return on assets at the least possible risk to the state, as well as to manage the state's many other financial assets and liabilities. It is crucial that the state maintain a good credit rating so that its debts remain affordable.

In Nevada the biennial budget is determined by the revenue forecast of the Economic Forum, a panel of five citizens appointed from the private sector. Expenditures are then limited to 95 percent of the revenue forecast, and any residual balance at the end of one biennium becomes available for the next budget. In addition to being limited by the revenue forecast, the budget is also limited by an expenditure cap established by the 1979 legislature, a cap that limits the long-run growth rate to the sum of population growth and price inflation, and that has never been binding. While some actions between legislative sessions are decided by the Interim Finance Committee, serious shortfalls in projected revenue usually lead the governor to call for a special session.

Figure 2.2 shows the forecasted revenues for the legislatively approved general fund budget in the 2007–9 biennium.

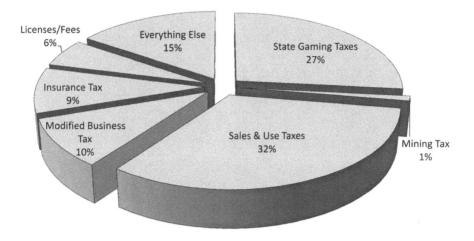

FIGURE 2.2. Nevada General Fund Revenues in 2007–9 Budget.
Source: Courtesy of *Revenue Reference Manual,* Fiscal Analysis Division, Nevada.

Nevada is one of nine states without a personal income tax, and one of only six without a corporate income tax, though three of those states still levy a gross receipts tax on business. In general, states without an income tax tend to have other revenue sources. Alaska and Texas, for example, get significant state revenue from oil. While Nevada is one of the world's largest gold producers, the state constitution constrains mining taxes to 5 percent of net proceeds. But Nevada has casino gambling, and a 7.75 percent tax on gross gaming revenues accounted for the lion's share of state revenues for much of the postwar period. Because the state has lost its monopoly on legal gambling to other states, Native American reservations, and international locations like Macau, this tax revenue now no longer keeps pace with the state's spending.

While the state's counties receive most of their revenue from property taxes, a third of the state's general fund revenue comes from sales and use taxes, as the state gaming tax declined to only slightly more than a quarter of state revenue. Figure 2.3 shows how the tax base for these two revenue streams has changed since 1980, adjusting for price inflation and the number of state

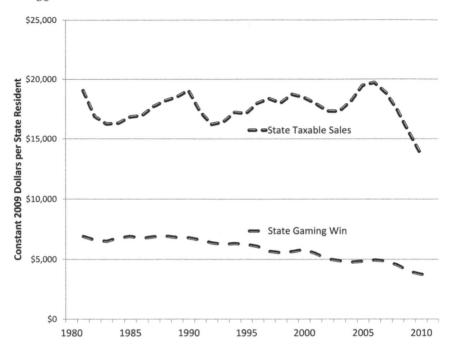

FIGURE 2.3. Nevada's Tax Base, 1980–2011. *Source:* Author's calculations from the State of Nevada Department of Taxation and the Nevada Gaming Commission.

residents. Sales taxes have proven to be very sensitive to the over-all state of the economy, particularly with the rise in untaxed ser-vices and Internet sales where sales tax is often uncollected, and real taxable sales per capita declined by 30 percent statewide during the Great Recession.

The next two largest sources of state revenue were the mod-ified business tax and a tax on insurance premiums. The former originally grew out of a small business tax per employee, and then was modified under Governor Kenny Guinn (1999–2007) into a tax on payroll. During the financial crisis, while Jim Gibbons (2007–11) was governor, this tax was modified again to become more progressive and raise more revenue. These modifications became known as the "sunset tax," because Washoe County's state senator William Raggio originally designed them to expire at the end of the biennium.

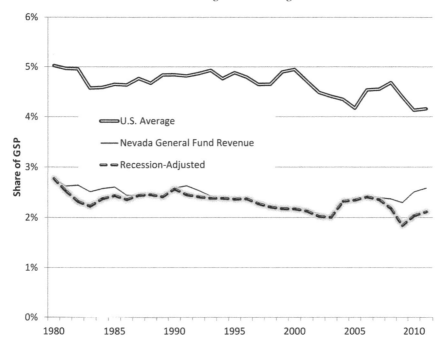

FIGURE 2.4. General Fund Revenue as Share of GSP, 1980–2011. *Source:* Author's calculations from the Nevada Legislature and National Association of State Budget Officers Web Sites.

Relative to those of other states in the union, Nevada's general fund is a relatively small share of the state economy, and it has not grown as fast as the economy. Figure 2.4 shows general fund revenue as a share of GSP since 1980. Dividing by GSP can be misleading during recessions, since if the pie shrinks, a piece that isn't any larger might still be a larger share. To correct for this, Figure 2.4 also shows an adjusted share that limits the GSP denominator to population growth and price inflation during severe economic downturns.

The mismatch between Nevada's economy and the tax base has been studied many times. In 2003 Governor Guinn started his second term in office with an attempt to finally address this mismatch and to restructure the tax system. Prior to becoming governor, he had built an impressive resume in both public education and the private sector, but he had never before held elective office.[2] This might explain why he was willing to take on the task, as well as why he was unable to achieve most of what he proposed. Still, the tax changes led to a rebellion from some members of his party. Once passed, they also led to a big increase in state revenues, which rose in 2003–5 by 44 percent over the prior biennium, almost twice as fast as the rise in GSP. As a result, the state began to run a surplus, and rebated $300 million in vehicle registration fees in fiscal year 2005.

When the economy went into recession in 2008 and tax collections plummeted, the pushback against Governor Guinn's tax restructuring would come back to haunt the state, since some Republicans saw the recession as an opportunity to cut state government further and roll back the taxes. Governor Guinn's successor played a key role. As a Republican assemblyman from Washoe County, Governor Gibbons had made his reputation by spearheading a change to the state constitution to require a two-thirds vote for any tax increase, and had signed several pledges to never increase taxes.

This chapter includes seven columns I published on the state budget during the crisis. One of these was coauthored with the late William Raggio, a Republican who served many years as party leader in the state senate. These columns make the argument that states are often forced to do the wrong thing during recessions, particularly when there is a lack of understanding how the budget works.

❯❯ Treasurer's Vignette: The Mendoza Line

Cash normally drops during the summer months as a new fiscal year begins. Departments draw down on their appropriations and revenues have yet to really start coming in. But in the summer of 2009, after the legislators had gone home, the cash in the state's coffers began to slip away at an alarming rate. Nothing was coming in to replace it. In late July I called a former budget director to get advice and express my concerns.

"No need to worry. Happens every year. Just hold tight," was the response.

We waited and watched as it continued to drain out. I asked my staff to figure out just how low we could go before we were at risk of not being able to pay the state's bills. $200 million—that was it.

We began to call it our Mendoza Line, after Mario Mendoza's famously low batting average. We hovered with our noses just above the mark until the end of September, a little over a year after Lehman's went belly up.

I came into my office at ten to nine on a Thursday morning to find five of my staffers waiting. "Guys," I said, "you look like you're about to go to your own funeral."

"196."

"What?"

"196. We're at $196 million," said my cash management deputy.

"You don't know that," I said. "There's always stragglers at the end of the month. Dollars to donuts someone's forgotten to key the data in. Come back Monday and tell me where we're at."

I sent them out of my office, closed the door and stared at the wall. Truth was they were panicking and I didn't want them to see that I might be, too. I needed until Monday to figure out what to do and I hoped and prayed we could eke by yet again.

On Monday my staff met me at the door. "Everyone's updated their numbers."

"Okay, where are we?"

"195."

"Good grief!" However, I had had the weekend to mull things over. "We're going to slow roll it," I told my staff. "Call any department that has a good-size appropriation and has drawn down a large part of it. Tell them they need to move some of it back to the general fund until they actually have invoices."

"How?"

"Tell them it's that or we're at risk of another special session."

We also had a big bill coming from the distributive school account. Since sales taxes were low the state had to make up the difference, and it was costing about $300 million a quarter. I instructed staff to call the two largest school districts and get an agreement that we would pay them monthly, not quarterly. Again I told them that if we couldn't make things work, I would have to go to the governor and there was a risk he'd move for another special session.

By the end of Tuesday we had forged agreements, paid the state's bills, and kept ourselves afloat. To stay above the Mendoza Line, we kept that policy in place for the better part of a year.

1. The State's Fiscal Situation (2009)[3]

Nevada's economy is in trouble. From 1990 to 2005 we had the fastest-growing economy in the country, and our unemployment rate was usually a little below the national average.

But in the past year our total personal income has declined 6.4 percent, the largest drop in the country, and our unemployment rate is one of the country's highest.

Our economy has been overly dependent on construction and tourism, the most of any state, and both sectors were particularly hard hit by this Great Recession. Although tourism might recover somewhat as the recession comes to an end elsewhere, our construction sector is coming down from a booming decade that was simply not sustainable.

What worries me, and should worry you, is that our state revenue is extremely undiversified, with a significant portion coming from taxes on gaming and hotel rooms. This tax base had been shrinking even before this recession.

In the mid-1980s gaming revenue totaled 17 percent of our state's economic output, but by 2007 it was only 10 percent (and only 8 percent this year). Over the same two decades, total casino revenue—including rooms, food, and beverage sales—declined by a third as a share of our economy.

With a comparable drop in taxable retail sales, our state government has seen its revenue sliced thin. General fund revenue for this past fiscal year was 12 percent lower than in the two years prior, when it peaked.

Thanks in part to stabilization funds from the federal government, the legislature passed a general fund operating budget for 2009–11 that was only 4 percent lower than the previous budget, although higher education was cut much deeper.

Revenue continues to fall below the reduced Economic Forum projections. According to the Budget and Planning Division, we are about $65 million below projections for the first three months of the new fiscal year, a shortfall that is only 1 percent of the current general fund budget, but would be 8 percent if it continued for the twenty-one remaining months in our current two-year budget cycle.

Meanwhile, Governor Jim Gibbons still insists that state government has a spending problem, not a revenue problem. This only makes sense if you understand him to mean that any state spending whatsoever is a problem. If you believe that there are essential public goods that must be provided—that public education, for example, is a worthwhile endeavor—then you should be concerned.

Did you know that Nevada's general fund is limited by law to grow no faster than inflation plus the state's population growth? The state's general fund was $390 million in the 1975–77 budget, about 2.8 percent of Nevada's total economy.

Because our population and the consumer price index are each about 4.4 times higher than thirty-four years ago, this caps our general fund expenditures at about $7.5 billion for the current two-year budget cycle.

Our general fund budget for the 2009–11 biennium is actually only $6.5 billion, which sounds like a lot but translates to only 2.4 percent of our projected economic output during these two years. How can the governor think this spending is out of control?

As I have said before, Nevada already has the smallest state government in the country, whether you measure it by the number of government employees (as a share of population) or by general fund expenditures (as a share of our economy). How much smaller should it be?

Of course, while the general fund represents the "discretionary" spending under the control of the legislature, it is only a portion of the entire budget. The state also manages other independent funds with dedicated revenues, such as the highway fund, and receives at least $1 billion in federal funding that it uses for Medicaid, highway construction, and other federally supported programs.

In addition, local governments such as Clark County and Las Vegas have their own budgets that are not under direct legislative control. Our state and local governments together still produce less than $10 billion per year, about 7.5 percent of our total economy—a proportion that is still one of the lowest in the nation.

Could our state government be more efficient? All human institutions are inefficient to some extent, including those in the private sector. Public agencies are harder to manage, and it is harder to measure good performance in the public sector.

Legislatures put more restrictions on state agencies, and as a result they are less nimble and often more bureaucratic. Legislatures also tend to spend money on programs that provide more political goodwill than economic benefits.

Even so, the idea that there is enough excess capacity to allow for further budget cuts without reducing valuable public services is a fallacy. Furthermore, when private firms reduce their workforces, it is usually because they have fewer customers; when the public sector has its budget cut, it usually finds itself with more people looking for help, people the federal government does not allow us to turn away, as well as more unemployed workers going back to school, and so on.

So what should we do about the decline in state revenue? The legislature has already cut most budgets, and included a furlough program for state workers. Now the governor has asked all state agencies to plan for additional cuts as high as 10 percent of the general fund allocation. In higher education, we will now have to cut deeper into meat and bone.

What becomes of our state if our K–12 system becomes even weaker, or if our higher education system—already the smallest in the nation—is forced to cut enrollments?

Gibbons is right that tax increases are a bad idea during a recession, although any economist can tell you the fiscal effect on the state's economy is less with tax increases than it is with cuts in government services. Borrowing during good times is usually not a good idea, and many will correctly point out that it is part of what got the country, and most of Nevada's homeowners, into this mess.

Borrowing during bad times, however, makes more sense, although of course it would have been better to have saved money for a rainy day. If you lose your job, you don't consider it a good idea to sell your car, clothes, and house and then live on the street, at least not if you ever want to get another job.

Similarly, the state needs to preserve its key assets, and it is not a good idea to let our educational system and other infrastructure deteriorate further—not if we ever hope to bring new businesses into the state.

It is ironic that state governments are effectively counteracting the stimulus efforts of the federal government. Cumulatively, state and local governments purchase 50 percent more goods and services than the federal government.

By cutting spending and raising taxes, state governments are dampening growth in their states that could have been fostered by the federal tax cuts and increased spending. The only reason this situation is not worse is that a large portion of what the federal government has spent so far has been given directly to the states.

How do we get through this crisis without doing long-term damage? Nevada might not need a bigger government, but it cannot afford a smaller one.

Nevada does not need higher tax rates, but it does need a broader, more-diversified, and less-unstable tax base. The governor and the legislature need to take the time to do the hard work of creating a new tax structure instead of resorting to campaign slogans.

We should delay actual implementation of any new taxes until the state economy has recovered, but institute a reporting requirement so businesses can better prepare, and so our state government can more easily borrow against that future revenue.

We also need to figure out what the next step is for our economy. Nevada has relied on casinos since 1931, and for the past decade we also relied on construction. If neither of these will carry us into the future, might it be time for us to reinvent ourselves once more?

2. State Cuts Are a Drag on the Economy (2010)[4]

Cuts to state and local governments have been a big factor in the slow recovery from the Great Recession. Over the past year state and local governments have cut 274,000 jobs, about half of what the private sector has added. Meanwhile, federal employment has remained relatively steady, except for a temporary surge of hiring for the decennial census.

As the state with the economy that went from first to worst, Nevada's budget cuts have been pretty deep, though they would have been much worse without federal government aid. In the next legislative session, however, this stimulus money will have run out, and the taxes we implemented in 2009 will expire. Although the projected budget gap is only about 1 percent of our state's overall economy, it is almost half of our state's general fund.

Many Nevadans are finally realizing that with gaming and tourism on the decline, we can no longer rely on taxing people from out of state, and we have to find a better way to pay for what we need ourselves. A recent poll found that two thirds of Nevadans were willing to consider some increases in state taxes to replace these lost revenues.

For a state that has long tended to be suspicious of government, what might account for this turnaround?

One possibility is that it has become obvious to many that Nevada really has a very small government, one that is even smaller than it used to be, and it doesn't provide much in the way of public services.

We rank among the smallest states in the number of state and local employees per capita, particularly in education. We have fewer teachers per person than the average state, and we have the smallest higher education sector in the country. To call us the Mississippi of the West in education does an injustice to Mississippi.

The largest part of the state's general fund budget is spent on supporting K–12 education; those expenditures continued to rise as the number of children in the state has increased (even though our support is still behind the average state). The state is obligated to spend more, not less, because it has to make up the difference as the property tax collected by local governments and the local school support sales tax revenue have declined.

Spending on human services is the second biggest part of the budget, and this spending has grown due to rising health-care costs and increased caseloads due to the nation's highest unemployment rate.

Together, these two parts make up almost 70 percent of the current general fund budget, up from 60 percent a decade ago. As a result, the decline in the total budget has fallen most heavily on the remaining portions, especially on support for higher education. In Nevada we treat higher education like a luxury good instead of an investment.

Those who think any amount of public services is still too much have pointed out that the state budget grew faster than the overall state economy in the first part of this past decade. But take a longer look, and you will find that the state budget has been declining as a share of either our GSP or our personal income. Our state's budget was a smaller share of our economy in 2007 than it was three decades ago, and by 2009 it was much lower still. Nevada's government still looks small if you also toss in monies spent by local governments, or the matching monies spent on highways, education, and Medicaid that come from the federal government.

Of course, people tend to need more public services in recessions, and so ideally state and local governments should be islands of stability in a turbulent economy. Instead, the requirement for a balanced budget when people are paying less in taxes means cutbacks at exactly the wrong time. Instead of remaining stable, Nevada's state budget has declined by more than our average private income, which further destabilizes our economy. This not only reduces the number of jobs and the overall amount of spending, it also leads to the loss of the public goods the state provided in the first place, some of which—like education—are crucial to our long-run recovery.

3. To Fix Nevada, We Need to Work Together (2010)[5]

For most of our history Nevada has hitched its cart to just one industry at a time—mining, divorce, gambling, and then construction. Now folks ask whether gaming or construction will bounce back, or if renewable energy can save us.

There is no silver bullet. Gaming might bounce back a little, but it is now a global, competitive industry. And renewable energy might provide our economy with a boost, but I am not sure it will create many in-state jobs.

Instead, we have to do the hard work. We can't bribe firms to move here with the promise of no taxes, but we can attract them if we provide a workforce that will make them profitable. We have to stop thinking of education as a consumption good, and instead see it as an investment. The payoff will take time, but in the best-performing states and countries, education and worker productivity matter a lot more than tax rates. New industries will come from new ideas. So, the resources we need are the people who create new ideas and solutions, and the workforce to implement them.

Regarding Nevada's budget crisis, we've been looking at this the wrong way. Our political tribalism blinds us to the fact that we have more in common than not. We are like Giants fans who choose to hate the other team, and forget to just love baseball. Good plays can be made by players on both teams, and good policies can come from both parties. Bad policies, too.

We can't spend our way to prosperity or solve problems just by throwing money at them. But we also can't cut our way to prosperity. Businesses don't prosper by saying they can't afford to invest, and neither can the state.

Nevada Republicans and Democrats will have to work together, and not retreat to their partisan positions and their tired old slogans.

Republicans will need to concede that we might need to find new revenues to make up for the ones few people are paying any more. We need to figure out a better tax structure than the one we have. An efficient tax has low rates but a broad base. Getting the lion's share from a declining industry such as gaming is bad policy, as is taxing only merchandise but not services, and taxing only merchandise sold in brick-and-mortar stores.

Similarly, Democrats need to concede that there are bad policies we have enshrined in state law that can make our state budgets grow too fast. The university system has a defined contribution for retirement, not a defined benefit, and the entire state government should move toward that. We need to take steps to reduce the ever-expanding costs of providing medical care. Collective bargaining rules have meant that some public-sector employees are paid more than labor market conditions would require, especially for some sectors of local government. This needs to be addressed. Tying pay to performance is usually a good idea too, if we can measure performance.

We need to start by deciding what it is we need the state to provide, and figure out how to provide it the best way. Then we need to figure out how to pay for what we need the state to provide. We can't just stop providing human services, especially when unemployment is so high. We can't abandon our responsibility to educate our citizens. We can't empty out our prisons, stop trying to prevent crime, or stop putting out fires. We need to figure out what type of society we want to create, how our K–12 system can compete nationally, and how our universities can produce the research our state needs and keep our best students in the state.

If we aren't willing to dig in and do this hard work, together, without political tribalism, then we ought to all just give up now and move. The last person who leaves can turn back our statehood back in.

4. State Fiscal Crises, the Depression, and Now (2010)[6]

This recession might not be comparable to the Great Depression in its depth and sheer misery, but it is comparable in some of its causes as well as in its unusual length. In Nevada our GSP has stopped falling, but unemployment keeps breaking post-Depression records.

Among the major contributors to the Great Depression and its painfully slow recovery was a fiscal crisis in the states. State and local governments have constitutional limits on how much they can borrow. Although this restriction works well in limiting government during normal times, in a downturn it adds fuel to a fire we would rather put out. Our income falls, so we pay less in taxes. Tax revenues fall, so public spending is cut.

Recessions are a chance to prune, and a fiscal crisis can force the public sector to stop doing things it should not be doing, or should be doing better. As the crisis gets deeper and longer, however, it forces cuts in increasingly vital services. The decline in public spending also hurts the private sector that sells goods and services to these governments and their employees, and the vicious cycle continues with more layoffs.

In judging whether government had any effect in helping the economy recover from the Depression, most people focus on what Hoover or Roosevelt did or didn't do. But federal government expenditures were less than 3 percent of GDP in 1929. Local governments alone spent twice that, and state and local governments together accounted for three quarters of public spending.

The drop in state and local government expenditures canceled out a significant share of the effect of increased federal expenditures on national GDP. Because property taxes did not bounce back until the 1940s, the state and local fiscal crisis continued for years. When the federal government began to provide grants to states, most of them were for new poverty relief efforts, not for normal expenditures such as education and public safety.

The long fiscal crisis of the 1930s pushed many states to restructure their tax systems. Nevada legalized gaming and became dependent on that for state revenue, while many states implemented sales and income taxes to replace property taxes. States also became much more dependent on the federal government to collect taxes for them, which come back to the states through grants.

As much as any other state, Nevada is now facing a fiscal crisis of a similar magnitude. The revenues we became dependent on after the 1930s have declined, and are not likely to fully bounce back. The three most recent sets of budget cuts not only are reducing the public goods provided to the state, but are also adding further downward pressure on spending in the private sector. Time will tell whether we have learned anything from experience in our response.

5. Private Sector Needs a Vital Public Sector (2010)[7]

As Democrats and Republicans prepare for what will be a very difficult budget session, we need to remember that our state motto is "Omnia Pro Patria," not "Omnia Pro Party." We might have some fundamental disagreements, but for the good of the state we need to work together.

First, Nevadans need to understand that the state is both smaller and more complicated than they think. Whatever they might think about the pay of firefighters in Las Vegas, Nevadans should understand that city and county government are different entities, with their own governments, revenues, and budgets. Within the state, Nevadans should realize that K–12 education, NSHE, and the various state agencies all operate under very different rules, with different pay and benefit plans. Nevadans should also realize that not all parts of the budget have grown the same:

the state's contribution for K–12 and human services combined has grown from 60 percent of the budget to 70 percent over the past decade, mostly for good reason.

Whatever they might think about the federal government, Nevadans should realize that the state government is different. Nevada's state government is one of the country's smallest, and the state takes on responsibilities that local governments often cover (e.g., community colleges). In the total number of state and local employees as a share of resident population in 2007, Nevada ranked dead last. We could have added 10,000 state and local employees and we *still* would have ranked last.

Democrats need to concede that some parts of the state budget could use reforms. While higher education has a defined-contribution retirement plan, many state employees are members of the Public Employee Retirement System, a defined-benefit plan. This latter plan probably needs to be replaced over time. The state might need to take steps to limit the growth of its contribution to the Public Employee Benefit System, which has been rising for years as medical costs continue to skyrocket, but this needs to be done gradually. If pay ever rises again, automatic step increases and cost-of-living increases might need to be replaced with pay increases tied more closely to performance. And the state law that enables collective bargaining for county and city governments might really need to change.

We all need to drop the notion that pay and benefits for state employees is about fairness. As an economist, I would argue instead that pay and benefits should be determined by what it takes to attract and retain trained and productive workers. If there are state jobs for which we are paying more than necessary, then we should reduce state pay. But where we are not paying as much as our competition for similar personnel we need to be willing to pay more.

Republicans need to understand that making these cuts could affect the growth of the state budget in the future, but they won't create much in savings now. Republicans in general, and the governor in particular, need to step away from the precipice and concede that we need taxes to replace the ones that people are no longer paying, and we need to design a better tax system to collect the revenues we need. We have depended too long on gaming revenues paid mostly by people from out of state. We have lost our monopoly and we have to figure out how to start paying our own taxes.

Republicans need to concede that its small public sector is necessary to the prosperity of the private sector. The idea that Nevada will prosper without either is absurd. Nevadans need to realize that the cuts so far have been significant. There was never much fat there in the first place, and there is certainly not much left to cut without doing real damage to the state.

A good tax structure should have low rates so these taxes don't distort private incentives, but be broad-based instead of focused on just a few sectors. Extending the sales tax to services, Internet sales, and other currently exempted sectors is an option. Reducing what the mining industry can deduct to calculate its net proceeds is an option. Most states have a corporate income tax, so we could implement one at a very low rate and still remain a low-tax state. Extending the modified business tax from just payroll to all value-added is another option.

Nevada already limits its general fund expenditures to grow no faster than population growth plus price inflation over the long run, but if and when the state economy and its budget revenues recover, we need to think about doing a better job building up a real rainy-day fund in case this ever happens again. We also need to realize that there might be things we could invest in, if we could ever afford to invest. There are things we could do to attract businesses that would really help with our employment situation, but we can never seem to afford them.

6. Changing Our Thinking on the Budget, with State Senator William Raggio (2011)[8]

By asking how much we have to cut to meet projected revenues, we are thinking about the state's budget completely backward. This approach assumes that the state provides services that are luxuries, like eating out at a fancy restaurant, which we can afford to cut when our revenues fall. This is wrong.

The state provides essential services that the private sector doesn't. We must educate our children in a K–12 system that prepares them for a productive life in the modern world. We must maintain law and order, courts and prisons, highways, and functioning state agencies. We must provide help to those who are unable to care for themselves. And we must have good community colleges and universities available for our brightest students, especially if we want Nevada to have a bright future.

How do we best provide these essential services? Can we provide them better, and at a lower cost to the state? Are there things we don't need to be doing, or are paying too much for? And are there other things we should be doing, with a good return on investment for the state?

We should be asking these questions regardless of whether we have a recession. We should always be looking for efficiencies. We need to address what Nevada can promise for state employee retirement and benefits. Other recommendations of the Sage Commission should be considered, where they are practical.[9]

Only after we figure out what we need to provide and how we can best provide it should we figure out how to pay for it.

We already have a small state government. We already limit the growth of our state general fund to inflation plus population growth over the long run, a limit we have not exceeded in more than thirty years. We already provide the bare minimum of the services essential to a functioning state. We need to stop thinking of a recession as a convenient way to force us to make it even smaller.

We should fund local government in a more fair way. Shifting responsibilities doesn't save any money, but only forces local government to increase other taxes instead. We should address state rules for collective bargaining, especially the "last best offer" rule, to make it easier for local governments to address their own budgets.

We now know that our tax structure needs to be overhauled, and we have many suggestions on the shelves. We have not yet faced up to the impact of losing our state's monopoly on gaming. We have not yet faced up to how services and Internet sales are an increasingly large and untaxed portion of the economy, relative to brick-and-mortar stores. We know we should have broader-based taxes with low rates.

This restructuring is a difficult task for a part-time legislature to accomplish in a very limited time. We both hope that Governor

Brian Sandoval will lead us to do what we all know needs doing, for the long-run good of the state of Nevada.

7. Can We Find a Way Forward? (2011)[10]

Nevada's current economic situation is like that of the Donner Party, a friend said. Our food is gone and snow is still falling. Some of us will make a break for it, but those of us left behind must choose between foraging for more food or eating our young.

This is a critical moment for Nevada. Do we watch helplessly as we spiral downward, or step up and invest in those things that will keep Nevada a state worth living in?

Most of those investments will be private, and we must do more than just hope our no-tax climate will magically attract firms willing to hire Nevadans. If that worked, we would already have the most diversified economy in the country.

However, some of the essential investments, such as education, are public. Gutting public infrastructure will not make Nevada a better place to live, nor a better place to start a firm. Many proposed cuts are penny-wise but pound-foolish, and we risk damaging our state for decades.

As we act, we should acknowledge the public sector needs to do some things better, and that its critics have legitimate concerns mixed in with their misinformation. Our politicians need to seek a compromise that finds revenues to maintain essential state services and improve public education, but that also implements reforms that prevent taxes from increasing in the future.

To begin with, we need to broaden our tax base. Relying only on sales of goods and gaming for our taxes is like Mississippi relying only on sales of cotton. Times have changed.

A recent study by two UNR professors, Sonja Pippin and Mehmet Tosun, shows that a tax reform that extends the sales tax to many services could raise enough revenue to fill the entire budget gap. Even the Nevada Policy Research Institute supports a broader tax base through a tax on services, if it is accompanied by a reduction in overall rates, which we can do once the economy stabilizes.

We could forage for other sources of revenue, too. We could tighten up on some other sales tax exemptions, such as those for soft drinks and many prepared foods, and we could eliminate many of the deductions that the mining industry takes from its net proceeds tax. We could either extend the current modified business tax or replace it with a more balanced business tax.

Governor Brian Sandoval doesn't want to raise taxes in a recession, although the alternative of sacrificing higher education and other state services would be even worse for the economy and our potential to attract new businesses.

The governor has proposed borrowing against the state's insurance premium tax, a plan that legislative Democrats argue is unwise. It would borrow from already-committed revenue and thus hurt our credit rating, raising our cost of borrowing. It would be like buying groceries on a check loan that you repay with next month's grocery money.

Yet consider this alternative: If the legislature passes a tax on services but delays it for a couple of years, this would give us time to figure out how to best collect it, and we would avoid raising taxes during the depths of Nevada's depression. If we borrow against this future revenue to fill the current gap, we are just smoothing out when we spend it. We would not have to repay from monies we won't have, and we would not risk our credit rating.

So that this does not lead to unnecessary future expenditures once the economy recovers, Nevada has a law that limits long-run growth of general fund expenditures to population growth plus inflation, relative to a 1979 base. Although we shouldn't increase expenditures just because we have the revenue, we should build up a significant rainy-day fund for the next time. We might even use that rainy-day fund for seed money loans to attract employers to Nevada.

Once debts are repaid and a rainy-day fund is on track, then we should reduce rates on existing taxes to a level sustaining a stable state government, one that grows only as fast as the economy over the long run, and that provides the minimum of what Nevada needs.

Should some of the budget gap be addressed with spending cuts? Yes, but not with arbitrary across-the-board cuts that are imposed regardless of value. We should demand specific proposals for cuts, for cases where the value produced for the state is not worth the cost, and improve the incentives of state employees and managers to report spending that is not in Nevada's best interest.

Next, we need reforms to slow the growth of future state spending, and to address any misuses. If some state or local employees have been promised future benefits far in excess of what they contribute, we should fix this. If state work rules allow some county employees to make far more than intended, we should fix this. We can consider transitioning more employees to a defined-contribution plan, and reexamine some of our collective bargaining rules. But we should also acknowledge that most employees have merited their benefits, and we should not lightly break commitments to those who have contributed in good faith.

State pay can also be addressed. Most state employees are willing to accept the governor's proposed 5 percent pay cut, if it allows us to keep doing our jobs. Once the economy recovers, this pay can be restored. Beyond that, however, future pay increases should not be across the board for all state employees alike. Instead, pay increases should be linked to market conditions for similar employees in other states, or in the private sector. And where performance can be reasonably measured and evaluated, merit pay increases should be preferred to automatic cost-of-living adjustments and longevity pay.

Let's stop putting ideology over the needs of the state, and let's quit punting our problems to the next legislature. Let's combine reforming and stabilizing the tax base with realistic cuts and reforms that prevent future tax increases when the bill for our short-term thinking comes due. When rescue finally comes, let's make sure we are not surrounded by large piles of small bones.

Notes

1. J.J. Lew, "The Easy Cuts Are Behind Us," *New York Times,* February 5, 2011.

2. See J. Ralston, *The Anointed One: An Inside Look at Nevada Politics* (Las Vegas, NV: Huntington Press, 2000).

3. Originally published as E. Parker, "State Must Be Smarter, or Start Over," *Las Vegas Sun,* December 27, 2009.

4. Originally published as E. Parker, "Falling State Budgets Are a Drag on the Economy," *Nevada Appeal,* October 17, 2010.

5. Originally published as E. Parker, "To Fix Nevada, We've Got to Do the Hard Work Together," *Reno Gazette Journal,* November 10, 2010.

6. Originally published as E. Parker, "State and Local Fiscal Crises, the Depression and Now," *Reno Gazette Journal,* June 16, 2010.

7. Originally published as E. Parker, "Private Sector Needs Vital Public Sector to Thrive," *Nevada Appeal,* December 5, 2010.

8. Originally published as E. Parker and W. Raggio, "Changing How We Think about the Budget," *Las Vegas Sun,* January 23, 2011. The late Senator Raggio represented Washoe County for many years, and was the leader of the Republicans in the state senate. This article was published simultaneously in the *Reno Gazette Journal.*

9. Governor Gibbons established the Nevada Spending and Government Efficiency Commission in 2008 as a nonpartisan group of professionals who volunteered their time to seek ways for Nevada government to save money, work more effectively, and perform more efficiently. The commission produced six reports and more than forty recommendations.

10. Originally published as E. Parker, "Can We Find A Way Forward?," *Las Vegas Sun,* February 27, 2011.

CHAPTER 3

Cutting State Spending

I don't want to abolish government. I simply want to reduce it to the size where I can drag it into the bathroom and drown it in the bathtub.

— GROVER NORQUIST[1]

Introduction

By most reasonable measures, Nevada has a relatively small government. In 2015 public employment—federal, state, and local— accounted for only 12 percent of total employment in Nevada, but 16 percent nationwide. In this measure, as in many others, Nevada ranked forty-ninth out of fifty states. However, less than a quarter of this public employment is for the Nevada state government itself; most public services are provided by local government at the city and county levels, and apart from military bases Nevada has relatively few federal employees.

As a share of the state's economy, Nevada's state budget is also one of the smallest in the nation, even though small state economies tend to have relatively larger governments. In the 2013–15 biennium total general fund revenue totaled $6.4 billion, or $3.2 billion per year, which worked out to about 2.4 percent of GSP. Of course, the state also receives federal funds equivalent to roughly 2.2 percent of the economy, and another 2.1 percent from dedicated funds such as the highway construction fund financed by gasoline taxes. Including these additional funds raises the size of government, but does not change Nevada's ranking relative to other states.

When property values began to decline after 2006, people began putting off their home purchases, and stopped buying household goods to put in them. Housing starts plummeted, and construction workers began to lose their jobs. As the previous chapter showed, the Great Recession led to a dramatic decline in sales tax revenues and exacerbated already-declining gaming revenues.

The federal government regularly issues Treasury bonds to finance expenditures when tax revenues decline. In contrast, state and local governments lack the ability to easily borrow for general fund expenditures, and are often constitutionally constrained from doing so. When revenues decline, states sometimes borrow from their other accounts until those revenues recover; if they are wise they also have a healthy rainy-day fund to stabilize expenditures. If the recovery takes too long, however, those other sources run dry and the state is forced to either raise revenues or cut expenditures. When Nevada finally came to this decision point, the debates were fierce.

Some saw the crisis as too good to waste, and wanted to use the opportunity to force a reduction in the size of state government. Those with this perspective tend to think public spending is generally wasteful, and those activities would be better shifted to the private sector or eliminated entirely. Others saw this as a need for shared sacrifice, and were offended by the possibility that the private sector might suffer while the public sector prospered.

A common storyline concerned a family gathered around the kitchen table after Dad loses his job. The family had to make difficult choices, it was argued, and could not continue on as before. Of course, nobody meant to imply that the family should take their kids out of school and live on the street, or that Dad should not look for a new source of income.

In economic terms, the alternative argument can be put into either microeconomic or macroeconomic terms. The microeconomic argument focuses on what economists call "public goods," meaning things of value to society that markets cannot easily profit from producing. The macroeconomic arguments focuses on the fact that one person's spending is another person's income.

The big policy choices, however, are mostly for nation-states that have control over their own fiscal and monetary policies and that have the credit rating to borrow from private capital markets. Although Nevada had some ability to borrow for long-term investments, capital expenditures, or other limited purposes by using such things as revenue anticipation bonds, mostly the state had to choose between finding new revenues to replace the sources that were drying up or cutting budgeted expenditures. With such a small state government in the first place, this led to very difficult choices.

This chapter contains three treasurer's vignettes, plus seven columns published between 2008 and 2011 on the choices facing the state. One of these columns was written with Professor Stephen Miller, then chair of the Department of Economics at the University of Las Vegas (UNLV). Another was written with Professor Tom Harris, the director of the Center for Economic Development. All of these columns concern the impact that cutting state spending has on the rest of the state's economy.

>> Treasurer's Vignette: Down for the Count

Between 2007 and 2011 the biennial legislature met annually. The legislators would head into the building with dread, not knowing how to balance a budget with volatile and often dribblingly low state revenues and extremely long unemployment and welfare lines.

There was no appetite to raise revenues and so they badgered legislative staff and the governor's budget office to find money where none existed. They sought to use federal stabilization funds to backfill holes in the education budget. Accounts were scrubbed and money was shuffled between capital and operating accounts. Employees were furloughed and lines got longer and in-boxes filled up. Hiring froze and budgets were shorn.

And, of course, calls were made. It was late one session that I received a call from legislative staff informing me that they needed $15 million.

In truth, all the money in the state treasury should be accounted for. That is to say, if you take all the state's expenses and all the state's revenues they should match. That is what is meant by a "balanced budget." So I could not simply pull out the state checkbook. If there is a surplus it means more came in than was forecast, and we were nowhere near that scenario.

Early on I had been able to identify funds because of unnoticed accounts and hardworking staff, but we had also used up most of the state's creative juices. However, the request was serious, if not desperate, and so my staff and I huddled and searched for ways to find money.

Looking at extra interest earnings in the bond fund and ensuring that businesses who had customers in Nevada turned over their unclaimed property, we were able to say that over the course of the next two years we could come up with an additional $5 million a year. That was it.

But it wasn't. The morning after the end of session, I woke up to a message on my cell phone from a legislative staffer. "We put you down for twenty," it said. In a panic I called my staff. Had someone changed what we had said? Was there some modification I wasn't aware of?

But my staff were as shocked as I. Calling around to members of a legislature that has ended means leaving messages and getting no replies.

For the better part of a day my staff and I were on the phone trying to get hold of someone, and when we finally did we were told, "The session is over, closed, done." The budget had been submitted. There was no going back.

"But we do not have $20 million," we cried.

They wouldn't hear it, couldn't hear it. Because when all was said and done they prayed for manna from heaven; when it didn't come, they dropped to their knees, bowed their heads and whispered, "Sine die, sine die."

1. Nevada's Problem Isn't Spending (2008)[2]

When the Nevada legislature meets next month, some believe its objective should be to dramatically reduce state spending. Governor Jim Gibbons says we have a spending problem in this state, not a revenue problem, and his opinion is shared by more than a few others.

Any government is too much for some people, but we can get some perspective on this issue by comparing Nevada's government to those of other states.

According to the most recent version of the Census Bureau's *Statistical Abstract of the United States,* only 5.5 percent of Nevadans work for the state or local governments, the lowest share in the fifty states by far.[3] Only a fourth of these are state employees; the rest work for local governments. Almost half of the total are employed in K–12 education, and 10 percent in higher education. The rest work in local police and fire protection, corrections, parks, highways, and so on.

The shares of the population working in K–12 and in higher education are also the lowest in the country; those low shares are the primary reasons why the total number of government employees in Nevada is so low.

Nevada also spends relatively less per person on government, even though both our average income and our cost of living are about 10 percent higher than the national average. As a share of total state income, Nevada's state government spending is the lowest in the nation.

Adding in spending by local governments, Nevada ranks forty-eighth in government spending as a share of income. This is especially surprising because smaller states tend to spend relatively more because of diseconomies of scale.

The Tax Foundation reports that Nevada has the next-to-lowest tax burden in the nation, just slightly above Alaska. That ranking is roughly where we have been since the 1970s.

We also received less federal aid than all but one other state, as either a share of income or per capita. Alaska received the most per capita and spent the most, except for Wyoming. Alaska also derives significant tax revenues from the production of petroleum, whereas Nevada's government derives very little from mining.

Even though our overall tax burden is low, because we don't have a state income tax, either personal or corporate, we have to collect it from somewhere. We collect a larger share of state and local revenue from property and sales taxes, and our state collects about twice as much, as a share of the budget, in license fees. The rest, of course, comes from taxes on gaming.

This tax structure also results in a pretty regressive system, in which poorer Nevadans pay relatively more tax. According to a recent census estimate, a family of four in Los Angeles would pay almost 10 percent of its household income in state and local taxes, regardless of whether it made $25,000 per year or $150,000 per year.

In Las Vegas, by contrast, the poor household would pay the same 10 percent in taxes, but the better-off family would pay only 4 percent in state and local taxes. In other words, a family with six times as much income would pay only 2.4 times as much in tax. In only four other states—Florida, Missouri, Wyoming, and Alaska—do the wealthier pay a lower share of their incomes to their state and local governments.

A popular report from the Las Vegas Metro Chamber of Commerce suggests that Nevada's government employees are overpaid, but that report compares apples to oranges—there are few keno runners in government, and few professors in casinos—and the *Statistical Abstract* suggests other conclusions.

Though local governments seem to pay more, Nevada's state employees earn almost exactly the national average, even though our cost of living is higher. At UNR the average employee is paid only slightly better than at comparable universities, but not enough to make up for the higher cost of living.

Nevada's two universities are striving to improve the quality of the education we offer our students, and trying to keep more of our best students in Nevada. Unlike most other states, Nevada has no private universities, so this is an important responsibility.

As my colleague Stephen Miller, chairman of UNLV's Department of Economics, has pointed out, when our best high school graduates think they can get a better education elsewhere, they go out of state and rarely come back. This affects our state's future economic growth as well as its future tax revenues. We can't get those talented students to stay in state if we can't afford to hire and keep smart professors from out of state.

We have some capable students studying at our two universities, but Nevada is last in the percentage of its population graduating from high school and last in the number of students who attend college, and only three states—West Virginia, Arkansas, and Kentucky—have a smaller portion of the population with college degrees.

Although inadequate state funding is not the only reason for poor educational attainment, it does not help, and dramatic cuts in what funding we do get are likely to leave us at the bottom. The social return on investment in higher education is significantly higher than the cost. Unless we can better educate our workforce, we are simply not going to be able to compete.

As an economist, I have no particular love of taxes, and there are usually ways any state organization could better manage the taxpayers' dollars. But there are also many things the private sector cannot efficiently provide. Like national defense, affordable and available public education is one of these. Too little government can be just as bad for economic growth as too much.

I don't really want a big state government, but we shouldn't make the smallest state government in the country even smaller. Further significant budget cuts will severely damage our state's educational system and its economy.

We should not make our problems even worse—not if we want Nevada to remain a desirable place to live.

2. How Much More State Government Can Be Cut? (2009)[4]

Two weeks ago I contributed a column to the *Las Vegas Sun* regarding the relative size of Nevada's state government. Former state senator Bob Beers responded in a column that was published last Sunday in the *Las Vegas Review-Journal*.[5] I want to thank Mr. Beers for his response, even if he mistakenly thinks I was wrong or reporting selectively.

I insist, emphatically, that I was telling it like it is. There is a lot of misleading information out there about the size of government in Nevada and the state's tax system, and I appreciate the chance to educate a wider audience than I have in my economics classes at UNR.

Mr. Beers says I did not give details on my sources, but newspapers appreciate brevity. Had he asked me, I would have gladly shared my sources and calculations, and, like any professor, I appreciate people checking my facts. I am easy to find online for anyone with access to a search engine, especially if you spell my name correctly, and I have made the data available on my website.[6]

Mr. Beers reports that state revenue was higher than the number I reported for expenditures. Nevadans might remember that we were near the peak of the housing bubble a few years ago, and revenues were unusually high. Rather than saving the surplus for a rainy day, Governor Kenny Guinn and the legislature chose to give many of us a pretty significant tax rebate. So I said I was reporting expenditures, which were more representative of the actual state budget than revenues.

Additionally, Mr. Beers reports that the data he found did not exactly match what I reported. In the month between when I downloaded the data and my column was published, it seems a new edition of the *Statistical Abstract* came out.

I have checked these new data, and include them, with updated calculations, on my website. Nothing really changed. As in prior years, Nevada still ranked fiftieth in the nation in the relative number of state employees, total state and local government employees, and employees in higher education, as well as forty-ninth in the nation in employees in K–12 education.

Skeptical readers might think these outcomes depend on which years we choose, since budgets can vary from year to year, so let us compare five-year averages instead.

For 1977–81 and 2003–7, years I chose for no other reason than because they are the start and the end of the data I have been able to collect so far, the results are surprising.

As a share of Nevada's total output, on every measure I have collected—state and local output, total state expenditures, general fund revenues and expenditures, and even tax burden—Nevada's government became smaller.

Even if we adjust only for population growth and changes in the consumer price index, and not rising real incomes as we should, Nevada's general fund expenditures fell over time. Real general fund revenues per capita were a little higher, but as I said above, revenues were unusually high during the housing bubble.

Although Mr. Beers admitted I might be right about the relative number of employees in state government and the higher education system, he argues that we are overpaid. He reports that government employees make significantly more in Nevada than the national average, but the data he cites—Table 448, column M—include earnings only of local government employees, which are three quarters of the total.

I think that is relevant for county commissions and city councils, but not for the legislature. For the quarter of employees working for the state, average earnings are equal to the national average even though Nevada's cost of living is higher than average.

Regarding how our state and university benefits compare with those of other states, I don't yet have a good quantitative set of cross-state data on this, but I will keep looking. What I have found so far suggests state employee benefits are neither better nor worse than in other states.

If Mr. Beers has the data I seek, I would appreciate his sharing them with me. We compete in a national marketplace, and our benefits are reasonably competitive but not more than that. We should not compare our benefits against those offered by casinos, but against those in other states and other universities.

As I recall, on his own original Web posting Mr. Beers said that I think we should "further expand government" (as well as a few other things I don't need to repeat that seem to push the bounds of professional dialogue). I don't know how he reads that in what I wrote. I certainly doubt that my former economics students—there must be several thousand working in Nevada by now—would say that I advocate big government; rather, I am quite critical of its inefficiencies.

Instead, I wrote that we should not make the smallest state government in the country even smaller because it would damage the future of the universities and the state. These are not equivalent statements.

I know this will be a difficult year for the legislature and the state, and hardship cannot be avoided. You would be surprised how many faculty members at my university supported forgoing our cost-of-living increase in July, but the legislators decided that they could not do that. My university has already cut roughly 10 percent from its budget, and valued programs and employees have been axed, but the numbers the governor has asked for in the next budget are simply catastrophic.

A cut of 20 percent, 30 percent, or more is not shared hardship; it is the size of the Great Depression. It only makes sense if you truly think that the state should not fund higher education, or much else for that matter.

Finally, it was not my intent to offend any Nevadans who earned their degrees online or at small private colleges when I wrote that Nevada has only two universities. I certainly support the desire of anyone to improve himself or herself through education, but I also assume anyone who has graduated from either UNR or UNLV knows that a university is not comparable with these other institutions. The fact that Mr. Beers suggests they are equivalent causes me some concern. Is that his objective for our state universities?

>> Treasurer's Vignette: If the Tree Falls

One November, before the legislative session began, we anxiously went before the credit rating agencies with a bond issuance.

Moody's, Fitch, and Standard & Poor had been downgrading states with gusto, but certain projects needed capital so we pulled together as many positive facts as we could and sat down for interviews, one after another. They went surprisingly well. Moody's threatened us with the need for a more extensive review, but backed down when we reminded them that its own affiliate, Moody's Analytics, had gone before the state's Economic Forum and given a rosy picture of Nevada's future. Our rating stood, AA+, and we were happy.

But then, early in the legislative session, Moody's called, asking for the state's budget. "We're in the middle of a legislative session," we told them. "We won't have a budget until June, but the law requires a balanced budget and that's what you'll get. Besides, what's the concern? We're not issuing any bonds right now."

But Moody's kept calling back. They asked for more and more information until they sought a formal call. My staff and I gathered in my office to hear the bad news: we had been downgraded to AA.

I was furious and told Moody's so. We weren't the cause of this financial crisis and Nevada was doing a pretty darn good job. In fact, if we were pointing fingers, then Moody's should remember its own role in giving sound ratings to junk bonds in return for fat fees. We didn't need a rating, and Nevada wasn't issuing. We hadn't sought this review. Moody's was just trying to rebuild its reputation by downgrading the little guys. It was an embarrassment.

I ended the call when they were midsentence. We sat.

"I don't think people hang up on Moody's," someone said.

"Probably not," I replied.

But once staff left my office, my bravado left me and I burst into tears. I called my mentor, Frankie Sue Del Papa.

"We were downgraded," I sobbed. "We've worked and worked to keep our rating. We'll never get it back. It's just awful!"

"Oh, hon," she replied. "No one even knows what you're talking about. Don't worry, it'll be fine."

She was right. The news came and went and no one cared. Not the legislature, not the governor, not the press.

3. With Override of Veto, a Sigh of Relief (2009)[7]

Recently the state budget was finally passed over Governor Jim Gibbons's veto. We should all breathe a sigh of relief. The governor said that increasing taxes is a bad idea, but cutting state expenditures to the extent he proposed, especially in higher education, was an even worse choice.

It is indisputable that Nevada's general fund has long been the smallest in the nation, relative to the size of our economy, and only half the national average. This share has been on a downward trend for decades.

Because our tax base is heavily dependent on merchandise sales and casino revenue, two sectors that have been disproportionately affected by this recession, our state's general fund revenue has fallen from about 3 percent of state GDP to about 2 percent. Our revenues thus declined by a third, the most of any state. But as a share of our GDP this was only a drop of 1 percent, and other states have bigger relative budget gaps. It is also important to understand that our state revenues declined much, much more than our economy as a whole.

Should we have increased taxes? Most taxes are inefficient, economists argue, because they have incentive effects that discourage people from potentially productive activities. However, this is more than offset when the government is able to provide socially valuable goods that the private sector can't provide in sufficient amounts. Public education is one of those goods.

Taxes are also less inefficient if they are broadly applied and rates are not too high. Although the taxes our legislature imposed are only second-best solutions, they are not likely to be very burdensome to the economy, given our already-low overall rate of taxation.

A tax increase reduces disposable income, and thus reduces private spending. The governor is right that this is a bad idea in a recession. But cutting government spending is an even worse idea in a recession, unless you believe the state provides absolutely nothing of value.

You lose the same amount of private spending as with a tax increase, plus you lose what government bought or provided in the first place. Consider that public employees and private contractors are Nevadans, too, and they are working for you.

Most people don't realize that state and local governments, in aggregate, spend more on consumption and investment than the federal government; this was even more true during the Great Depression. At a time when the federal government is trying to stimulate the economy, the states are unintentionally making it worse because they are generally constrained to balance their budgets. Economist and *New York Times* columnist Paul Krugman has called this problem "fifty Herbert Hoovers."

Unemployment in Nevada, which usually hovers at or below the national average, has risen dramatically in the past two years to 10.6 percent of the labor force in April, compared to a national rate of 8.9 percent that same month (now 9.4 percent for May, which is not as bad as many expected).

Personal income in Nevada, which grew by 5.5 percent in 2007 and 3.1 percent in 2008, was projected by the Economic Forum in December to rise by 1 percent in 2009. That was probably too optimistic, but I have seen no sane economist project average income declines of more than 5 percent in 2009, and incomes should improve in 2010.

Of course, this is only the average, and although many are doing okay (other than watching their 401[k]s wither away and their homes go underwater), others are disproportionately hurt. Much of the construction sector, for example, has seen its business completely dry up.

Are state budgets, and state employees, sharing this pain? The governor asked state workers to take a 6 percent pay cut, which the legislature reduced to 4 percent with an unpaid furlough of one day per month for most workers. The governor's budget called for a cut of a third in the total higher education operating budget, which the legislature reduced to about 11 percent.

Although we are not hurting as much as the construction or tourist sectors, higher education is facing cuts that are certainly more than the average Nevadan is expected to bear.

Some think higher education spending is out of control. In Nevada it has only kept pace with the rest of the economy. Not coincidentally, our state's proportion of the population with a college education has remained stagnant, while in other states it has increased significantly.

The total operating budget for NSHE, including the state's general fund contribution and the tuition and fees paid by students, was about 0.6 percent of our GDP in 1985, the year I entered graduate school. After having peaked at about 0.7 percent in 2003, it was back down to the same 0.6 percent ratio this past fiscal year. It will be lower next year as a result of these cuts.

Are the cuts real? Thankfully, our universities and community colleges have been preparing for this for a year, and we are working to make our institutions more efficient. Over the past year these institutions have closed centers, increased teaching loads, encouraged early retirements, eliminated many valuable student services, and terminated hundreds of productive people.

Those who have left are not being replaced. Meanwhile, most institutions have more students to teach than before, not fewer, which is very different from the experience of the private sector in a downturn.

We are now making more cuts. But it could have been so much worse had the executive budget been approved. We would be closing whole colleges, not just programs, and turning away students by the hundreds.

But it is not so much about cuts, or how many jobs have been saved, as it is about Nevada's future. Many of us have chosen this profession over usually-more-lucrative private-sector jobs because we believe in the value of a public education. At UNR and UNLV we are trying as hard as we can to create universities that Nevada can be proud of, universities that will attract our best high school students and keep them in our state after they graduate.

This matters because education is very important to our economy. One study cited recently in the *Wall Street Journal* noted that our country lags behind a number of other countries in education, and estimated that our country's educational gap costs us as much as $2.3 trillion per year, about 16 percent of our GDP. Nevada has the biggest educational gap in the country, and it makes it hard for us to attract and keep new business in the state.

Many—though certainly not all—of those who argue that we should have cut spending more than 11 percent do so because they oppose public education and public services on principle, and think this was a good opportunity to make our government even smaller. For the rest of us, we should be grateful the legislature was able to override the governor's veto.

4. Spending Cuts Won't Solve Nevada's Ills (2010)[8]

The governor says that, like any family, we all must live within our means. How can you live within your means if your means are in free fall? A breadwinner who has lost his or her job will cut frills, but what parent would tell their kids, "Hey, we can't afford to feed you anymore"? You would use your savings until you could find a new job, or borrow what you could, and you would look for new sources of income.

Education is not a frill for Nevada. We have the smallest state government in the country, the lowest number of public employees, among the lowest high school graduation rates, and the fewest kids in the country who go on to earn a two- or four-year degree.

Gaming has been falling as a share of our economy for decades. Our sales taxes focus on durable goods that people aren't buying, and we exempt many goods and most services. Our mining industry pays less than 2 percent of its proceeds for what it removes, which is much less than it would pay in any other state. We are one of the few states in the country without a corporate income tax, but we are still rated as a poor place for business because we lack an educated workforce.

Raising taxes in a deep recession is a bad idea, but cutting spending is an even worse idea. Recent estimates have calculated that tax increases to cover the projected deficit would cost the state almost $500 million in GDP, but spending cuts would cost the state more than $1 billion. This would result in another eight thousand unemployed in the private sector, once you take everything into account, on top of those jobs lost in the public sector.

Our general fund has already dropped to about 2.2 percent of our state GDP, and we are now told to cut it even more, to fill a revenue shortfall that works out to about $13 per person, per month. Taxes to fill this hole would not really be a burden on the economy, and borrowing to fill it would not be a burden on the future.

Nevada has been hardest hit in this depression because our state economy was much more dependent on gaming and construction than any other state's, and these sectors suffered most. But total personal income in Nevada fell only 6 percent from peak to trough, and actually rose slightly in the second and third quarters. State revenues have fallen much, much more than that, because our tax revenues are even less diversified than our economy.

We need to get through this biennium without damage to education that will be hard to undo. We should cut where it won't do too much harm, borrow what we can, and tax if we must. We must then come up with the political will to create a more stable tax base once this recession ends, with low rates but a broad base, so we don't always remain at the bottom of every measure.

5. Nevada's Fiscal Structure, with Stephen Miller (2010)[9]

Nevada continues to face one of the most difficult fiscal situations of any state in the country, but we are not alone. According to the Center on Budget and Policy Priorities, the recession created budget gaps in most states. In addressing these gaps, forty-two states cut spending while thirty-three increased taxes and other revenue. The American Recovery and Reinvestment Act also provided important funding that assisted states in closing about 33 percent of their gaps.

Nevada, however, fell into the deepest hole. From the end of 2007 through the middle of 2009, Nevada's personal income declined by 6 percent, twice as much as in any other state. Over the same period, Nevada's revenue declined by more than 12 percent, twice the national average decline for state and local government tax collections.

Our most recent legislative session balanced the budget with cuts in program spending, salary saving through furloughs, and temporary increases in taxes. The recent special session cut programs even more. While the American Recovery and Reinvestment

Act prevented even more drastic expenditure cuts or tax increases, we will not likely see additional relief from the federal government going forward. Unless the Nevada economy recovers more quickly than most analysts anticipate, the legislature will face an even more difficult task in balancing the next biennium's budget than it faced during the last session.

Nevada's biennial general fund budget is roughly $7 billion, which works out to about 2.5 percent of total state output, or a little more than $100 per person per month. Current estimates report a $3 billion hole, all things included; this is a huge portion of the total budget but a small portion of our overall economy.

Why are tax revenues declining so much more in Nevada than elsewhere, and can we expect them to ever recover? Our state depends heavily on gaming taxes, and related taxes on hotels and restaurants, because visitors pay a large share. Gaming in Nevada was once a profitable monopoly, but that monopoly is gone and these revenues have been declining as a share of our economy for decades.

We also depend heavily on the sales tax. For a time, the boom in housing construction and the added money spent on furnishings for new houses covered the relative decline in gaming receipts. The Great Recession hurt these revenues disproportionately, but few people expect they will bounce back to former levels. Tax revenue lagged behind economic activity because activity shifted from taxed to nontaxed areas.

We no longer can continue to plug budget holes with quick fixes that do not address our longer-term problems. Instead, we must make long-needed modifications in the existing tax structure that will provide a better revenue stream going forward. We could accomplish this with new taxes, such as personal or corporate income taxes, but a less dramatic approach would instead broaden the bases for existing taxes.

With Nevada's propensity to tax narrow parts of the economy, recent structural changes in its economy mean that we no longer collect the revenue to maintain necessary state services. This unstable structure demands immediate attention.

This inherent problem means the legislature revisits the revenue issue on a regular basis, tinkers with existing taxes, and adds new wrinkles. Nevertheless, several prior tax-funded studies commissioned by the legislature yielded the same forgettable result. We know we need change, but legislators fear the political consequences of seeming to favor "big government," even though Nevada runs the smallest state general fund in the country, as a share of our economy, and even though Nevada successfully constrained the growth of the total general fund expenditure for decades to no more than population growth plus inflation.

We need serious consideration of several changes in tax structure. Here are three examples:

First, the explosion of Internet purchases has shifted a high percentage of transactions from those that yield sales tax revenue to those that do not, and has created a big hole in this revenue source. Nevada and twenty-two other states have already passed legislation to conform to the Streamlined Sale and Use Tax Agreement, a pact to simplify, standardize, and modernize sales tax collections to prevent a federal prohibition on Internet taxes. This needs to be implemented and expanded so we can better collect taxes on this rapidly growing share of our sales.

Second, consumption spending nationwide has shifted from goods to services over recent years, but the latter is largely exempt from the sales tax. The sales tax levy should fall equally on both goods and services, and our tax structure should reflect the overall economy. Extending the sales tax to services, however, requires careful consideration of what constitutes final, rather than intermediate, transactions. Moreover, when considering this extension, we should also reconsider the existing exemptions to the sales tax to make sure they still make sense.

Third, the modified business tax collects revenue from wages and salaries. More broadly, taxing wages and salaries comprises a part of the value added by firms. Replacing this tax with a value-added tax on firms would expand the base to include nonwage and salary income, such as rent, interest, and profit.

The economy changes as production and consumption patterns adjust to changes in technology, competition, consumer preferences, and demographics. A well-designed tax system needs to adjust in concert with the changing economy.

>> Treasurer's Vignette: Putting It on Ice

One summer the refrigerator in my house stops working, without warning, complaint, or even a cough. It's the end of July and the inside of the fridge is dark, wet, and sour.

I head to Sears to buy a new one, but they are so expensive! The salesman laughs and says, "Too bad your fridge didn't wait a few weeks. We have a big sale coming up at the end of next month."

I look at him. "How big of a sale?"

"Hmm," he says. "Pretty big, with 50 percent off on a lot of these babies."

I would have to wait twenty-four days, so I think about this. I think about milk. I think about butter. I think about eggs. I think I don't actually need a refrigerator: I just need to keep things cold for twenty-four days. I just need ice.

"Thanks," I say. "See you in twenty-four days."

I go to the supermarket and buy six large blocks of ice. I go home and put two in the freezer and four in the fridge set on baking pans, leaving very little room for things like milk and butter and eggs. I remove the ice cube tray from the freezer to make room for more food, and shut the door. I think, twenty-four days; this will have to do.

When John (my first husband) comes home, he is not impressed. This will never work, he tells me, but I am not listening.

"I need a drink," he says. He grabs a glass, opens the freezer, and shouts, "We have all this ice and no ice cubes!!!"

"Only twenty-four days," I say.

We finally get our new refrigerator, and a few months later, as we are all in yet another special session, I am sitting in my office thinking about refrigeration.

This is how my mind works. It is December, I think. The budget is short. The budget is short because the law requires us to keep 5 percent of the budget in reserve. We don't have 5 percent. The legislature needs time to raise revenues and decrease expenses to create a balanced budget. Then I think, the legislature needs to get to regular session, and that is only two months away.

And I realize we don't actually need 5 percent in cash: we just need access to it for the budget. We will never actually spend it. At home, I think, I brought in ice for twenty-four days. If I had a big emergency at home, I would use a line of credit. I need to put the budget on ice, even if it meant we had no ice cubes.

I call up my staff, and after a lot of arguing they found a way to arrange a line of credit for the state, and that bridged the legislature from the December 2008 special session through the end of the regular session in 2009.

We put the budget shortfall on ice, and we never touched the money.

6. Taxes and State Economies, with Tom Harris (2011)[10]

Since Nevada has a very small government, and was the fastest-growing state for decades, did the former cause the latter?

Actually, it's not likely. Examine the statistics comparing the real growth of a state's GDP to the share of GDP provided by state and local governments for all states over the past forty-five years, and you will find no correlation. States with relatively smaller governments have not tended to grow any faster than other states.

There is, however, a strong statistical relationship between a state's real GDP growth rate and the lagged growth rate of its state and local governments. A fall in state and local government spending in one year tends to be followed by lower economic growth in the next year.

Why is this? One way to look at it is that state and local governments provide essential public goods that cannot be adequately provided by the private sector, such as roads and education. While higher taxes often create some disincentives for private investment and growth, many of these public goods are necessary investments for the private sector to function.

For example, interstate and state highways increase productivity by making it possible for retailers such as Wal-Mart to incorporate just-in-time inventory management. Otherwise, stores would have to hold large inventories, decreasing profits while increasing consumer prices. Similarly, without good public education, the private sector lacks the educated workforce it needs.

You can also consider what economists call spending multipliers, which are particularly important in a recession. If the state spends less to fix a bridge, this means less revenue for a construction company, fewer jobs, and fewer purchases of material from other companies and subcontractors, so those other companies also have fewer jobs. Firing an elementary school teacher means less money is spent by that teacher on rent, food, and other goods.

In Nevada good estimates are that a $100 reduction in state and local spending reduces Nevada's GDP by $162, and reduces household income by $136. Firing 100 state or local employees reduces Nevada's total employment by 153 workers.

Meanwhile, an increase in taxes to fix that bridge or keep that teacher reduces the money firms can pay to their workers or to their stockholders, and taxpayers have less to spend on purchases in restaurants, furniture stores, and the like. Increasing state and local taxes by $100, however, reduces Nevada's GDP by much less than $100, though it depends on the type of tax.

In short, the multipliers for state and local government spending cuts are larger than the multipliers for tax increases. Economists teach this to every first-year student in macroeconomics, and estimates from real data consistently find it to be true.

7. Is Nevada's Public Sector Too Big? (2011)[11]

As we head into a very difficult budget discussion, some Nevadans continue to disagree about whether we have a spending problem or a revenue problem. Before we decide whether tax increases or spending cuts are best for the future of Nevada, we should first settle the question of whether Nevada's public sector is too big, once and for all.

State government spending has been growing faster than our overall state economy, some argue, and they call anybody who disagrees with them a tax-eater. We need to take their argument with a grain of salt, for several reasons.

First, state spending varies year by year, and it is easy for a state-hater to make a case by picking low starting and high ending points that do not reflect long-run trends. Second, growth rates are often high when the base is small: a penny is a bigger share of a dime than of a quarter. Third, this argument fails to consider what the money was spent on, and whether those things were necessary or beneficial. Finally, this argument usually ignores the last three rounds of budget cuts that hit the state.

Yes, it is true that budgeted general fund expenditures were a larger share (2.9 percent) of GSP in the peak of fiscal year 2008, compared to 2000 (2.1 percent), or even 1994 (2.4 percent), so expenditures grew faster than the economy. But even the 2008 peak was less than the 1979 share (3.3 percent), which is the base period used by Nevada Revised Statutes (NRS) 353.213, the law that limits general fund growth. And even then, our general fund share was still among the smallest in the nation.

Some argue that Nevada is actually average, in terms of its public spending per capita. Horrors! What they don't mention with this trick is that Nevada had, at least through 2008, a cost of living that was closer to California's than to Mississippi's, along with a higher total per capita income and wages for most blue-collar occupations that were substantially higher than average. Put this into real terms, and we were nowhere near average in the size of our public sector.

Consider public employment, the essential measure of government size. The 2011 issue of the Census Bureau's *Statistical Abstract of the United States* has data for state and local employment in 2008. Before budget cuts began, Nevada had the fewest state and local government employees in the nation, relative to population, even though other states with our population and geography tend to have relatively larger governments. We would have had to hire 8,000 workers just to be the second-smallest in the nation, and 26,000 to just be average. And that was before budgets were cut, cut again, and cut some more.

Yes, these relatively few public employees were well paid, at least on average. The *Statistical Abstract* reports that the average wage for Nevada's state employees was about 7 percent higher than the national average in 2008, while city and county employees earned 20 percent more. However, the American Chamber of Commerce Researchers Association calculates that Nevada's cost of living was about 10 percent higher than the national average, so our state employees were really paid about average.

Averages disguise variation. State corrections officers made about 30 percent more in Nevada than they would have elsewhere, while local firefighters, especially those in Las Vegas, made higher incomes than firefighters elsewhere. Salaries for K–12 teachers, however, were at the national average. And while college professors like me were well paid, we earned about the same average salary we would make at other similar universities in other states. One-size-fits-all generalizations aren't helpful, and neither are one-size-fits-all policies.

Add in furloughs, layoffs, and all the other budget cuts doled out over the past few years, and we can be confident that, when new comparable data become available, Nevada's public sector will remain among the smallest in the nation, even before we contemplate the cuts Governor Sandoval has proposed. So can we now move forward with more-meaningful arguments?

Notes

1. S. Galupo, "The Norquist Anti-Tax Pledge Is Cracking—and That's a Good Thing," *American Conservative,* November 26, 2012.

2. Originally published as E. Parker, "Comparisons Show Spending Isn't Nevada's Problem," *Las Vegas Sun,* December 21, 2008. A short version of this was published in the *Reno Gazette Journal.*

3. Census Bureau, http://www.census.gov/library/publications/time -series/statistical_abstracts.html

4. Originally published as E. Parker, "How Much More of State Government Can Be Cut?," *Las Vegas Sun,* January 4, 2009.

5. B. Beers, "Statistics and Nevada's Tax Burden," *Las Vegas Review Journal,* December 28, 2008.

6. See "Dr. Elliott Parker, Professor of Economics, Director of the University Core Curriculum," http://www.business.unr.edu/faculty/parker.

7. Originally published as E. Parker, "With Override of Veto, a Sigh of Relief," *Las Vegas Sun,* June 7, 2009. A shorter version of this column was published in the *Reno Gazette Journal* on May 31.

8. Originally published as E. Parker, "Spending Cuts Are Not the Solution to Nevada's Ills," *Nevada Appeal,* February 10, 2010.

9. Originally published as S.M. Miller and E. Parker, "Nevada's Fiscal Structure in Need of an Overhaul," *Las Vegas Sun,* April 11, 2010. Professor Miller was the chair of the Economics Department at UNLV.

10. Originally published as T. Harris and E. Parker, "What Is the Effect of Taxes on State Economies?," *Reno Gazette Journal,* January 12, 2011. Professor Harris is the director of the Center for Economic Development at UNR.

11. Originally published as E. Parker, "Is Nevada's Public Sector Too Big? Facts Don't Back It Up," *Nevada Appeal,* February 6, 2011.

CHAPTER 4

Cutting Higher Education

Higher education is confronting challenges, like the economy is, about the need for a higher number of more adequately trained, more highly educated citizenry.

— MARGARET SPELLINGS[1]

Introduction

Relative to other states, Nevada has a very small public higher education system. Unlike most other states, it has no private colleges or universities of any real size. This is the result of both supply and demand, as well as a result of Nevada's history.

On the supply side, Nevada has positioned itself as a low-tax state, and many have moved here to avoid taxes in their home states, where their children possibly have already been educated. This means tight budgets for education at all levels. On the demand side, upper-income Nevadans often send their kids to out-of-state colleges, and historically lower-income Nevadans were able to earn a decent living working in casinos without an education, and many felt no need for their children to go to college. Nevada's rapid postwar population growth meant that most educated Nevadans—Kate and me included—were educated elsewhere. Many had little interest in or support for state institutions.

Higher education budgets began to grow during the boom, and were then trimmed back during special sessions as tax revenues failed to live up to the Economic Forum's projections. For the 2009 legislative session, Governor Jim Gibbons (2007–10) proposed deep cuts to higher education, by up to half for the university's state-supported budget, in spite of growing enrollments. In a podcast, Governor Gibbons argued that Nevada was generous in supporting higher education, since it spent a larger share of the budget on it. My response was publicized by veteran political commentator Jon Ralston, and the governor ceased making that particular argument.

By the end of that legislative session, Washoe County state senator William Raggio's "sunset tax" softened the cuts somewhat. The governor vetoed the legislative budget, and then his veto was overridden. Still, the system's universities and community colleges took in a series of cuts that forced the laying off of many of their faculty and staff, and the closing down of entire departments. In a rare move, UNR fired a large number of tenured faculty. The damage was greater than that, of course, because a large number of top faculty were poached by other universities, particularly those faculty who were bringing in millions of dollars for grant-funded research.

Governor Gibbons was challenged in 2010 by Brian Sandoval, a former federal judge, and found himself in the unusual position of being an incumbent governor defeated in his own party's primary. In his first biennial session, Governor Sandoval showed himself no more willing to address the basic budget problems of the state than Governor Gibbons had been, and it was only when a court ruled against one of his proposals late in the session that he relented in allowing the sunset taxes to be continued.

By the 2013 session the crisis had eased, at least for the universities. Revenues were finally growing again, and NSHE was able to pass new funding formulas that allowed the universities to keep more of the tuition paid by out-of-state students. For the smaller and more rural colleges, however, this only led to more cuts. Even now, in 2016, we continue to repair the damage done by those cuts.

This chapter begins with the letter I wrote to Governor Gibbons responding to his podcast, mentioned above, followed by two articles written with Bruce Shively, the budget director of UNR. These were written for faculty, citizens, the board of regents, and even legislators who wanted to better understand how higher education budgets worked. I then include five columns written in defense of NSHE, including one that was written two years later as a letter to Governor Sandoval, who was proposing similar budget cuts.

1. A Letter to Governor Gibbons (2009)[2]

Dear Governor Gibbons:

I just read the text of your podcast, and I am afraid that I must say it is misleading. You said, "Nevada spends more general fund tax dollars on higher education than most other states," but this is not actually true.

A poor man spends a bigger portion of his income on food, but that does not mean that he eats more than others. Nevada's higher education system gets a larger portion of its budget from the state, but that does not mean it spends more to educate its students. As a share of state GDP, Nevada has the smallest general fund in the country. Nevada is also fiftieth in the country in higher education spending as a share of state income, fiftieth in the country in the number of higher education employees as a share of population, at the bottom in the number of students who attend college, and below the national average in higher education spending per student, even though our cost of living is relatively high and smaller states typically spend more per student than big states.

You said that higher education has the ability to raise its own revenue, but this is misleading as well. It is true that our tuition is relatively low, and this has been a long-standing policy of the state as it tries to move up from the bottom in the number of students who attend college. The regents can raise tuition, but if we tripled it next year we would not come close to filling the gap, since we would push out many of our students. Other revenues—like dormitory fees, tickets to sporting events, and so on—go to pay expenses associated with those revenues, and do not generate substantial residuals. Research grants go to fund research expenses, and if we tried to spend those funds on instructional costs the legal consequences could be severe. Your budget would not increase those other revenues, but instead would decrease them. It will cost us our most productive researchers who bring in the most outside funding, it would scare away potential donors, and it will encourage our best students to go elsewhere.

You said that you are proposing only a 36 percent cut, not a 50 percent cut, but this is also somewhat misleading. Yes, there is a 36 percent cut in the total NSHE general fund budget, but some programs within NSHE are left relatively untouched. Athletics, for example, did not have its budget changed much at all. But the cuts you proposed for the main campuses of UNR and UNLV are much, much larger than the average for the system as a whole. Relative to our total state GDP, the cuts are tiny—roughly a quarter of 1 percent—but relative to the total amount the university has to spend on instruction the cuts are simply devastating.

To survive and prosper in a knowledge economy, Nevada must better educate its citizens. Regardless of your political disagreements with our chancellor, you must see that a good university system is crucial for our future.

Sincerely,
Elliott Parker
Professor of Economics
University of Nevada, Reno

2. College Budgets for the Perplexed, with Bruce Shively (2009)[3]

The *Reno Gazette Journal* published a story last month on a rise in donations to UNR, and some readers wondered whether this could help offset the reduction in state funding that the governor has proposed. In justifying his proposed cuts to higher education, the governor explained that the university system had other revenues besides the state's general fund. Can other revenues be used to replace state funding for the university?

As a public institution, the university's budgets are public information, and these are available online.[4] However, just because this information is easy to find does not mean it is easy to understand. This is because state legislatures use the budget to control the activities of the university, to ensure that monies are spent as the state intends. In this report we will try to provide an introduction to the university's many different budgets so the answers to these questions can be better understood. In addition to defining the eight areas of university budget responsibility, we explain the differences between operating budgets and self-supporting budgets, grants and contracts, student tuition and fees, and the capital improvement budget. We hope that this explanation will help readers understand whether the university is able to use other sources of revenue to cover instructional costs. Finally, we take a look at the big picture.

Defining the Eight Areas of University Budget Responsibility

The legislature gives our university the responsibility for administering eight different budget areas. In addition to (1) the main campus operations of the university, the president administers separate budgets for (2) the University of Nevada School of Medicine (hereafter the School of Medicine); (3) intercollegiate athletics; (4) the University of Nevada Cooperative Extension (hereafter Cooperative Extension program); (5) the Nevada Agricultural Experiment Station; (6) the State Health Laboratory; (7) Business Center North; and (8) statewide programs, including the Nevada Bureau of Mines and Geology, the Seismology Lab, Extended Studies, the Nevada Small Business Development Center, and other programs providing statewide outreach. Each of these budget areas has a state-funded operations budget, and most have one or more self-supporting budgets, as we will explain below.

State agencies like the university operate on a fiscal year from July 1 to June 30, and the legislature sets the budget two years at a time based largely on its projected revenues. Although the board of regents has an oversight responsibility for the university, it does not have taxation authority and must rely on the legislature to appropriate revenues and authorize expenditures. Any unspent revenue from state-funded budgets cannot be banked for future use, but must instead be returned to the state.

Operating Budgets

For fiscal year 2009, which was set by the 2007 legislature and started on July 1, 2008, the eight operating budgets for UNR totaled approximately $279 million. As figure 4.1 shows, the state-supported operating budget for the main campus was $197 million, or 70 percent of the total. The School of Medicine accounted for

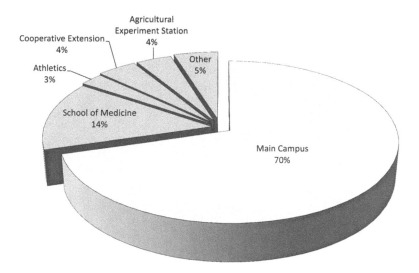

Cooperative Extension
4%

Agricultural
Experiment Station
4%

Athletics
3%

Other
5%

School of Medicine
14%

Main Campus
70%

FIGURE 4.1. State-Supported Operating Budget for the University of Nevada, Reno, Fiscal Year 2008–9. *Source:* Courtesy of the Nevada System of Higher Education annual budgets.

14 percent of the total, and all other operating budgets together accounted for 16 percent of the total. Intercollegiate athletics received $7 million in state appropriations, $2 million of which went to pay for athletic scholarships

For the main campus operating budget of $197 million, 46 percent went to pay for instruction, mostly for professor salaries; 21 percent went to pay for utilities and other costs of operation and maintenance; and 32 percent went to pay for everything else, including the salaries of administrators and their staff, student services, information technology, research administration, the university police, and scholarships. The majority of the state-appropriated operating budget is set by the legislature using a formula-driven approach. Once the total expenditure is determined, the state estimates the amount it expects the university to earn from other sources. The remaining amount necessary to fund the authorized expenditures is appropriated from the state general fund. For the main campus, these other revenue sources include student registration fees and out-of-state tuition (22 percent of the operating budget) and some investment income and

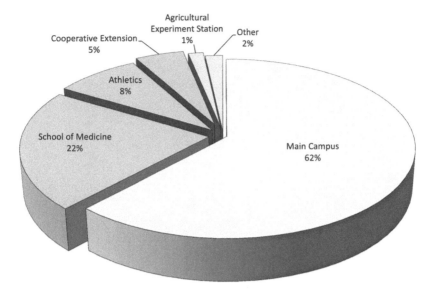

FIGURE 4.2. Self-Supporting Budget for the University of Nevada, Reno, Fiscal Year 2008–9. *Source:* Courtesy of the Nevada System of Higher Education annual budgets.

miscellaneous revenues (1 percent). Thus, the official state allocation made up 73 percent of the main campus budget in fiscal year 2009, and 79 percent of the total for the eight different operating budgets.

Self-Supporting Budgets

The second category of university revenue, the self-supporting budgets, is shown in figure 4.2. These budgets are under university administration and must be approved by the board of regents, but they do not depend on state appropriations. On the main campus, self-supporting units include the residence halls, food services, parking services, and the student health center; these units charge fees for services they provide.

For fiscal year 2009, self-supporting budgets totaled $202 million in the eight areas, or roughly two fifths of the combined budget. About a fifth of this, $35 million, was garnered through student fees, another fifth was from gifts and investment income, and almost a third was from sales and services. Intercollegiate athletics brought in $17 million through its self-supporting budget, or 70 percent of its total revenue, a share that compares rather well to that of other universities. The School of Medicine also received more revenue from its self-supporting budget than from its operating budget. Indirect facilities and administration cost recovery accounts from grants and contracts are also considered part of the self-supporting budget, as we will explain.

It is important to understand that revenues from these self-supporting budgets cannot easily be directed to support other activities. Many self-supporting units receive no state funding, and rely entirely on generated revenues to support their operations. In most cases, self-supporting activities carry minimal cash balances. Redirecting substantial funding from these accounts to offset state budget reductions would mean that several of the self-supporting activities would, very shortly, cease to be financially viable.

The residence halls and parking services both currently generate residual balances, but these funds are intended to be used for the construction and financing of important new facilities. For example, Argenta Hall and both the West Stadium and Sierra Street parking structures were constructed entirely with self-generated revenues, without any participation from the state, and current fees are servicing the debt for these projects.

The School of Medicine receives most of its revenue—roughly $45 million for the first two thirds of the current fiscal year 2009—through a separate budget for its clinical practice plan, which is organized as a 501(c)(3) corporation called Integrated Clinical Services. A large proportion of this 501(c)(3)'s revenue is then transferred into the self-supporting budget to support the salaries of those on the School of Medicine medical faculty who provide medical services to the community.

Private donations to the university are also connected to self-supporting budgets. These donations are usually made to the University of Nevada Reno Foundation, which reports to the administration and the board of regents, but some are made directly to the regents or to the Athletic Association of the University of Nevada. The university's endowments from private donations are managed in a separate budget, and then these funds are distributed when appropriate to the self-supporting budgets of different parts of the university. Private donors generally earmark their do-nations for specific purposes, and few donate to the university just to help cover operating costs. Some give to specific programs, some for specific purposes, and many give money for student scholarships. We cannot use these funds for other purposes, not without violating the trust of our donors and, perhaps, the law.

Another significant funding source for self-supporting bud-gets is dedicated student fees. One third of student registration fees is designated for a variety of special purposes, while the re-mainder is appropriated by the state. The greatest use of these nonappropriated student fees is for access-related financial aid programs. Other uses include capital construction costs for the Knowledge Center (library) and the Crowley Student Union, support for the Associated Students of the University of Nevada activities, student union operating expenses, intercollegiate ath-letics, and, unfortunately, servicing the debt for the Fire Science Academy.[5] Graduate students pay a comparable fraction, more than a third of which goes for financial aid, with some of the re-mainder going to the Graduate Student Association. Students are sometimes also charged set fees for the unique cost of specific courses, and any fees so collected must be used for the purposes designated.

Grants and Contracts

The third category of revenue, grants and contracts, is the most heavily restricted of the three. Grants and contracts are awarded competitively by organizations external to the university, most notably by the federal government through agencies such as the National Science Foundation, the National Institutes of Health, and the U.S. Department of Energy. Most grant-funded research is done in the fields of medicine, engineering, and the physical sciences, as well as in agriculture through the Nevada Agricul-tural Experiment Station. Expenditures from grant and contract funding, which table 4.1 shows are projected to total $85 million for fiscal year 2009, are restricted by the granting agencies and can be expended only for the expressed purposes specified in the grant award, on budgeted expenditures like lab equipment, gradu-ate research assistants, and wholly grant-funded research faculty.

Table 4.1. Summary of University Revenue, Fiscal Year 2009

	Fiscal 2009 Operating Budget	Fiscal 2009 Self-Supporting Budget	Fiscal 2009 Combined Budget	Projected Fiscal 2009 Grants and Contracts
Academic Programs				
Office of the Provost	4,979,030	24,949,070	29,928,100	258,000
Liberal Arts	26,385,138	1,543,687	27,928,825	2,601,031
Science	19,417,986	3,472,057	22,890,043	19,793,419*
Engineering	11,140,613	1,969,871	13,110,484	10,260,546
Division of Health Sciences	9,346,952	2,521,807	11,868,759	6,517,920
Education	9,212,390	1,933,337	11,145,727	3,801,116
Business	9,474,595	960,856	10,435,451	2,181,463
Agriculture, Biotechnology, and Natural Resources	4,313,117	790,086	5,103,203	
Journalism	1,935,582	888,830	2,824,412	5,000
Extended Studies	686,336	1,094,674	1,781,010	529,549
Academy for the Environment	585,560		585,560	324,992
Subtotal Academic Programs	97,477,299	40,124,275	137,601,574	46,273,036
Administration and Finance	50,840,628	14,009,535	64,850,163	20,000
Student Services	8,958,612	45,086,039	54,044,651	7,523,005
Info. Technology, Libraries	19,949,426	4,108,223	24,057,649	179,100
Research	3,697,653	11,411,749	15,109,402	897,427
Office of the President	3,183,119	7,667,252	10,850,371	
Development and Alumni Relations	3,987,880	2,740,760	6,728,640	
Scholarships	5,942,623		5,942,623	
Reserves	2,475,317		2,475,317	
University of Nevada, Reno (Main Campus)	196,512,557	125,147,833	321,660,390	54,892,568
School of Medicine	39,058,043	43,997,424	83,055,467	21,551,164
Intercollegiate athletics	7,054,213	16,685,759	23,739,972	
Cooperative Extension Service	11,833,480	9,759,898	21,593,378	2,092,857
Agricultural Experiment Station	10,940,073	2,973,511	13,913,584	6,038,263
Statewide programs	8,892,041	1,485,614	10,377,655	
State Health Laboratory	2,129,397	1,390,131	3,519,528	
Business Center North	2,681,831	626,061	3,307,892	
Total	279,101,635	202,066,231	481,167,866	84,574,854

Funds from grants and contracts are not available for other purposes, such as instruction, and cannot be used in any way to offset
state budget shortfalls. The fines and other legal penalties from
any misuse are prohibitive.

In addition to authorized expenditures, the university receives
an additional portion of most grants, called facilities and administration, for overhead. While the federal facilities and administration rate is usually 40 percent, many granting agencies demand
much lower rates. For fiscal year 2009, the university expects to receive about $14 million in revenue from this source, about 16 per-
cent of expenditures; it is then included in the self-supporting
budgets. This indirect cost recovery helps the university pay for
things like research administration, the maintenance of current
research facilities, and the construction of new buildings for research purposes. Some of it is also allocated by the university for
new faculty start-up costs, like equipping a laboratory, or is allocated to the colleges and departments that produce the research
to offset their administrative costs.

Student Tuition and Fees
In fiscal year 2009 the university taught roughly 13,000 undergraduates and 3,000 graduate students; these students paid roughly
$85 million in tuition and fees, not including almost $30 million
for on-campus room, board, and books. In addition to a number
of fixed mandatory fees, Nevada residents paid a registration fee
(in-state tuition, really) of almost $130 per undergraduate credit,
which rises to $145 per credit for fiscal year 2010. Graduate stu-
dents pay 50 percent more per credit, and every semester non-
residents pay an additional $6,170 each in tuition, though there
are nonresident discounts for "good neighbor" counties in California, children of alumni, and the Western Undergraduate Exchange program.

The university has a "letter of intent" agreement with the state
on how these student fees are allocated. Roughly a third is kept by
the university through designated special-purpose fees, and are
included in the self-supporting budget. The rest, including out-of-
state tuition, is subtracted from the operating budget to determine
the state's general fund allocation. In fiscal year 2009 this included

$34 million from the state portion of registration fees plus almost $12 million in out-of-state tuition and a few miscellaneous fees. Students in the School of Medicine paid 6 percent of this portion of the operating budget, and the other 94 percent came from students on the main campus.

The state uses a weighted average of enrollments for the past three years to project student enrollments forward. This projection helps the legislature to determine the formula for the university's operating budget, particularly the instructional portion; the legislature has been setting the university's total operating budget to 85 percent of the formula amount (though this is proposed to drop to 55 percent under the governor's budget). The projected enrollment is also used to project the tuition revenue the state will deduct from the total; the effect of any increase in tuition on student enrollments is not taken into consideration in this projection.

Do students benefit when the board of regents increases tuition and fees? Not always, and clearly not in the present environment. The way the budget process works at the state level is that a series of formula calculations determine the overall expenditure level, or operating budget. Once the expenditure level is determined, the legislature allocates university revenues, which consist mainly of appropriated student registration fees and nonresident tuition, and then allocates from the state general fund to make up the difference. In this way, tuition and fees serve as a direct offset to the state general fund. If any increase in tuition leads to a fall in the number of students enrolled, then this will actually reduce the university's overall operating budget in the future, and not just the state's general fund contribution.

The more tuition and fee revenue is available, the less of a general fund allocation is required. The board of regents has already approved a 5 percent increase in student fees and might yet adopt additional increases for fall 2009. The best-case budgeting scenario, while not as draconian as the governor's recommendation, still forecasts total expenditure authorizations well below the budgets funded for the current fiscal year. Consequently, students will be paying more for substantially reduced services, while receiving nothing in the way of improved services for increased tuition. This biennium, increased student tuition and fees will serve only to fill a hole left by declining state revenues.

The revenues the university receives from students can be affected by many things, including the cost of tuition, the state of the economy, an increase in the GPA admissions requirement, a reduction in the funding of the Millennium Scholarship program (which is not indexed to inflation or increases in tuition), or the creation of a new state college. Some of these are not under our control. The university has suggested correcting the way the state accounts for student tuition and fees so that the university can benefit from any increased tuition. The legislature, however, has not yet been willing to allow the university control over increases in its own student revenues.

The Capital Improvement Budget

In addition to the state-supported operating budgets, self-supporting budgets, and grants and contracts, the university has a separate capital improvement budget for the construction of new buildings. Usually, these budgets are set by the legislature, and the university is expected to raise additional funds from private donors, facilities and administration allocations from grants and contracts, and even student fees. These capital budgets are project-specific, meaning that these funds cannot be spent on other categories or projects. Readers of the local newspaper who ask how the university can be cutting its budget, eliminating its programs, and laying off faculty and staff while it is also constructing the new math and science building need to understand that these funds come from a completely different budget, and are not the result of misplaced priorities.

The Big Picture

As table 4.2 shows, the governor's budget proposal of January 2009 included cuts of $76 million in the university's operating budget. The governor has defended these cuts by arguing that state appropriations are only one of the university's many sources of revenue; indeed, as a share of the combined operating and self-funded budget, the proposed cuts for fiscal years 2010 and 2011 are 22 percent below the 2009 budget. Some of the governor's

TABLE 4.2. Relative Magnitude of Governor Gibbons's Proposed Cuts

	PROPOSED CUTS	2009 BUDGET STATE FUNDS		2009 BUDGET OPERATING BUDGETS		2009 BUDGET OPERATING + SELF-SUPPORTED	
Univ. Nevada, Reno	−71,795,243	144,152,936	50%	196,512,557	37%	321,660,390	22%
School of Medicine	−1,762,823	36,333,039	5%	39,058,043	5%	83,055,467	2%
Cooperative Extension	−1,002,531	9,976,270	10%	11,833,480	8%	21,593,378	5%
Agri. Exp. Station	−436,628	9,686,428	5%	10,940,073	4%	13,913,584	3%
Statewide programs	−953,757	8,892,041	11%	8,892,041	11%	10,377,655	9%
Intercollegiate athletics	−53,359	7,054,213	1%	7,054,213	1%	23,739,972	0%
Business Center North	−278,668	2,681,831	10%	2,681,831	10%	3,307,892	8%
State Health Laboratory	−128,219	2,129,397	6%	2,129,397	6%	3,519,528	4%
Total	−76,411,228	220,906,155	35%	279,101,635	27%	481,167,866	22%

supporters have even included contracts and grants in their calculations, while the university's defenders have noted that the proposal is a 50 percent cut to the state's support of the university's main campus operating budget, where most instruction is carried out, while leaving other budget areas relatively unaffected.

The governor's budget proposal results in an overall 37 percent cut to the operating budget of the main campus, assuming the legislature and the board of regents allow these cuts to be implemented as proposed. As a result of the external restrictions associated with grants and contracts, and the fiscal limitations of self-supporting functions, these cuts fall almost exclusively on the university's instructional and support budgets, and academic programs will inevitably be damaged. Other than implementing dramatic increases in student tuition and fees, the university has limited options when cuts approach these levels. It is hard to imagine any way to implement these cuts without doing long-term damage to the state, the university, and its students.

3. Higher Education Funding, with Bruce Shively (2009)[6]

For most of its first century, NSHE consisted of only one institution, which was originally located in Elko as the State University of Nevada. The university graduated its first class of three students from the new Reno campus in 1891. Almost 120 years later the university graduates roughly 2,000 students per year, and has a total enrollment of almost 14,000 student FTES (full-time equivalent).

After the Second World War, however, the state's population grew rapidly, and new educational institutions were created. The university's sister campus, UNLV, began as an extension effort of the Reno campus in the 1950s. It became independent as Nevada's Southern University in 1965, and in 1968 the board of regents granted it equal status with UNR. The Desert Research Institute was created in 1959 to focus on specific areas of grant-funded research, becoming independent from the University of Nevada in 1969. Community colleges were also created around this same time, beginning in 1967 with Nevada Community College in Elko, later Great Basin College. Though still referred to in state law as the board of regents of the University of Nevada, this elected body now oversees an NSHE consisting of eight different institutions of higher education.

At present, the state-supported operating budget of UNR's main campus totals almost $200 million per year, 22 percent of the total NSHE budget. In addition, as noted above, UNR also has separate budget authority for the School of Medicine, intercollegiate athletics, Cooperative Extension, the Nevada Agricultural Experiment Station, the State Health Laboratory, Business Center North, and statewide programs. All together, these eight operating budgets account for 32 percent of NSHE's budget.

UNLV has an operating budget that accounts for 31 percent of NSHE's total, plus authority over intercollegiate athletics, statewide programs, the Boyd Law School, the School of Dental Medicine, and Business Center South (see figure 4.3). All together, these account for 35 percent of NSHE's budget. The five other colleges—College of Southern Nevada (CSN), Truckee Meadows Community College, Western Nevada College, Great Basin College, and Nevada State College in Henderson—have a combined operating

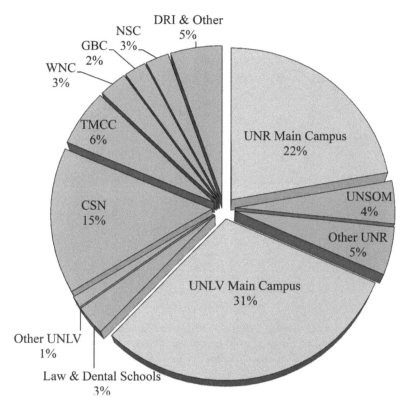

FIGURE 4.3. Nevada System of Higher Education 2008–9 Operating Budgets. *Source:* Courtesy of the Nevada System of Higher Education annual budgets.

budget of roughly $250 million, or 28 percent of the total. Finally, the state-supported operating budgets for the Desert Research Institute, system administration, Student Computing Services, and everything else account for the remaining 5 percent of NSHE's total.

Between 1985 and 2009 NSHE's total operating budget grew from $102 million to $886 million, and some have suggested that this is extraordinary growth. To put this in its proper context, however, we need to adjust for inflation, population growth, and rising real incomes. As a share of state GDP, therefore, the total operating budget for higher education in Nevada has remained constant over the past quarter century, but with much fluctuation.

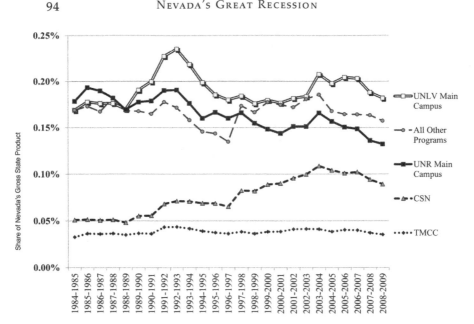

FIGURE 4.4. Nevada System of Higher Education State-Supported Operating Budget, by Fiscal Year, as Share of Nevada GSP. *Source:* Courtesy of the U.S. Bureau of Economic Analysis and the Nevada System of Higher Education annual budgets.

The total share had grown from 0.60 percent in 1985 to 0.71 percent by 1992, then fell back to 0.58 percent in 1997. By 2004 it had risen again to 0.71 percent, only to return again to 0.60 percent in the current budget year. Recent budget cuts requested by the governor mean that the actual expenditures for 2009 will come in significantly below this original budget, but these figures are not yet widely available.

UNR's share of this total spending declined considerably, from 45 percent to 32 percent over the same period, or from 30 percent to 22 percent if we consider only the main campus. In 1985 UNR's operating budget was larger than UNLV's, even if we exclude the related operating budgets for athletics, the School of Medicine, Cooperative Extension, and so on (figure 4.4). In 2009 UNLV's budget was almost 40 percent greater than UNR's. Las Vegas, however, has been the center of growth in the state, and enrollments at UNLV and CSN have grown rapidly. With an enrollment of almost 20,000

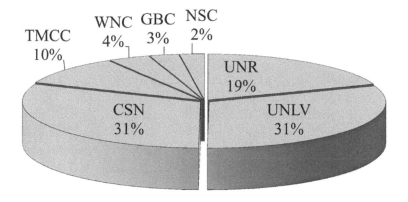

FIGURE 4.5. Nevada System of Higher Education, Student FTE Enrollment, 2007–8. *Source:* Courtesy of the Nevada System of Higher Education annual budgets.

student FTES, UNLV now accounts for 31 percent of total state enrollment, equal to that for CSN and considerably larger than that for UNR. As a result, some members of the legislature and the board of regents have wondered if UNLV was being treated fairly.

The legislature tried to address this concern with reliance on a formula-based approach to funding higher education. The current funding formula is the result of the 2001 Committee to Study the Funding of Higher Education in Nevada. The purpose of this committee, which was chaired by state senator William Raggio and that included several members of the board of regents, was to develop funding formulas to ensure the equitable distribution of funds for NSHE institutions.[7] The study also included the development of peer groups for each institution; the implementation of the funding formula largely resolved many legislative concerns at the time.

What emerged from the funding study was a formula that uses common calculations, as well as a common set of drivers, to develop institutional appropriations. The formula relies on student enrollments, shown in figure 4.5, and other factors to cover salaries for new faculty positions, fringe benefit rates, student faculty ratios, library volumes per degree program, the number of classified employees per faculty member, and even the number of square feet per custodial employee. The formula even includes a salary equity pool to rectify historical differences between UNLV and UNR in average salaries for existing faculty. The formula was supposed to achieve internal equity between the two universities, and considerable effort was even made to improve equity among other NSHE institutions.

The committee was also clear that equity did not necessarily mean equality, and institutions would receive different funding based on the mix of programs and the extent to which they engaged in graduate education. The formula recognizes, and funds, differences in mission among the two universities, the state college, and the community colleges. The student faculty ratios for lower division instruction at the universities are the same as those used for the state college, and nearly equal to those used by the community colleges. (The community colleges have a more favorable student–faculty ratio for lower-division high-cost programs than do the two universities.) In addition, the cost classifications for the various academic programs are also similar for all institutions. Science and engineering courses are considered high-cost courses, while English and foreign languages are considered low-cost courses, regardless of whether they are taught at the universities, the state college, or the community colleges.

The "guts" of the funding formula is a sixteen-cell matrix. This matrix is divided into clinical; high-, medium-, and low-cost programs; and lower-division, upper-division, master's, and doctorate levels of instruction. Institutions receive funding based on the distribution of students between high- and low-cost programs and the concentrations of students at the lower-division, upper-division, and graduate levels of instruction. The members of the study committee, Senator Raggio in particular, clearly recognized that those institutions with a greater proportion of their students enrolled in high-cost programs (e.g., science and engineering) have higher costs of instruction than those institutions with greater concentrations of enrollment in business and the social sciences. Similarly, costs increase by level of instruction. Graduate instruction is more costly than lower-division instruction. The current formula attempts to provide funding appropriate for the types of programs and levels of instruction offered at the various

NSHE institutions. Equitable funding within a mechanism that recognizes mission differentiation is a major goal of the formula.

The current funding formula also includes economies of scale, particularly related to administrative costs, and provides increased operations and maintenance (O&M) support for aging facilities, which is an issue for an increasing number of NSHE campuses. The formula also recognizes the need for increased instructional and support costs associated with students with disabilities. Similarly, the library formula calculations provide increased library resources required by graduate instruction based on the number of master's and doctorate programs at each institution.

Finally, the funding formula is responsive to shifts in enrollment, using a three-year weighted average for enrollment. Growing institutions are rewarded for increasing enrollments, whereas institutions whose enrollments are declining will ultimately receive fewer resources. UNLV, for example, experienced significant increases in funding because of strong enrollment growth in the 2002, 2004, and 2006 biennium periods. Not only does the formula react to overall changes in enrollment, but it also responds to shifts in enrollment within a unit. If a campus experiences a shift in enrollments from low-cost programs to high-cost programs, the formula will react appropriately and produce increased funding. Resources thus follow student enrollments in the current funding formula.

The three-year weighted average is based on actual enrollment data rather than institutional projections. The use of institutional projections prior to the adoption of the formula resulted in a tendency for some institutions to overestimate their enrollments, and the discrepancy between funded and actual enrollments created significant credibility issues for NSHE. As structured, the three-year weighted average serves to buffer sharp increases or decreases in enrollments. This feature of the formula has lessened the initial impact for campuses experiencing declining enrollments during previous legislative sessions.

Nonetheless, the total operating budget per student is still higher at UNR than it is at UNLV, even when we subtract the other areas of budget responsibility that are not primarily engaged in the instructional mission. To better understand why, it is important to

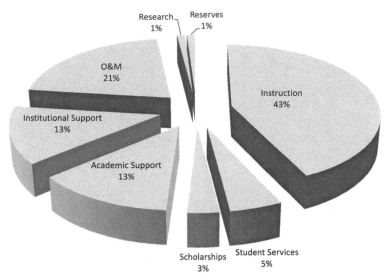

FIGURE 4.6. University of Nevada, Reno, Campus Operating Budgets, by Type, 2008–9. *Source:* Courtesy of the Nevada System of Higher Education annual budgets.

recognize that the operating budget covers different categories of spending, including instruction, research, public service, academic support, institutional support, O&M, scholarships, and reserves. Academic support includes such areas as the budgets for the offices of the provost and the deans, instructional technology, and campus computing. Institutional support includes the offices of the president and vice presidents, along with other administrative functions such as budgets and finance, personnel, alumni relations, and campus police. Of these, instruction is the largest component of the budget at UNR, followed by O&M, which includes utilities, custodial services, groundskeeping, plumbing, and so on (figure 4.6).

UNLV's budget is divided into the same general areas, though there are small differences in what is included where. The first major difference between UNR and UNLV is that UNLV spends a smaller proportion (17 percent) on O&M, largely because UNR has older, less-energy-efficient buildings, and UNR must also manage the extensive facilities of the School of Medicine, Cooperative Extension, and the Nevada Agricultural Experiment Station. UNR also spends a larger proportion on institutional support (8 percent). As a result, UNLV spends a larger proportion of its budget on instruction (51 percent) and student services (6 percent).

Why does UNR spend more on institutional support? As with O&M, one reason is that UNR administers a larger proportion of other budgets, including faculty and personnel services for the School of Medicine, which has a self-supporting budget that is much larger than its state-supported budget. The other operating budget areas for UNR total 45 percent of the main campus budget, while UNLV's other budget areas total only 13 percent of its main campus budget. It is also likely that there are some economies of scale in administration, as well as in O&M, since UNR spends less in total on these areas than does UNLV.

Disparities in per student FTE funding are largely reduced if we look at only the costs of instruction. UNR and UNLV have almost identical budgets per student FTE for instruction, even though UNR has a higher ratio of graduate students.

Both universities have greater costs per student FTE than the community colleges. Partly this is because the formula funds higher levels of instruction, particularly graduate courses, at higher rates. The community colleges, however, are also given proportionately fewer full-time positions. Even though full-time faculty there are expected to teach more courses than in the universities, due to differential research expectations, these colleges are expected to rely more on part-time faculty who earn considerably less per section. The colleges also appear to have some economies of scale in instruction, with the largest of them having the lowest cost per student, and Great Basin College the highest of them. Meanwhile, Nevada State College has an instructional cost per student FTE that is closer to that for the universities.

A weakness of the current formula structure is that it includes the entire operating budget, whether funded by the state or by student tuition. This has reduced the incentive of institutions to increase tuition to cover a larger share of expenditures or to provide a better education for students. Since higher tuition and fees will ultimately reduce the number of students attending, this therefore reduces total funding for the universities. Students who pay more are not likely to get more, because state support for the university will ultimately fall significantly more than tuition revenues rise.

Although the formula is not perfect, it has nonetheless helped to reduce disparity between the two universities in instructional funding. As the system of higher education has grown, UNR has claimed a decreasing proportion of the total state-funded operating budget. It would be a poor choice for those advocating to educate more of Nevada's underserved population to try to set the institutions to fighting each other. Infighting over resources might benefit political interests, but it would not serve the interests of either university, and is not justified by the available data.

›› Treasurer's Vignette: A Practical Man

May is college savings month, and the Treasurer's Office manages the so-called 529 college saving plans and prepaid tuition funds. May 29 is, for obvious reasons, 529 day. My staff and I take every opportunity to drum up awareness for our college savings programs.

We decided to host an annual contest for children in kindergarten through fifth grade, entitled, "I want to go to college to be a...." Any child in Nevada could submit either a picture or a paragraph on the subject, and six winners annually would get a college savings account opened in his or her name with an initial deposit of $529. Not too shabby, if you ask me.

The names of the children were put on bits of paper and scrambled in a bowl. We would then head to the staff break room. Pushing aside packets of mustard and pickle relish, we would nervously point to each other to do the choosing because, if we could have, we would have chosen every child. These contests were a favorite for all of us.

That year, one of the winners was a fifth grader from out near Mesquite. She wanted to be a teacher. At the ceremony we invited her U.S. congressional representative to present her with a large blown-up check.

When she arrived, I noticed her shoes looked new. Her dad, her mom, her brother, and her uncle all attended. We had balloons and ribbons and cake. She asked if it would be okay if she changed her mind on what she wanted to be, and we reassured her. With a wide smile, she told me she wanted to go to college in Nevada.

After we presented the check, everyone headed for a piece of cake, and I met with her father because he needed to fill out some forms to open the college savings account for his daughter. But as I spoke to him, he put his hand on my shoulder and said, "That's all right; we don't need to open an account."

I wasn't quite sure what he was saying. I asked, "Do you already have a college saving account?"

"No," he said, "but she's not going to college, so there's no need to set it all up. She was real excited to win the contest and her mom wanted her to have the ceremony, that's all."

I got it. I came from that family. He was a practical man, and knew just how far to let his daughter dream before it became just silliness. He wasn't going to break his little girl's heart by giving her false hopes. I suddenly saw my father in him, and he would not budge in spite of my entreaties.

The American dream for men like him is not the same as the one most of us grow up with. His American dream includes a job, but it doesn't include college—not for him, not for his kind. His low expectations for his family's future hurt me deeply.

That evening I went back to the hotel, but I could not get that little girl out of my mind. I was angry and tearful, and it was too close to home. So I called my staff and told them to drive out to that little girl's home in Mesquite, while the rest of us went to the next town for the next winning child's ceremony.

"Whatever it takes," I told them. "Don't leave until they've opened the account. Tell them even one semester at community college is better than none. Do not leave until they agree."

As always, my staff rose to the occasion. They spent two and a half hours sitting at the family kitchen table, telling her family over and over in many, many different ways, that yes, it is possible. Finally, with her mother on their side, her father opened the account.

But don't cue the music just yet. More and more I have run into Nevadans who believe they are just being practical because they accept that the offer we make as a country remains just out of reach. One savings account is not an answer. If you want to put the American dream within reach, one account will not get you there. Every child will need to hear the message that it is possible.

4. Nevada Undercuts Its Future (2010)[8]

When the special session of the Nevada legislature ended two weeks ago, the budget for NSHE was reduced by another 7 percent. Before our faculty and students had time to express our appreciation that the cuts were not much worse, we began to learn exactly which colleges, programs, and positions were slated for elimination, and it took our breath away.

At UNR our total operating budget has been reduced by 13 percent over the past two years, while our enrollments continued to rise. The first two rounds of our cuts applied to administrative and support functions, and now we are weighing proposals to close the College of Agriculture, Biotechnology & Natural Resources; shrink the College of Education; eliminate the French, German, and Italian programs; and end many graduate degrees, among other things. These proposals must be reviewed by the faculty and approved by the president; however, if they aren't implemented, other cuts will be proposed.

UNLV, CSN, and other institutions have taken similar reductions and will be making similar decisions. The state's contribution to NSHE's budget has fallen by a third over the past two years. Increased student tuition and federal American Recovery and Reinvestment Act money have filled about half that hole.

There has been much hardship in Nevada and around the globe as a result of this recession (which I have argued elsewhere is technically a depression). After rising by an annual average of 9 percent over the previous fifteen years, personal income in Nevada has dropped by 6 percent since the end of 2007, more than twice the decline of any other state.

Good people have lost their jobs as people have stopped spending, unemployment remains high, and the bad effects cascade. The legislature did the best it could in a bad situation, and nobody thinks the state should be immune from cuts.

Before you assume I am just whining, let me explain that although I feel terrible for my colleagues, I am more concerned for the rest of us, and for our state. Our faculty are smart, productive people, and most of those whose departments are eliminated will land on their feet. In fact, some of them, especially those who bring considerable research money into Nevada, are being re-cruited by universities in other states.

So why do we need public universities in the first place? Free markets are wonderful at giving more to those who already have, and private universities such as Harvard and Stanford are among the best in the world. But as my colleague Maureen Kilkenny, a respected economist in one of the departments slated for elimina-tion, says, "Markets can do nothing for people with nothing." For those who lack education, skills, or family wealth, the free market offers little hope for improvement. By paying taxes to provide edu-cation, we help to level the playing field.

Universities provide the best education to students because most of their faculty actually create knowledge. The more people learn, the more capable they are to of making good decisions and finding good jobs, and the easier it becomes to turn hard work into a better life. Those who become educated usually earn more, and contribute in turn to the revenue necessary to run the state and educate others.

Other states have a large number of private universities. Rela-tive to public universities, private universities pay their faculty roughly 20 percent more on average, and spend significantly more per student. Those same states also invest significantly more in their public universities.

As a share of national income, higher education spending in the United States tripled from 1960 to 2005, rising to 2.9 per-cent of our total national income. Higher educational enrollments rose almost as fast. The number of college degrees conferred grew almost fourfold relative to population, and the share of gradu-ate degrees doubled. This accumulation of human capital is one of the reasons our national economy has done so well over the long run.

How does Nevada compare? In 1985 the total NSHE operating budget was about 0.63 percent of our GSP. By 2008 "B.C." (before the cuts) this ratio had peaked at 0.65 percent, still the lowest share for higher education in the country.

When these cuts go into effect, this ratio will be at its lowest level in several decades. College enrollments have been a flat share of Nevada's population over the past couple of decades, while the share of college enrollments increased for the country as a whole. The lead that other states have over us is widening.

It takes money to make money, but in the midst of this budget crisis we are not making good investments. We are cutting colleges, classes, positions, and salaries. It will hardly be a surprise when we discover our most productive people have gone elsewhere, and our students have received a poorer education.

Unless they have little need for skilled labor, business owners who might have considered moving to Nevada will surely change their minds, because a good education system is an essential component of their quality of life.

5. Public Education Is in Short Supply (2010)[9]

Until the bubble in our housing market burst in 2006, and our economy went into a tailspin, young people without a college degree could earn a decent living in Nevada. Casinos and construction offered relatively well-paying jobs for these workers. So perhaps it made some sense that Nevada consistently ranked at the bottom in high school graduation rates and the percentage of residents with a college degree. Perhaps we have simply had less demand for education.

But there is also a supply side. According to the Census Bureau, in 2006 Nevada had the lowest number of employees working in public education of any state, relative to population. In public K–12, we had 25 percent fewer employees than the national average. In public higher education, Nevada had a third fewer employees per capita than the national average, even though we rely much less than most other states on private colleges.

How do we compare to our neighbors to the west and the east? We compete with California for students, and the prices Californians pay for things significantly impact us here. But Utah is also a good comparison because it has a population that is only slightly larger than ours, and faces many of the same geographic challenges as Nevada. Utah is also not as wealthy as Nevada or California.

It is no surprise that Nevada has significantly fewer employees in public education than California or Utah. What is surprising is that Utah has more than twice as many people working in public higher education than Nevada, even though Utah also has private universities such as Brigham Young University. Utah has put many more resources into higher education, and a much larger share of Utahans have college degrees.

Things have gotten much worse for Nevada since 2006. The state's economy has been the worst performer in the nation, and the state's tax revenues have declined much more than our state's economy. Higher education has taken a disproportionate share of this budget hit.

NSHE has lost a fifth of its state-funded operating budget in the past two years. At UNR we have 350 fewer employees, we shut down programs, and we fired productive faculty, even as our number of students has grown. We now have the largest and best-prepared freshman class in our history, and more of our students are graduating than at any time in recent memory, but if more cuts come we will be hard pressed to keep serving them.

The state economies that are now recovering fastest are those with a more educated workforce. If we ever hope that we will be able to reinvent our economy in the future, we need to be able to educate our students. We need to maintain a higher education system that will attract our best students, rather than chase them off to other states.

6. Cutting Budgets at the University of Nevada, Reno (2011)[10]

I knew little about UNR when I joined the faculty in 1992. I soon learned it was a school on the rise, albeit in a state that didn't take higher education seriously.

In 1999 Nevada still ranked forty-ninth in the country in the number of public higher education employees per person, with four employees per thousand people. Although NSHE received an above-average share of state general fund dollars, this translated into a total operating budget of only 0.60 percent of GSP, one of the smallest shares in the country. The only states with similar numbers for public education had large numbers of private colleges and universities.

Even though NSHE had an open enrollment policy and a policy of low tuition enshrined in state law, Nevada had the lowest proportion of college students in the nation. Most of our best students

left us for college elsewhere, and few returned. The best who remained were as good as students at top universities, but they
weren't as challenged as they should've been because their competition wasn't always as good. Though some at UNR worried we
would chase students away if we demanded too much from them,
many faculty pushed and pushed for improvement, and gradually
they made it a better university.

With Governor Guinn's Millennium Scholarship program, a
growing economy, and legislative support, an effort was made
to turn this low enrollment around. NSHE's operating budget increased by 8.5 percent per year from fiscal year 1999 to fiscal year
2009, growing almost a full percentage point faster than our overall economy. UNR's budget grew, too—not as fast as the rest of NSHE,
but enough to keep up with inflation and our enrollment growth.
We hired new faculty, and we were increasingly able to compete
against much bigger universities for the best. Our entering fresh-
men improved. And we slowly became one of Nevada's gems.

How much of a difference did this growth make? By 2008
NSHE employment had grown to 4.1 per thousand persons, although it was still in forty-ninth place nationwide. The total NSHE
operating budget rose to a peak of 0.65 percent of GSP. UNR attracted record numbers of National Merit scholars, and we were
eventually recognized as a first-tier school and a Carnegie research university. We increased our enrollment by two thirds, and
increased our graduation rates. Our freshman retention rate increased to 80 percent, even though the share of them eligible for
Pell Grants more than doubled. We even fielded a decent football
team. UNR became a university I would be proud to have my children attend.

When the recession hit and the state began to pare its budgets, higher education took a relatively bigger hit. At UNR, our
total operating budget is almost 15 percent less than it was two
years ago. Students are paying substantially more in tuition and
fees, but this only made a small dent in the $45 million decrease
in the state's general fund contribution from fiscal year 2009 to
fiscal year 2011.

Now Governor Sandoval has proposed more cuts. The proposed general fund contribution to UNR will be 50 percent less in

fiscal year 2013 than in fiscal year 2009, even though our enrollments keep rising, and the total operating budget will be 35 percent less. Adjusting for inflation, that would be a combined budget cut of 46 percent per student.

The university is not a set of LEGOs that we can take apart and quickly rebuild. The damage we will do to Nevada's university system will take decades to undo. While a few of our best faculty have left already, most have remained because they like it here, and because they hope things will improve. If enacted, this budget will make sure any such hope in our future is misplaced.

›› Treasurer's Vignette: A Material Form of Hope

In trying to do what I could to get more families saving for college, I wanted to offer up hope in a tangible form, to provide a guide rail that a child and her family could hang on to as they picked their way along the difficult and overly narrow path from have-not to opportunity. As best I might, I wanted to help put the American dream squarely within the reach of everyone.

I once read that the false prophecies of hope come in three different ways.[11] First there is the hokey hope that tells you that you, too, can join the ranks of the wealthy and privileged, if only you work hard and play by the rules. This is Horatio Alger's version of the American dream, and in time we realize how tall this tale is.

Second is the mythical hope created by celebrities. Every young athlete just knows that he or she is destined for professional sports. Every teenage singer practicing in front of the mirror is certain that the future will include a lucrative recording contract and adoring fans. In time, most of us grow out of that, too.

Finally, there is the hope for easy answers and sudden solutions. We offer a path out of malignant poverty so far out of reach as to leave matters completely beyond our control. This hope convinces you that only a revolution or the second coming will save you. It is a hope that is very much deferred, and to paraphrase Langston Hughes, hope deferred is no hope at all.

The material forms of hope are realistic and achievable, but they require more than just hard work. In my own life the most material form of hope came through education. Or, as my Mexican

American father put it, "You want to be a duck, best learn to quack like one." Education gave me the ability to quack with the confidence of one who can reach out and pull that American dream right in.

Thus, when my chief of staff came to me with the idea of creating college savings accounts for all the state's children, I was willing to move mountains to make it happen.

The idea was simple: We would open a small college savings account for as many Nevada children as we could, and launch a massive marketing campaign to send these kids the message that an education beyond high school was not just a dream. We would encourage their parents to save, and we would promise matching funds to help a family along the way. There was research showing that this could make a real difference, and we could do it without using taxpayer money.

My campaign team told me it was not a good idea politically, and they strongly urged me to drop it. I pondered their comments for maybe half an hour, and then replied that if this meant I lost a race, so be it.

I also had objections from some members of one large school board, who claimed that I wanted to open such accounts only to improve my political prospects. I suggested that if they really wanted to, they could drop their school district from the plan, and deal with the consequences. I probably was not very polite.

Along the way, we also encountered problems with federal privacy rules, shoddy student data files, and incompatible software between school districts and the state. When we sent out the first account statements to each family, 15,000 were returned because of bad addresses. We had to hire a firm to tell many of these schools where their own students were living.

In the end, we got agreement from the state Department of Education, the superintendents and school boards of each of the seventeen school districts, and many, many, principals and teachers who committed hours and hours of their time and resources to help make this program a reality. We also obtained a grant of $20,000 from Charles Schwab Bank to help fund the program, and assistance from both the United Way of Southern Nevada and Junior Achievement of Northern Nevada.

What does it mean to a family to know that they have a college savings account for their child?

A woman in Ely burst into tears, much to the embarrassment of her husband, because her uncle had told her that if she got a college account for her child he would put some money into it. She had never known how to get one.

A mom and grandma arrived toward the end of one of our events, literally running toward me, holding bills in their hands, saying, "Are we too late? We have the money to match. Can my daughter have a college savings account? Please, dear God, don't tell us we are too late."

A five-year-old in Elko grabbed onto my trousers and said, "Please, please can I still go to college even if my mom doesn't know what college is?"

Over and over again people cried, or clapped, or grabbed my shoulders to give me a hug. What can I tell you? Nearly 90,000 children in Nevada now have college savings accounts, and we are one of the first states in the nation to offer college savings accounts state-wide. When I left office the families that had contributed the most to those accounts were from Title I schools, the poorest of the poor. We should not give up on these children.

I remember the day I first realized that I would go to college. I crawled into my bed and hid my face in my pillow, sobbing with both pain and happiness as I imagined that my future might be better than the life I grew up in.

7. A Letter to Governor Sandoval (2011)[12]

Dear Governor Sandoval:

I have just been asked by my university's faculty senate to chair a committee with an awful job. Over the next month we will review program closure proposals, trying to get part of the way to the budget cuts you proposed. I would like to ask you to please make this awful job unnecessary.

We call this process curricular review. We are deciding which faculty to fire, and which students will lose their degree programs. These are productive faculty who work hard, and we have been cutting budgets by firing many good people over the past four years. This is really getting old, and it is completely reversing years of effort to make Nevadans proud of their oldest university.

My university alone has already lost 350 positions, mostly very educated people who then left the state—and Nevada already has too few of those. Now we have 150 more jobs on the block, and many more to come since we are less than halfway to your target. We aren't that big of a university, and these cuts are starting to cripple us.

You are mistaken when you say these cuts are best for the state's economy. As an economist who looks at the data, I know these cuts are bad for the economy. Cutting state expenditures during a recession makes the economy worse, not better.

We know that education matters for the future of the state, both K–12 and higher education. Without our monopoly on gambling, Nevada doesn't have many resources, and nowadays the most productive resource is the knowledge and skills of our workers. And it will take many years to undo the damage we are doing now.

This is a death spiral. If we gut higher education, productive people and productive investment will flow out of the state, not in.

We know this is not a temporary problem. Gaming is a much smaller share of our economy than it used to be, even though our state budget still largely depends on it. We have known for years that we need a tax system that better reflects our economy, a tax system that can apply low rates to a much, much broader base. Yet we keep procrastinating on the solution.

The budget problem is not too big to solve. While the state's budget gap is a large fraction of the general fund, it is only 1 percent of our state economy. For the average resident, it is roughly the cost of eating out once a month.

So why not find a compromise, for the good of the state? Pass better taxes but delay them, so you don't raise them during a recession. Instead, borrow against these future taxes to get us through our current crisis without doing too much long-term damage. Then negotiate other reforms that will help control costs, so we don't have to raise taxes even more in the future.

You seem like a reasonable person, not an ideologue. I assume you have good intentions. Can you please help us, and not lead us off the cliff?

Sincerely,
Elliott Parker, Professor and Chairman
Department of Economics, University of Nevada, Reno

8. Going the Wrong Way (2011)[13]

Since the legislature adjourned sine die, many have written about their relief that the state budget will not be as bad as expected. Governor Brian Sandoval has been praised, and criticized by some in the far-right wing, for finally being a little reasonable, once the judiciary made it clear that his budget was built on false premises.

Of course I share the relief, and agree that it could have been worse. But it also could have been much, much better. Had the governor signaled his reasonableness before the last minute, he would have done less damage, and could have driven a much better bargain with the legislature. We could have used more-thoughtful reforms, less last-minute scrambling, and less swinging of the scythe.

Nevada needs tax restructuring. Our tax base no longer reflects our economy, and we need a broader, more-stable tax base that will allow us to lower rates on those few things we do tax. We need the legislature and the governor to give this more thought, and to quit thinking that procrastinating for one more biennium is a successful plan of action.

Nevada's biennial general fund expenditures are budgeted to fall from $6.9 billion to $6.2 billion, a cut of 10 percent in state spending. For comparison, our GSP fell by 6.5 percent from peak to trough in this recession, and our personal income fell by 7.3 percent.

This general fund budget is less than 2.5 percent of our expected GSP over this period, hardly what we would call big government. But Nevada already had one of the smallest general funds, and the fewest public-sector workers, in the country.

In the short run, this reduction in state spending means fewer jobs in the private sector, too, and the impact could be surprisingly large. Estimates based on the experience of all states over the past forty-five years find that, on average, such cuts are likely to reduce the state economy by 2 percent below where it might have been. That suggests a $5 billion loss in economic activity over the next two years, a frightening prospect in our current depressed state. Of course, it could have been worse, right?

Business investment tends to flow downhill, to where other firms are investing, to where an educated labor force works, to where good customers live. Since we have lost our gaming monopoly, we need to find a new economic engine in this state, and we won't find it without a vibrant system of higher education.

Instead, we have done our best to rock NSHE back on its heels, to chase away some of our best and brightest people, and to undermine the motivation of the rest. And we created a Knowledge Fund to spur innovation that we don't even have the knowledge to fund.

At its peak a few years ago, NSHE employed 0.4 percent of Nevadans; its total state-supported operating budget was about 0.65 percent of GSP. Even after a decade or more of growth, Nevada was still forty-ninth in the nation in public higher education spending, though we lack the significant private universities other states have.

Since that peak NSHE has lost 20 percent of its state funding, and now it is losing 15 percent more. While this is not as bad as the 36 percent proposed by then-governor Jim Gibbons and the 29 percent proposed by Governor Sandoval, it is still heading in the wrong direction. Some can be made up for with higher tuition and fees, but not as much as people seem to think.

Most attention focused on the K–12 system, which affects many more kids. But NSHE has taken bigger cuts than any other major state institution, this round and cumulatively, and at times we seemed to be almost invisible.

Higher education institutions are now getting ready to give out pink slips. UNLV president Neal Smatresk announced that 215 more jobs will be lost, along with 18 academic programs and

9 departments. UNR will be cutting a slightly larger share, though our enrollment has continued to grow; 414 positions have already been lost, and we expect to lose almost 200 more. CSN and other Nevada institutions are making similar cuts, all subject to a vote of the board of regents.

Sure, money isn't everything, and many will still be working hard to provide the best education we can with what we have to work with. Sure, there will be some cost efficiencies gained, but much damage has been done, damage that will take a decade or more to undo, at least.

Universities improve by attracting top people from out of state, and by becoming attractive to our best students to keep them in state. Now some of our top faculty have left, or are planning to leave. Our ability to keep our best students has diminished, and if they leave they are not likely to return.

Nevadans need to wrap their heads around the fact that the future of our state depends on a better tax system to support a functioning state government, especially a functioning system of higher education. To attract investment and employers, we need this much more than we need to stay an extremely low-tax environment. Cooperation between the governor and the legislature has only reduced the sharp angle of our downward spiral.

Notes

1. Margaret Spellings served as secretary of education under President George W. Bush.

2. This letter was printed in J. Ralston, "Econ Prof Tries to Teach Gibbons Some Economic Realities on Higher Ed," *Las Vegas Sun,* February 12, 2009.

3. This is based on an unpublished white paper, E. Parker and B. Shively, *University Budgets: A Guide for the Perplexed,* UNR, March 23, 2009. Mr. Shively is the associate vice president for budget, planning, and analysis at UNR.

4. See "Planning, Budget & Analysis," UNR, http://www.unr.edu/vpaf/pba /budget/

5. The Fire Science Academy was established by the board of regents in Carlin, Nevada, and was never able to generate enough revenue for the university to cover the cost of construction and operation. President John Lilly used a special student fee on the main campus to cover the debt burden. The university was eventually able to get approval for selling the facility to the Nevada National Guard.

6. This is based on an unpublished white paper, E. Parker and B. Shively, "Funding, Fairness, and the Formula: The University of Nevada, Reno, in the System of Higher Education," UNR, April 17, 2009.

7. Legislative Counsel Bureau Bulletin 01-4, "Committee to Study the Funding of Higher Education in Nevada," January 2001, https://www.leg.state.nv.us/Division/Research/Publications/InterimReports/2001/Bulletin01-04.pdf; p. 39.

8. Originally published as E. Parker, "Nevada Undercuts Its Future with Budget Cuts in Higher Education," *Las Vegas Sun,* March 14, 2010.

9. Originally published as E. Parker, "Nevada's Public Education Is in Short Supply," *Reno Gazette Journal,* October 13, 2010.

10. Originally published as E. Parker, "University of Nevada, Reno, Can't Withstand Proposed Cuts," *Nevada Appeal,* February 20, 2011.

11. For an explanation of the types of hope identified here, see J.M.R. Duncan-Andrade, "Note to Educators: Hope Required When Growing Roses in Concrete," *Harvard Educational Review* 79, no. 2 (Summer 2009).

12. Originally published as E. Parker, "Time to Find a Compromise for Good of State," *Nevada Appeal,* March 27, 2011.

13. Originally published as E. Parker, "Going the Wrong Way," *Las Vegas Sun,* June 12, 2011.

CHAPTER 5

The National Economy

Keynes did argue—and persuasively—that to cut public expenditure when an economy has unused productive capacity as well as unemployment owing to a deficiency of effective demand would tend to have the effect of slowing down the economy further and increasing—rather than decreasing—unemployment.... But I would also argue that the unsuitability of the policy of austerity is only partly due to Keynesian reasons. Where we have to go well beyond Keynes is in asking what public expenditure is for—other than for just strengthening effective demand, no matter what its content.

— AMARTYA SEN[1]

Introduction

The National Bureau of Economic Research records thirty-three recessions since 1854, an average of more than one every six years. Since the Second World War these have become less frequent, the contractions have become shorter, and the expansions in between have become longer. The Great Depression seems like ancient history to most people, and many of us—including many economists—have forgotten the lessons it taught us.

I specialized in comparative and international economics, and normally would not have focused on the Great Depression. However, my interest in China led me into a new area of research, and I published a series of journal articles on recent price deflation in Japan and China. This led me back to studying the Great Depression and other historical business cycles in other countries. In the first of those articles, a colleague and I examined the international record and found strong evidence that deflations made recessions much worse, and that a little deflation was a lot worse than a little inflation.[2]

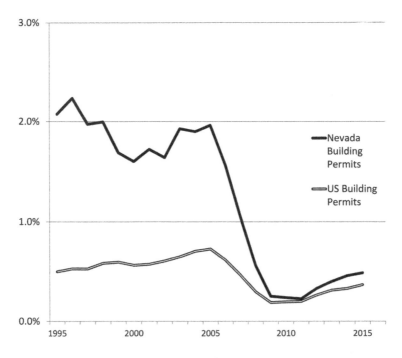

FIGURE 5.1. Building Permits per Resident. *Source:* Courtesy of the United States Census Bureau.

The Great Recession was what Richard Koo, chief economist at the Nomura Research Institute, called a balance sheet recession.[3] In an earlier chapter, figure 1.1 showed the housing price index for Nevada and the nation, adjusted for inflation using the consumer price index. The collapse of the housing bubble led to a financial crisis, and the collapse of financial asset values led firms, banks, and households to cut spending and try to reduce their debts. This set off a chain of events that led to the worst recession since the Great Depression.

The construction sector, in particular, was very hard-hit. Nationwide, both building permits and housing starts fell by 73 percent between the peak and the trough. In Nevada, where the construction sector was the largest in the nation, the decline was 87 percent. This can be seen in figure 5.1, which adjusts annual building permits by population. When housing prices were rising, Nevada was building houses at three times the national rate. Between 2006 and 2009 the state fell back to earth.

The late economist Hyman Minsky made a good case that financial crises tend to cause particularly nasty recessions.[4] Irving Fisher, an eminent economist from Yale in the early twentieth century, noted that debts become harder to repay when prices are falling, and firms begin to default on loans.[5] But the idea that government action could help in such a time was first articulated during the Great Depression by British economist John Maynard Keynes (pronounced like "canes").[6]

The Keynesian argument is that sometimes aggregate private spending falls too much, far below what the economy can potentially produce. Investment spending in particular is especially sensitive to herd behavior, and when spending falls many firms cut back on production instead of prices. Because one person's spending is another person's income, more people lose their jobs and spend less in turn. This is particularly problematic when inflation and interest rates are low, because interest rates don't usually fall below zero and businesses have many practical reasons to not cut wages and prices.

Unemployment rose steeply to its highest level in decades, particularly in Nevada, where the percentage of construction workers was highest (see figure 5.2). Economic output, as measured by real GDP per capita, fell dramatically below its potential in the United States, and remained there for years. In Nevada, of course, the fall was much worse, and the recovery much slower to begin.

The only way to stabilize the economy in bad times, Keynes argued, was for government to spend more during recessions to offset the fact that the private sector was spending less. Similarly, Keynes argued that government should spend less during good times to keep the economy from overheating and to build up savings for the inevitable bad times. With a countercyclical fiscal policy, public and private spending could become complements, not substitutes.

In the decades since the Great Depression many economists have pointed out a number of flaws in the Keynesian approach. In normal recessions, which tend to be short and shallow, the government could actually destabilize the economy by taking too long to act, and wages, prices, and interest rates could adjust to help restore equilibrium to the market. The notion that

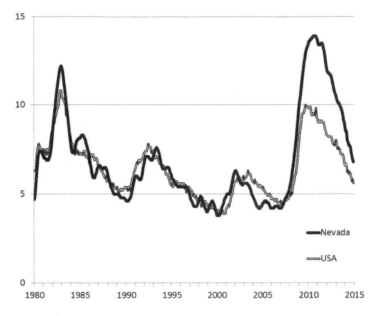

FIGURE 5.2. Unemployment Rates. *Source:* Courtesy of the Bureau of Labor Statistics, U.S. Department of Labor.

government knew enough to micromanage the economy smacked of hubris. Government spending on short notice was unlikely to go toward creating things of value to society. If the economy is not in a deep recession, government spending could crowd out the private sector in a variety of ways. Keynes did not appreciate the role of the central bank and the benefits of stable money and prices. Keynes focused on the demand side of the equation, without enough consideration for the incentives of the supply side. And so forth.

However, just because Keynes was wrong about some things does not mean he was wrong about everything, and the Great Recession met most of the conditions for a perfect Keynesian storm. Price inflation was close to zero, interest rates fell so low that people were effectively paying the U.S. Treasury to lend money to the federal government, unemployment skyrocketed, and everybody was cutting spending, yet wages and prices could not fall quickly enough to restore the economy to equilibrium.

This chapter includes eight columns I wrote between 2011

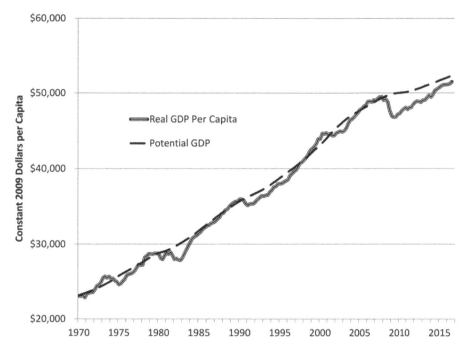

FIGURE 5.3. Real GDP per Capita and Potential GDP. *Source:* Courtesy of the St. Louis Federal Reserve Board Economic Research and Bureau of Economic Analysis.

and 2014 on the national economy, along with several vignettes from Kate about fighting the good fight in an impossible situation. The articles tried to correct a number of common misperceptions about the nature of this particular recession.

1. Why Hasn't the Economy Recovered? (2011)[7]

A recession is fascinating, in a morbid sort of way, for an economist. But I must admit that I am really getting tired of this one, and would like to get back to considering other problems.

Real GDP grew at an average 3.6 percent annual rate in the decade before 2000, and 2.4 percent annually in the seven years after, well ahead of the 1 percent average annual rate of population growth. It began falling in the first quarter of 2008, and by the second quarter of 2009 it was down 5.1 percent. Figure 5.3 shows this in real per capita terms.

Technically, the recession has now been over for two years already, though it doesn't feel like it. A recession is when the economy actually shrinks, followed by a trough and then a recovery. Since 2009 our GDP has grown steadily but slowly, and has almost reached the level it was at back at the end of 2007. Population has grown by 3 percent since 2007, however, so we are still really lagging.

For the past two years, average per capita income has increased, but not for the average person. Instead, most of the rising income has gone to the top 2 percent of the distribution, for people whose incomes come from capital gains and stock options. The unemployment rate has pulled back from its peak of 10.1 percent in the last months of 2009, but at 9.1 percent it still remains stubbornly high. Benefits have ended for many unemployed, and a significant number have simply withdrawn from the workforce—giving up, retiring early, or even going on disability to replace their incomes.

A recession caused by a financial crisis is simply different from most recessions: it is deeper and longer and harder to recover from. Immense damage was done by reckless lending behavior and home buying driven by the foolish belief that prices would always go up.

Most Americans lost a large fraction of their net wealth, and that has long-term effects on their consumption spending. The balance sheets of most financial institutions were so badly damaged by the dramatic growth of nonperforming loans that banks are still very cautious about lending. Banks are instead holding huge piles of excess reserves, with more than $1.6 trillion on deposit at the Federal Reserve alone. Firms don't hire when people aren't buying and banks aren't lending.

Before the recession began, private consumption and investment in new residential housing had reached record levels, and record shares of GDP. Our nation's total spending substantially exceeded what we produced. Americans stopped saving, and we chose to live beyond our means. We had to borrow from abroad to pay for what we bought. The federal government was doing it too, running large deficits as it cut taxes and fought two wars, borrowing during good times instead of putting something aside for a rainy day.

Perhaps a recession was due to pull us back to living within our means. Unfortunately, as we cut our spending, our income fell—and not coincidentally, since the less we spent, the more people lost their jobs. It becomes harder to live within your means when your means fall too. But this also means that we can't recover back to the economy we had, since that was clearly unsustainable.

This global recession was largely "made in America," but the waves it caused elsewhere keep rippling back and drowning our meager efforts at restoring confidence. Adjusted for inflation, our exports have grown by 22 percent since the recovery began, and are now at the highest share of our GDP ever. This has helped, but it has not been enough to close the foreign trade deficit.

Faster economic recovery would require more purchases of the goods and services we can produce, but if domestic consumption is unlikely to return to its former unsustainable levels, if banks aren't lending enough to fuel private investment, and if growth in foreign exports is limited by problems abroad, why isn't the government increasing its purchases to take up the slack?

The federal government has significantly increased its spending, as many people have argued. But where did that spending go, and why didn't it lead to a faster recovery?

National defense spending, which accounts for a fifth of the federal budget, has grown faster than the economy over the past decade. In real terms this spending grew by an average rate of 4.6 percent from 2000 to 2007, and 3.7 percent since, though most of the latter increase happened during the so-called surge in Iraq in 2008, and not during the recovery.

However, the lion's share of the federal budget goes to social spending, mostly what economists call transfers. For individuals, transfers are primarily social benefits like Social Security, Medicare, veterans' pensions, and unemployment benefits. The federal government also helps state and local governments pay for these things, as well as for highways and other spending.

According to the Office of Management and Budget, federal spending on everything else makes up only 11 percent of the total budget. This spending has fallen significantly since the recession began, even without adjusting for inflation or population growth.

Furthermore, the overall increase in federal spending has been mostly offset by decreases in state and local government spending. Subtracting out social benefit transfers to individuals, and adjusting for inflation, total government purchases of goods and services have risen by only a total of 2.2 percent since the end of 2007, less than half the rate of population growth over that period.

Thus, the growth in government spending has gone almost entirely into the pockets of those receiving federal benefits, not those who work for government or who sell products to the government. As with the many tax cuts in the stimulus package, these transfers have only further dampened consumer spending. Contrary to popular belief, the government has not actually been buying more goods and services, so how can it possibly make up for the decreased demand from the private sector?

2. Where We Went Wrong after September 11 (2011)[8]

A decade ago we stood at a crossroads, and we made a choice.

Our economic output had grown fast in the prior decade, faster than it had grown in any decade since the 1960s. Gross private investment reached 18 percent of GDP, its highest level since 1984. Total government expenditures—federal, state, and local— stood at less than 30 percent of GDP, its lowest share since 1979. The federal budget was in surplus, and Alan Greenspan, the chairman of the Federal Reserve Board, was cautioning Congress that we should not pay off too much of the federal debt, since the financial system needed U.S. bonds. What a difference a decade makes.

There were warning signs of problems to come. The stock market had just gone through a speculative bubble, especially in tech stocks. There were also signs of a housing bubble starting in California. Private consumption was rising, along with imports, as household savings rates fell. Americans were letting their assets do their savings for them.

The Gramm-Leach-Bliley Act of 1999 had repealed the firewall between investment banks and commercial banks, along with the conflict-of-interest provisions, which had been put in place by the Glass-Steagall Banking Act of 1933. We let mergers create banks that were too big to fail. Some worried that allowing Citibank, Bank of America, and other deposit-taking banks to trade in things like mortgage-backed securities and collateralized debt obligations might pose risks for the economy, and the Enron collapse showed big firms could engage in financial shenanigans that were not in the interest of their shareholders.

But nobody, outside of those people putting together White House briefings, knew that there were people about to hijack four planes and fly them into the Pentagon, the World Trade Towers, and, unintentionally, a field in Pennsylvania.

After the heartbreak of that day, we made a choice to go shopping. Had we been called to make a sacrifice, I am confident that most Americans would have proudly responded. We should have cut our demand for foreign petroleum, to reduce the money we turn over every day to people who hated us. Given the long slog ahead, we should have invested in our economy, our education, our infrastructure, and our people.

Instead, we cut taxes, and fought two long, unfunded wars with borrowed money. Instead of tightening our belts, we increased our consumption spending to all-time highs on borrowed money. What we borrowed from abroad created the largest trade deficit in our history. Instead of taking care to prevent another financial asset bubble, we allowed a new one to take hold in housing. Instead of working together as Americans, we used the crisis for partisan purposes. What were we thinking?

The housing bubble frothed, and then it burst. Financial firms made risky bets for short-term gain with other people's money. The damage done to household wealth led to a permanent fall in consumption, the damage done to banks still discourages them from lending, and the damage done to confidence still discourages private investment. Instead of a recession, we created a new depression. How can we fix it now?

Absent a time machine, there is no easy solution. We were consuming too much of our income, and so we can't count on consumption to recover and think that will be a long-run solution. We need investment, both private and public, but where do we get the money for it if we don't save, unless we borrow more from abroad? Export growth has been one bright spot during this slow recovery, but the economic problems abroad that this recession aggravated makes that hard to keep going.

When the private sector buys less of what we produce, a good fiscal policy would have the government step in and buy more. But in spite of what many people think, real per capita government purchases—including what government pays its workers and what it buys from private companies—are lower now than before the recession began. The federal government has bought more, yes, but most of this spending was on the military. State and local governments have bought less.

What the federal government did, however, is give more away in tax cuts and benefits. Certainly this helped to slow the decline in consumption, but it was hardly enough to replace the fall in private investment. Certainly the millions who received unemployment benefits needed them, but how much better would it have been not to destroy their jobs in the first place?

This weak combined fiscal policy response only slowed the bleeding, but it was not a permanent solution. In the long run, we need to save more and invest more, both public and private. In the short run, borrowing made sense to keep the economy from spiraling downward, but in the long run we need to save more, in both the private and public sectors.

We need to invest more, in both the private and public sectors, in factories, infrastructure, and education. That will take getting banks to start lending out their excess reserves. We need to export more, and stop importing more, but that will take a fall in the dollar's value that will be painful for us. We need to reestablish some sensible financial regulation to make sure we don't go through this again. And we need to act together, as Americans, and not make our economy worse in hopes of winning the next election.

A decade ago we had a choice, and we screwed it up. September 11, 2001, could have made us stronger, but we chose not to let it, and we blithely walked over a cliff. It is time to pick ourselves up, learn from our mistakes, and make better choices. Is anybody with me?

>> Treasurer's Vignette: Foreclosures and "The Senator"

When I was seven we lost our house. It was the only one we were ever to own while I was growing up. I remember a man came to the house dressed in a gray suit. I answered the bell and told my dad the president was at the door.

Papers were signed and that weekend my grandpa pulled up in a flatbed, not the best vehicle I would recommend on moving day. My brother was exactly eight days old and things were in disarray. Objects were thrown out that should have been kept (like my mother's spices), boxes were accidently dropped and words exchanged, but what I remember most was my four-year-old sister standing next to a doll's cradle in which my brother lay. My father brushed by it holding the end of a couch and it flipped, and my sister, at just the right height, held out her tiny hands and caught my brother perfectly, while my mother sat down in slow motion on the sidewalk.

Thus, when the foreclosure crisis hit Nevada, I felt especially compelled to help those who were losing their homes. I found out that the Michigan attorney general's office was hosting foreclosure workshops and, with the help of their staff, we came up with a proposal to do the same in Nevada. However, I had neither the staff nor the money to pull it off. So I went to the attorney general's office and offered them top billing if they would lend staff, and then went to Senator Reid's office and offered the same if they would provide financial assistance. The workshops would never have happened without them.

In two months we had scheduled free foreclosure workshops in Vegas, in Reno, and in Fallon. Senator Reid's office worked with banks and mortgage lenders so that invitations were sent to all customers who were at least three months behind in mortgage payments. Representatives from the HOPE NOW alliance, Neighbor Works America, and the local U.S. Department of Housing and Urban Development office also attended, to provide additional information and one-on-one counseling. The first workshop was at Cashman Center in Las Vegas.

On a Saturday morning in 2008 the mitigation departments of the financial institutions were setting up inside, while lines of homeowners snaked around the building outside. It was forty-five minutes before we opened the doors and the press arrived, cameras shouldered, trucks parked with large antennas, rolling live for the morning news.

A reporter I hadn't seen before walked over and held out his mic: "You're just doing this to get your name in the papers, aren't you?"

I was mortified. What if people were watching the morning news and would now decide not to come? My lame response, "No, of course not," did not dissuade him.

He pressed on. "I mean, you can't actually force the banks to do anything."

The reporter was sharp and crisp. He seemed to know what he was talking about, and I worried all our work would start to look like a political sideshow. I excused myself from the interview and found Senator Reid's staff.

Half an hour later the reporter was gone, a new one in his place. The new reporter wanted a story on my personal experience with losing a home.

Staff worked that day from seven in the morning until five that night and the lines never slackened. At a quarter to five that evening a woman started making a ruckus in the line as we began to tell people we would have to close the doors. She had gotten there late because she worked Saturdays. Her home was to be auctioned in four days.

People ahead of her agreed we should try to get her in. We contacted her bank. They called off the auction and started the mitigation process on her loan. In the end, she stayed in her home with new terms she could afford.

At each workshop there were more people than we could possibly help. The press never showed up in Reno or Fallon, but the lines were always long and the senator's staff was always there to make sure that what we could do was done.

3. We'd Forgotten What a Depression Looks Like (2011)[9]

If you think this recession has been going on far too long, you are right.

Economists define recessions as the period of actual decline in real economic activity, which we generally measure with GDP. This recession, which began in early 2008, was officially over by the middle of 2009. Adjusting for price inflation and population, real per capita GDP normally grows about 1.5 percent per year. Instead, it fell by 6.4 percent.

That doesn't sound so bad, considering that we were looking into a deep abyss in the fall of 2008.

But even though real per capita GDP has grown by 3.2 percent since the middle of 2009, we are still 8 percent below where we would have been without the housing and banking crisis that Wall Street helped create. Adding it up, we have lost almost $4 trillion in income since 2007. Since our annual GDP is $15 trillion, you can see we are talking about a lot of money. A robust recovery is still several years away, so this loss will only keep increasing.

Normally, recessions last a year or less, and recovery takes another year or so. Why is this recession so different?

Let me let you in on a poorly kept secret: this is a depression. Some economists prefer to call it a balance sheet recession, so we don't frighten the children (or consumers, or investors, or voters), and so people don't think we are comparing this to the whopper of the early 1930s, when government did everything wrong in response.

People assume a depression is just a word for a bad recession, but those who know the history of recessions define it as a downturn caused by a financial crisis. What makes that different?

In a financial crisis, banks and other financial institutions become extremely concerned about the poor quality of the debt they hold, and are afraid to take on any more risk. As a result, they collect reserves to offset their bad debt instead of lending it out. Firms won't hire or invest if demand is weak and they can't get loans.

Consumers lose much of their wealth in depressions, permanently depressing their spending habits. Because our financial crisis involved housing, the biggest asset most people own, homeowners are substantially poorer than they were five years ago. Firms that depend on old consumer spending habits struggle to survive.

Unlike recessions caused by tight money, depressions tend to push interest rates toward zero. Price deflation is also a danger, since falling prices make debt harder to repay and encourage banks to hold cash and bonds instead of making loans like they are supposed to do. Unless stopped, deflation creates more deflation, causing a downward spiral.

Governments tend to become the borrower of last resort in depressions, as investors flee other assets and look for somebody relatively safe to hold their money. As the Euromess is now demonstrating, however, even governments might not be safe bets.

When the recession is short, state and local governments with falling tax collections, increased spending needs, and balanced budget requirements can raid rainy-day funds and other balances. But if the recovery is slow, financial distress forces these governments to cut spending or raise taxes at exactly the wrong time. Though the private sector was hit first by the recession, the contraction of the public sector substantially slows down the recovery.

In normal times, things are different. When the economy is near full employment and markets are working well, an increase in government demand only crowds out private demand. Firms sell more to the government and less to private investors or consumers. If government borrows to pay for its spending, this bids up interest rates, reducing borrowing by the private sector. If those borrowed funds come from abroad, then exports fall instead, since every dollar we borrow from a foreigner is a dollar not spent on our goods. In normal times the multiplier is near zero, so that an extra dollar spent by government has very little net effect.

In a typical recession there is slack in the economy and crowding-out is not complete, so the multiplier is positive, if still not very big. But fiscal policy often requires a legislative decision, and implementation takes time; by the time government acts, the economy is well on its way to recovery. The private sector can generally create enough growth on its own, if government doesn't make things worse.

In a depression, however, the economy's normal recuperative powers are weak. Fiscal policy becomes the only tool government has left, even if its effectiveness is limited. In essence, government spending is a parachute slowing the economy's decline, not a rocket propelling us back to full employment. With it, the recession won't be as deep, but the damage is still substantial and recovery still takes years.

International evidence shows that recessions caused by financial crises are deeper and longer. Fiscal intervention can reduce the severity but can't make it all better. Even seven years later, on average, economies are 10 percent below where they should have been.

Why don't most people understand this difference? We have forgotten our past. Those who lived through the Great Depression will never forget it and know that this one now is much less nasty. But before that big one, depressions occurred with some regularity, and they were twice as long and twice as deep, on average, as recessions.

The institutions and rules we created after the big one prevented it from happening again. In time we came to think depressions were just a scary tale our grandparents told us so we would behave. Eventually, we came to believe we didn't need no stinkin' rules anymore, as the bandit in *The Treasure of the Sierra Madre* might have said.

Now most of us still don't know what hit us, or who to blame.

4. Hyperinflation? Take a Deep Breath...(2011)[10]

For several years, predictions about hyperinflation have pervaded the media. Yet consumer prices have risen only a total of 2.7 percent over the past three years, compared to 12.6 percent over the three years before, and 8.5 percent over the three years before that. Where is the hyperinflation, and why hasn't it shown up yet?

The Federal Reserve Act of 1913 created twelve regional banks, effectively owned by private member banks, plus a board of governors appointed by the president and confirmed by the U.S. Senate. This system has the power to create money by issuing credit in exchange for reserve assets. These assets once included gold, but the primary asset the Federal Reserve now purchases is government bonds, the debt of the federal government. In exchange, the Federal Reserve issues currency (i.e., the $970 billion in Federal Reserve notes currently outstanding, printed by the U.S. Treasury and deemed legal tender) and makes deposits in the reserve accounts of member banks.

When the financial sector melted down in 2008, the Federal Reserve did something unprecedented: it began to purchase massive amounts of government bonds, and even mortgage-backed securities and other nongovernment assets. The monetary base more than tripled as a result, rising from $870 billion in mid-2008 to $2.68 trillion now. By comparison, the monetary base rose by only a total of 8 percent in the three years prior.

Those with a simple mechanistic view of the economy see this expansion as inevitably leading to inflation, and these fears have been one of the major factors underlying the recent asset price bubble in gold. But these fears are largely misplaced, at least for the time being. What we are seeing is the complete opposite of hyperinflation.

Price inflation results when the supply of money outpaces demand, and people look to spend the excess money they don't want to hold. When hyperinflation takes hold, people are afraid to hold money and similar assets, and they spend what little money they hold as quickly as possible.

Money is not just currency. It primarily consists of deposits, which are created when banks make loans, people use that credit to buy things, and sellers deposit the money back in the bank. This goes on in a cycle called the deposit expansion process, and the total money supply is many times the original amount of credit issued by the Federal Reserve. The measure, called M2, currently stands at $9.5 trillion, about 3.5 times the monetary base.[11]

When banks stop lending, the money supply shrinks, and the result is price deflation like we experienced in the Great Depression. When prices fall and people aren't buying, firms can't pay back their loans, which makes banks even more fearful of lending. Unemployment rises, and the cycle continues.

The ratio of M2 to the monetary base was 8.1 in 2005 and 8.9 in 2008 when banks were still lending like crazy. Had the collapse in lending been allowed to spread, the price level might have fallen by more than half. Such a deflationary spiral would have made the Great Depression seem like a mere trial run for the big one.

What happens after a financial crisis is that government bonds become the only safe asset around, and the government becomes what the late economist Hyman Minsky called the borrower of last resort. In spite of the recent downgrading of U.S. Treasury bonds, they still look like a safe bet compared to everything else. Prices for long-term government bonds have risen, pushing annual yields for ten-year Treasuries below 2 percent. This would not be happening if major investors expected any significant inflation.

Now everybody wants to hold public debt, not private debt. They also want to hold money, not spend it or lend it. European government debt is not quite so attractive, due to chronic borrowers like Greece, and most other countries that might be considered safe places to park money don't borrow much, so there are few of their bonds to buy. The result is that the U.S. money supply can barely keep up with money demand, and price inflation slows as a result.

Are there future risks? Once banks have deleveraged most of their bad assets, and the economy has finally recovered, they should start lending again. Once investors are no longer afraid of additional bad financial news, they might be willing to hold other assets. Then, and only then, the Federal Reserve will need to back out of its current intervention, and bring the monetary base back down to normal by selling off some of its new reserves. As long as people can manage a little faith that the Federal Reserve can do this, there is no reason any of us should be hyperventilating about hyperinflation.

» Treasurer's Vignette: My Staff Takes a Stand

Meredith Whitney had become a star. First, she predicted problems with Citigroup, and the financial crisis. Then she began talking about states defaulting on their bonds. But when she decided to highlight what she viewed as the terrible economics of Nevada and its high level of debt and then compared us to Greece, she got under the skin of my staff. They demanded I respond.

"Nobody is going to listen to us," I told them.

They wanted me to go on CNBC, but I assured them that, not only did I not know whom to call, but no one at CNBC would answer my call if I did. Finally, to put an end to the argument, I told them to write a letter and we would send it to CNBC. The letter read like a treatise on municipal debt and I imagined it would be dumped in the trash if it was ever opened, but I had promised and so I sent it off.

However, my staff was on a crusade and had also taken to calling and e-mailing CNBC nonstop to demand the opportunity to present their views. Thus, a couple of weeks later, my staff crowded into my office with great excitement to inform me that I was going to take Meredith Whitney down.

"I'm going to do what?!"

"And you need an uplink," they chorused.

"What do you mean I'm going to take Meredith Whitney down? What are you talking about? And what in the hell is an uplink?"

I feared I was becoming like Mark Twain's celebrated jumping frog, but no amount of argument would deter them, nor would they agree to take my place. No, they were united in the belief that I could do it. All I needed was something called an uplink.

It turned out that the local PBS station had such a thing and it would allow me to be on CNBC from afar. They also had a makeup artist who needed to cake on so much foundation that my expression was immovable. My staff had come to see me perform and one had brought his son. They offered last-minute facts while I, tethered to the uplink, sat on a plastic chair in a cavernous room with lots of cables and an earpiece that kept falling out.

"Tell them how our debt service makes up only 3–5 percent of our budget!"

"Don't forget our debt is paid on 17 cents of $100 assessed value!"

"Debt service is only a little over $250 million a year!"

"Take her down! Let's do it!"

Sometimes the hardest thing to do in politics is translate the hard work of staff into words the public will understand. On the show, I said,

I can't speak for Ms. Whitney, but I do have to say it would be nice if she did a little homework, drilled down a little bit into what those numbers are.... It's as if she said, Well, a family of four makes $100,000 a year and they buy a house for $200,000, oh my goodness that's half their income. It's half the cost of that house, [and] they can't possibly afford it. But you and I know that's not [an] "apples-to-apples" comparison.... We have a double-A rating, and the reason we have that rating is the rating agencies say we have a moderate level of debt, very conservative fiscal practices.... Nevada holds back 5 percent extra revenue as a "shock absorber" and has an eleven-month reserve.... That is to say, if I collected no more, not a nickel, for the next eleven months, I could pay the state's debt, no problems.

When I got out of the way of the uplink, my staff was clapping and congratulatory. Throughout the day we heard from Nevadans who had seen the show and felt good about their state.

5. What Happened to Employment? (2012)[12]

Every president, regardless of party, tends to be judged by the electorate on how the economy performs under his watch, even though this performance is not entirely under the control of our elected officials.

The public sector—mostly local government, but also federal and state—employs only 16 percent of American workers and produces only 12–13 percent of our nation's GDP, so it is the private sector that really determines how our economy performs. Events from the past and from other countries also have a huge effect, but the government's budget decisions, regulations, tax rates, and other policies still matter.

People often focus on GDP growth, adjusted for inflation and sometimes population. In the recession we are now emerging from, real per capita GDP fell by 6.4 percent from the start of 2008 through mid 2009, and then began to slowly recover. A problem with GDP, however, is that it tells us nothing about how the income from what we produce is distributed. GDP can grow even when people are losing jobs, if the average income of those at the top is increasing faster.

People also focus on the unemployment rate, and the national rate rose from 5 percent in 2007 to 10 percent in 2010 before coming down. However, this rate is relative to those counted as either working or looking for work. When unemployment is rising, many unemployed workers get discouraged and stop looking. When the economy starts to recover, they reenter the market to look for work. As a result, the unemployment rate can lag behind the economy, and in the short run it can confuse us about the economy.

Actual employment is sometimes a better measure of economic performance, and this recession cost the U.S. economy almost 8.8 million nonfarm jobs in the two years from early 2008 through early 2010. This was about 6.3 percent of our total jobs.

This was much, much worse than any other postwar recession. In the early 1980s, during the first twenty-four months of President Reagan's first term, we lost 2.3 percent of jobs in what we then said was the worst recession since the Great Depression. In the recession of 1991–92, under the first President Bush, we lost only 0.8 percent of jobs, but he still lost his job to President Clinton. In the first two years of the second President Bush's first term, a recession cost us 1.7 percent of jobs, and in the third year employment barely grew by 0.1 percent.

In the last year of President Bush's second term, however, the economy hit a wall, and then it fell on us. In the year before he left office, the economy lost 4.5 million jobs, or 3.2 percent of total employment. Half of this loss occurred in the last three months, as we plummeted into the scariest recession in most of our lifetimes.

For the next year, President Obama's first year in office, the economy lost 4.3 million more jobs, though the rate of decline slowed after the middle of the year. Officially the recession ended in mid-2009, but recovery would be long and slow.

In the two years since, we have added back more than 3.6 million jobs in the private sector, while still losing 0.5 million jobs in the public sector. Counting the 5 million jobs that would have normally been added since 2007, we are still 10.6 million short of where we were. The number of unemployed grew because job growth wasn't enough for all the new entrants.

Figure 5.4 shows the percentage change in U.S. payroll employment for the seven longest business cycles since 1950, including

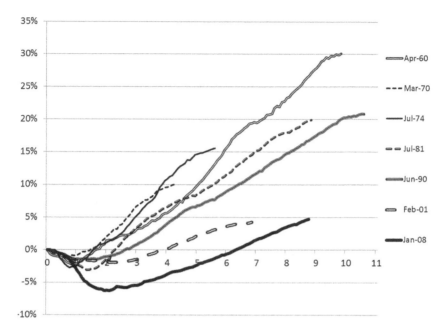

FIGURE 5.4. Employment Change in Postwar Recoveries. *Source:* Author's calculations from the Bureau of Labor Statistics, U.S. Department of Labor.

both the recession and recovery. It is pretty clear that the current one, which began in January 2008, is in a class all by itself.

This past year's private-sector growth rate of 2.1 percent finally exceeded the normal job creation rate, so we are starting to regain lost ground. At the current rate of private-sector job growth, if the public sector stabilizes this year and nothing else derails us, it will take America five more years before employment recovers, since we must also find jobs for all of those who would have normally entered the job market during this time.

In Nevada the tale is even tougher to tell. Nevada's real per capita GDP fell by a combined 12.6 percent in 2008 and 2009, and then fell again by 1 percent in 2010. Our unemployment rate rose from 5 percent in 2007 to almost 15 percent in 2010, before falling back to 12.6 percent now.

But the best measure of this recession's impact is that Nevada lost 80,000 jobs in 2008, another 87,000 jobs in 2009, and then another 18,000 jobs through September 2010. This added up to 14.3 percent of total state employment, a job loss of more than twice the national rate. Since then, we added back only 9,000 jobs, a mere 0.8 percent of jobs. At that rate of recovery, it will take Nevada almost thirty years to catch back up to where it was in 2007, even if nobody ever moves here again.

Most of this recent employment uptick has come in casinos, restaurants, and hotels, and almost all of that happened in Las Vegas. The rest of the nation is starting to recover, so folks are coming back to Sin City for their vacations and conventions. Indeed, Nevada's private sector has added 17,000 jobs in the past fifteen months, an increase of almost 2 percent.

Declines in public-sector employment, however, canceled out more than half of this past year's private-sector growth. The state, cities, and counties have shed 17,000 government jobs in Nevada since the middle of 2008, including 5,300 jobs in the past year alone, adding up to a net decline of 11.6 percent. If this stabilizes, now that tax revenues are starting to recover, then the current rate of growth in private-sector jobs suggests it will take only twenty years to claw our way back.

Although these employment numbers don't distinguish between good jobs and not-so-good jobs, or part-time and full-time employment, they still tell an important part of the story. Nationally, it appears we are finally and consistently headed in the right direction in employment. In Nevada we have started to add jobs back as well, but too few to feel any confidence. We need to be careful not to mess this up, and we need to pick up speed.

» Treasurer's Vignette: In the Ring

Nevada has long paid a premium on its bonds, paying more in interest than other AA bond issuers pay. Bond buyers view Nevada's bonds with suspicion.

Is Nevada really a good bet? In the midst of the financial crisis, we decided that, instead of hiding in the shadows, we needed to be more aggressive so that we didn't start to be seen as another Illinois or California.

Indeed, some education was in order, and my staff and I laid out a campaign to improve the reputation of Nevada's bonds. We successfully opened up a retail window for individuals to buy our bonds. Nevadans loved it. Then we went on a road show: Boston, New York, Philadelphia—throwing ourselves to the wolves to answer any and all questions related to Nevada.

Bond shops are invariably made up of almost all men, and to me it's as if they are posing for a Warby Parker photo shoot. They might want to look like they just got back from a trek through the Sierras, but had they ever really been to the West?

They wanted to know about revenues in April (we don't have an income tax), about balancing the budget via furloughs (correct), about the pension fund (employees pay half and don't get Social Security), about casinos cannibalizing themselves (and how many different boxes of Kellogg's are in your cupboard), about whether Vegas was passé (and yet they couldn't wait to go there for their friend's birthday bash), about Indian casinos (what about them?), about whether we would default on our bonds (they're triple-backed, I have eleven months of reserves, and no, Nevada can't default on its bonds), and finally about water.

To which, in exasperation to one group in Boston, I quipped, "West, water, war." And when they didn't laugh, I said, "That's from Mark Twain."

Once we got down to the lobby, my staff said, "Mark Twain didn't say that." "No," I said, "my mother's aunt did and she's a chicken farmer, so who better to know?"

We barely made the train from New York to Philly. It was past 8 PM, we hadn't eaten since breakfast, and we were tired. My chief treasurer bought a Pop-Tart, but then couldn't quite bring himself to open it. Instead, he asked my senior deputy whether she had ever thought about being a cage fighter.

"I think you'd be good at," he said. "You know, in the ring, duking it out. You could subscribe to some of their magazines to get started."

She narrowed her eyes and gave him a look. I pretended to be resting.

But the fellow across the aisle leaned over, "Are there magazines on cage fighting?" he asked.

"I think they're joking," I said, and then, "For crying out loud, eat your Pop-Tart."

"I think it's past the expiration date."

"Not possible. It says on the package: Fresh new flavor."

When we finally make it to our hotel it was past ten. The next morning we visited our last bond shop. These guys buy a lot of Nevada bonds but they were a missing player from our last sale and so we were particularly intent that they should know how valuable Nevada's bonds are.

After a good forty-five minutes of back and forth, the head of the department took his glasses off and gave me the smallest of smiles. "You know," he says, "nobody here ever listens to Meredith Whitney."

I smiled from ear to ear all the way home.

6. Not the Worst Recovery (2012)[13]

Is this the worst recovery in U.S. history? *CBS Evening News* anchor Scott Pelley claimed this recently, and television viewers have recently been treated to numerous commercials replaying this claim. The commercials, unsurprisingly, are paid for by American Crossroads, an anonymously funded super PAC created by Ed Gillespie and Karl Rove.

First, it is true by most reasonable measures that the Great Recession, which we are still recovering from, was the worst U.S. recession in fifty years. But U.S. history goes back much further, and there have been many worse recessions in our history, with much slower recoveries.

Does anybody remember the Panic of 1797? The Depression of 1815–21? The Recession of 1836–38? The post–Civil War Recession? The Panic of 1873 and the resulting Long Depression? The Panic of 1893? The Panic of 1907? The Depression of 1921? The Great Depression? I doubt folks did their homework.

How can we objectively measure the depth of a recession or the speed of a recovery? Pelley used unemployment rates. Though the national unemployment rate actually rose higher in 1983, to 10.8 percent versus a peak of 10.1 percent in 2009, it came down faster in that earlier recession. However, the unemployment rate is not available for most of our history, and it is hard to compare over time. It also rises when the long-term unemployed start looking for work again because the economy is improving.

Economists think a better measure is average economic output, as measured by real (i.e., inflation-adjusted) GDP per person. By this measure, the current recession was deep. From the last quarter of 2007 to the second quarter of 2009, average output fell by 5.9 percent (normally it would have grown by 2.9 percent over that period). The previous postwar record was minus 4.7 percent, set in the recession of 1957–58 (when the unemployment rate topped out at only 7.5 percent).

But this Great Recession pales in comparison to the Great Depression, when average output fell by almost 30 percent, unemployment rose to 25 percent over four years, and it took ten years before real GDP per capita reached its prior peak. There are at least five other, earlier recessions in which average output fell more than in our recent recession and in which real per capita GDP remained below its previous peak more than five years out.

It is simply not true that this is the worst recovery in U.S. history. Since this economy hit bottom in 2009, economic growth has been positive but unimpressive, and not enough to create the jobs needed for all those who lost their jobs plus those who enter the workforce each year. However, the economy will regain its previous peak in this quarter, a duration of less than five years.

There are at least four major reasons why this current recession and recovery is worse than most postwar recessions. None of these reasons has been addressed by the political commercials I have seen.

The first reason is that this was the first balance sheet recession since the Great Depression, not one of the garden-variety recessions that most of us have experienced. The recession that began in 2008 was caused by a bubble in the housing market that burst a couple of years before and a financial crisis that left us on the edge of an abyss. As both the Great Depression and Japan's lost decade show, recessions like this are almost always deeper and longer than most recessions, and much harder to recover from, no matter what the government does.

Home equity is the primary asset for most middle-class families, and the collapse in home prices substantially reduced the wealth of most Americans, affecting their spending. Businesses also found themselves with severely damaged asset values, and so they used their profits to pay down debt rather than hire more workers.

The second reason is that the biggest decline in the economy came from the reduced construction of new homes, and this residential investment has been very slow to recover. Business investment, by contrast, has mostly recovered to its prerecession peak. Does anybody really think residential housing construction was likely to bounce back quickly to prerecession levels?

Third, this recovery has been led by exports, but the financial crisis exacerbated economic problems in many other countries. Recessions elsewhere led to reduced tax collections, and many countries had to bail out their banks, too. The resulting budget deficits and bond market worries led to austerity policies that made these foreign recessions even worse. The result is that foreigners have lower incomes and are buying fewer of our goods and services. It becomes hard to sell what we produce when fewer people are able to buy, either here or abroad.

The fourth and final reason this current recession and recovery is worse than most postwar recessions is because this is the first postwar recovery in which real government purchases of goods and services—by state, local, and federal governments—actually shrank.

After the 2001 recession, real government purchases grew by about 5 percent per year. After the recession of 1991, these purchases grew by about 2 percent per year. In the recession of 1982–83, government purchases grew by about 5 percent per year. In the recession of 1974–75, it was about 3 percent per year. Such increased purchases by the government have always helped the economy recover.

In contrast, from 2009 to 2012 total government purchases, particularly those by state and local governments, fell. The federal deficit rose only because taxes fell and transfers rose.

It is ironic, then, that so many commercials argue the complete opposite.

If you remove government purchases from the equation and look only at GDP purchased by the private sector, you find that the private economy actually is recovering faster now than in the three years after the 2001 recession under President George W. Bush. However, the crash of 2008 left the economy at a much lower starting point than in 2001.

We need a debate over how best to lay the groundwork for future economic growth. We need, however, to stick to the facts and avoid unsubstantiated hyperbole disconnected from any real understanding of what has happened. I fear this is a lost cause until after the election is over.

7. The U.S. Economy in an Election Year (2012)[14]

We are now in the final month of a long election season, and in spite of the fact that Nevadans will continue to be bombarded by political advertising, most of us have already made up our minds on which candidates we support. If we are to have any hope of crafting sensible policy solutions after the election, however, it is important for us to separate the wheat from the chaff in this political discussion. We need some sense of history and perspective regarding the current economic situation in order to know how to proceed.

If you haven't figured it out yet, this was a very unusual recession. Severe depressions were regular events before the Second World War, but since then our recessions have been comparatively short and shallow, with most declines in economic activity lasting six months to a year, followed by faster growth that recovers lost ground.

But the buildup of mortgage debt prior to 2006 and the collapse of housing prices afterward played a huge part in the financial crisis, turning this recession into a near-depression; excessive private leveraging was not limited to housing. Since then, deleveraging by producers, tightened lending by banks, and reduced consumption by households, who felt much poorer due to the collapse of their home equity, all contributed to several years of dramatically reduced private spending.

In the face of all this, the federal government's record fiscal stimulus was not really as big as we think, particularly since state and local governments responded to declining tax revenue by cutting their spending to match. Most people are surprised to learn that the government now spends less on goods and services than it did when President Obama took office, if we include state and local governments. While some observers mistook federal hiring for the decennial census of 2010 as evidence of rapid growth, federal employment has increased by 12,000 jobs during Obama's entire term, a rise of only 0.4 percent, and a pittance compared to the 650,000 jobs lost in state and local governments.

Pundits talk about how policy uncertainty has depressed private investment spending, but this is misleading. Certainly residential investment in new housing has fallen dramatically since 2006, but the rest of investment has almost recovered back to prerecession levels, and industrial and commercial lending has now bounced back as well.

The economy could not recover to resemble its former self, and should not be expected to. The prerecession economy was largely built on rising private debt and excessive construction, while Americans were spending more than we produced by borrowing from abroad. Every dollar we borrowed from the savings of other countries was a dollar those countries did not spend on our exports. Our export sector did start growing faster after the recession, but this year the Euromess and the slowing Chinese economy have dampened that back down.

As private debt declined, government debt rose in response. Paying down debt through increased savings is good in the long run, but in the short run it makes a recession worse. It is not only sovereign public debt that matters.

Economists like to distinguish between structural and cyclical deficits. Tax revenues rise and fall with the business cycle, while some types of government spending rise during recessions automatically. Thus, recessions worsen government budget deficits, even if the government makes no effort to stimulate demand. If we followed a sensible policy, we would have taken advantage of the upper part of the business cycle to pay down our debt before the recession, so we wouldn't have had to do the wrong thing at the wrong time.

The structural part of the budget deficit is unsustainably high, but candidates and pundits who talk about the deficit sometimes remind me of Captain Renault in the film *Casablanca*, as they are shocked—shocked!—to discover we are suddenly running budget deficits under President Obama. Yet we turned surpluses into deficits back in fiscal year 2002, and the peak deficit year was fiscal year 2009, which began a month before the election. That deficit was projected to be $1.2 trillion before President Obama even took office, although when the stimulus passed in spring 2009 it rose to a bit over $1.4 trillion. Since President Obama took office, the budget deficit has come down only a little, helped along by more cuts to the payroll tax and federal support for state spending on Medicaid and unemployment benefits.

In a nutshell, the major source of the current structural deficit in the federal budget are the tax cuts we passed in 2001 and 2003, exacerbated by the rising cost of health care. Federal income tax receipts averaged 11.2 percent of personal income during President Clinton's second term, but averaged only 8.9 percent from 2003 to 2007, before the recession began. The lost revenue almost precisely equaled the average budget deficit under President Bush, even with increased military spending on two wars. By 2009, during the recession, federal taxes were down to 7 percent of personal income, the lowest share since 1950.

Including Medicare and Medicaid support, federal health-care spending grew steadily from 3.6 percent of GDP in 2000 to 5.5 percent in 2009, due to both an aging population and rising health-care costs. From 1990 to 2008 the consumer price index grew 2 percent faster per year for medical care than it did for everything else (that price difference has dropped to 1 percent since 2009).

The structural issue regarding Medicare costs is how they will affect future deficits if costs keep growing at this rate. But it is a mistake to focus only on the public sector. The United States currently spends about 18 percent of GDP on health care, twice as much as other developed economies. Shifting the cost from public to private without addressing the underlying problem does the public a disservice.

Under current law, the deficit is projected to be forced down dramatically next year, though few think we will actually go over this fiscal cliff. Most of the stimulus spending has already expired.

The income tax cuts and the more recent payroll tax cuts will also expire on January 1, and together these are estimated to bring in over $400 billion more in annual tax revenue. In addition, Congress passed an automatic sequestration last year that will cut $1.2 trillion in spending over the next nine years, including a 9.4 percent cut to defense (excluding military pay and benefits), and an 8.2 percent cut to nondefense discretionary programs.

There are only three problems with this fiscal cliff. First, implementing these spending cuts and tax increases might work when the economy is near full employment, but under current conditions they might push the economy back into recession, which could backfire on the deficit. Second, tax increases are politically unpopular, and we should expect to see the government scramble to reduce the number of people affected by it. Third, the sequestration cuts are intentionally arbitrary, and we should expect to see a major effort to change how many of the cuts are made. Still, a gradual implementation of tax increases and spending cuts once the economy is a little stronger would help us get the budget to a more sustainable level.

Debates over the optimal size of government are too often ideological, and we need to take a deep breath. The United States remains one of the most market-driven economies in the world; even though governments often become a larger portion of the economy during a recession, our government is still relatively smaller than in most other developed nations. Restoring Clinton-era tax rates does not lead to socialism, and efforts to reduce our health-care spending is not fascism.

We need some sense of balance regarding the public–private mix. Free and private markets usually work better than government, but not at all times and not in all areas. Government does not always have to be in conflict with the private sector, and sometimes can support and promote market activities. While there are lots of things we can do better, neither candidate, nor the parties each represents, has a monopoly on either bad ideas or good ideas. But until we can get to the point where we can agree on an initial set of facts and quit demonizing those who disagree with our interpretations, we will remain stuck in our respective corners.

8. Why Is Unemployment Still So High? (2014)[15]

The official U.S. unemployment rate began rising in June 2007 and peaked more than two years later at 10 percent, the highest peak since it reached 10.8 percent in 1982. Now, more than four years later, it stands at 6.7 percent. This rate is only slightly higher than the average rate of 6.5 percent since 1980, but still considerably higher than the 4.4 percent rate of May 2007, before the Great Recession began.

During this recovery the unemployment rate has fallen by an average of 0.8 percent per year. Contrary to popular opinion, this is not unusually slow. During the eight expansions since 1960 that lasted more than a year, the unemployment rate dropped by an average of 0.8 percent per year. Three expansions (1961–62, 1975–79, and 1982–89) had faster drops in unemployment, and four (1963–66, 1971–73, 1992–2000, and 2003–6) had slower drops. So one lesson is that unemployment is still so high only because the Great Recession was so deep.

Nevada, of course, was an outlier this time. Our unemployment rate rose from 4.2 percent to 14.0 percent in a recession lasting a year longer than in the rest of the nation; though it has fallen to 9 percent as of November 2013, it still remains tied for highest of any state. This status can largely be explained by the fact that we had twice as many construction workers as the rest of the country on average, and these construction jobs suffered disproportionately from the collapse of the housing market. Otherwise, we would have remained near the national average.

There are many unusual features of this recovery, just as the Great Recession itself was very unusual. The first is the contraction of public-sector employment due to imposed austerity, mostly in local government but also in state and federal government. During the eight years of the Clinton administration, total government employment rose by 240,000 jobs per year, all in local governments (the federal workforce fell by 45,000 jobs per year, exactly offsetting the increase in state governments). During the eight years of the George W. Bush administration, public employment rose by 220,000 jobs per year as jobs increased for all three levels of government.

During the five years of the Obama administration, by contrast, public-sector employment fell for all three levels of government, by a combined 140,000 jobs per year. This is the first time this decline has occurred since the end of the Second World War, and this difference alone accounts for 1.3 percent of the labor force. In other words, had public-sector employment expanded during the Obama administration at the same rate it expanded during the previous sixteen years, the unemployment rate would now be 5.4 percent, never mind the effect of 1.8 million more people having jobs with paychecks they could be spending on goods and services from the private sector.

A second unusual feature of this recession might be the number of workers forced to work part time when they would have preferred to work full time. The Bureau of Labor Statistics does not have good comparable data on this from previous recessions, but it currently estimates that these individuals rose from less than 3 percent of the labor force in 2007 to almost 6 percent in 2009. This rate, which is the difference between what the Bureau calls the U-5 and the U-6 rates, has been slowly dropping since 2009, and did not rise in response to the Affordable Care Act as some might have thought.[16] The Bureau also reports the number of discouraged workers and those marginally attached to the labor force. Together these numbers (the difference between the U-5 and the U-3 rate, which is the official unemployment rate) rose slightly during the recession, from about 1 percent to 1.5 percent, and has remained steady since.

A third unusual feature of this recession is the falling labor-force participation rate, which peaked in 2000 at 67.3 percent of the noninstitutional population before falling to 66 percent when the recession began, 65 percent when the recovery began, and 63 percent now. The labor force includes those who are employed plus those who are officially unemployed (and looking for work), so when people exit the labor force this reduces the unemployment rate without creating more jobs. The expiration of long-term unemployment benefits is likely to lead even more individuals to exit the workforce.

One important explanation for this is the retirement of the baby boom generation, a bulge in the population that began in

1946, slightly more than sixty-five years ago. Census projections show the share of our population in the prime working years of eighteen to sixty-four will drop by 3 percent from 2010 to 2020, and another 3 percent by 2030, before stabilizing. This alone will slow growth, since fewer people will be working. While this exit of baby boomers appears to explain much of the decrease in the labor force, anecdotal evidence suggests that not all of this is voluntary. Many people near retirement age had hoped to keep working, and many of them might have inadequate savings to retire in any comfort.

A fourth unusual factor is the relatively low rate of inflation in the expansion, the lowest in any expansion since the 1950s and 1960s. This particularly matters because the distribution of income is widening, and there is more downward pressure on lower-end wages from rising international competition, technological changes, and social changes like the falling power of unions.

Low inflation does not really matter when wages are relatively stable or incomes are becoming more equal over time. But when there is downward pressure on wages at the lower end, then low inflation makes adjustment difficult. Economists call this "downward-wage rigidity." Employees often tolerate stagnant wages when prices are rising, even though it means their real wage is falling. But there are many things that prevent decreases in nominal wages, including implicit contracts. Employers who cut wages often find that morale suffers and worker productivity falls, costing them more than reducing the wages saved. If nominal wages don't fall when labor demand decreases, then this puts upward pressure on the unemployment rate and makes recovery more difficult.

In the 1950s economists called the relationship between the unemployment rate and the inflation rate the "Phillips Curve," after the New Zealand economist who noticed a regularity in more than a hundred years of British inflation and unemployment data.[17] By the late 1960s some economists thought this meant that ever-higher inflation could push unemployment rates way down, a simplistic view that Milton Friedman effectively disproved. By the time I was in graduate school, nobody taught the Phillips Curve anymore, and it was assumed that there was no relationship what-soever. But there does appear to be a relationship nonetheless, at least at very low rates of inflation. High inflation might not lead to low unemployment, but very low inflation (and especially de-flation) might help cause higher unemployment, at least in the short run.

Of course, economists have identified many reasons why actual price deflation can slow growth, usually associated with how it affects interest rates. When inflation is low or negative, for example, the cost of holding cash is low and banks have less in-centive to lend. The demand for money rises at the expense of other types of financial assets, and because most of the money supply is created by the lending behavior of banks, the money supply can grow too slowly even when the central bank is priming the pump. Consumers have less incentive to spend now and more incentive to wait, which reduces the demand for the products workers produce. The result is a downward pressure on demand.

Recessions can be caused by many things, but when they are caused by financial crises, recoveries take longer and lost ground is rarely recovered. The Great Depression was the last time such a recession occurred in the United States. Because this reces-sion devastated the net wealth of many households, especially in Nevada where two thirds of home mortgages were under water, the impact on consumer spending was long lasting. Deleveraging by households, firms, and financial institutions took several years; the downward pressure on prices made wage adjustment harder; and austerity imposed by state and local governments made it worse.

Japan experienced this for more than two decades, and only now appears to be changing course. Because countries like Spain and Greece share a common currency with Germany and its phobia of inflation, they have had a more difficult time get-ting their real wages back down after their boom years. And in the United States the long recovery continues. We can only hope now that neither external events nor our own taciturn foolishness make it any harder for us to finally get our unemployment rates back down.

Notes

1. A. Sen, "What Happened to Europe?," *New Republic,* August 23, 2012.

2. See F. Guerrero and E. Parker, "Deflation and Recession: Finding the Empirical Link," *Economics Letters* (2006). See also Cargill and Parker, "Why Deflation Is Different."; T. F. Cargill and E. Parker, "Price Deflation and Consumption: Central Bank Policy and Japan's Economic and Financial Stagnation," *Journal of Asian Economics,* 2004; T. F. Cargill and E. Parker, "Price Deflation, Money Demand, and Monetary Policy Discontinuity: A Comparative View of Japan, China, and the United States," *North American Journal of Economics and Finance* (2004); F. Guerrero and E. Parker, "Deflation, Recession, and Slowing Growth: Finding the Empirical Links," *ICFAI Journal of Monetary Economics* (2006).

3. Koo, *The Holy Grail.*

4. Minsky, *Stabilizing an Unstable Economy.*

5. I. Fisher, "The Debt-Deflation Theory of Great Depressions," *Econometrica* 1, no. 4 (1933): 337–35.

6. J. M. Keynes, *The General Theory of Employment, Interest, and Money* (London: Palgrave, 1936).

7. Originally published as E. Parker, "Why Hasn't the Economy Recovered?," *Nevada Appeal,* September 6, 2011.

8. Originally published as E. Parker, "Where We Went Wrong after Sept. 11," *Nevada Appeal,* September 11, 2011.

9. Originally published as E. Parker, "We'd Forgotten What a Depression Looks Like," *Las Vegas Sun,* November 27, 2011. This was also published as "Why Is This Recession Different?," *Nevada Appeal,* November 20, 2011.

10. Originally published as E. Parker, "Hyperinflation? Take a Deep Breath[ellipsis]," *Nevada Appeal,* October 9, 2011.

11. The Federal Reserve System defines M0 as the notes and coins in circulation, and M1 as M0 plus demand deposits (i.e., checking accounts) and travelers checks. The most common measure of the money supply is M2, which includes M1 plus savings accounts and other "small" deposits under $100,000.

12. Originally published as E. Parker, "National Unemployment: Where Have We Been, and Where Are We Going?," *Reno Gazette Journal,* February 22, 2012.

13. Originally published as E. Parker, "It's Not the Worst Recovery. Really," *Las Vegas Sun,* August 12, 2012.

14. Originally published as E. Parker, "The U.S. Economy in an Election Year," *Washington Watch,* October 2012.

15. Originally published as E. Parker, "Economic Recovery Update: Why Is Unemployment Still So High?," *Washington Watch,* February 2014.

16. The Bureau of Labor Statistics, U.S. Department of Labor, defines six unemployment rates. U-1 counts only persons unemployed for fifteen weeks or longer, while U-2 adds in recent job losers. U-3 is the official rate,

and includes those who are actively looking for work but haven't recently worked at all. U-4 adds in discouraged job-seekers who have not been looking recently, U-5 adds in other persons more marginally attached to the work-force, and U-6 adds in those working part time who are seeking full-time employment.

17. A.W.H. Phillips, "The Relation between Unemployment and the Rate of Change of Money Wage Rates in the United Kingdom, 1861–1957," *Economica* 25, no. 2 (1958): 283–99.

CHAPTER 6

Federal Fiscal Policy

In 1790, the nation which had fought a revolution against taxation with-
out representation discovered that some of its citizens weren't much hap-
pier about taxation with representation.

— LYNDON B. JOHNSON[1]

Introduction

Many discussions about taxes begin with the assertion that they
are rising out of control. In the past thirty-five years, the revenue
collected by the U.S. government—federal, state, and local—has
grown more than fivefold. Income taxes are the largest source of
federal government revenues, followed by payroll taxes for social
insurance programs. Corporate income taxes and other federal
taxes make up a small share of total federal revenue, and federal
revenue makes up the majority of all taxes paid to all levels of government. Figure 6.1 shows how much the federal government collects if we adjust for price inflation; since 1980 the total has grown
by 166 percent.

The problem with presenting these data in this way is that we
fail to account for the gradual annual increase in the U.S. population, and for rising real incomes that affect how much federal,
state, and local governments must pay to their employees to compete with the private sector. We can divide by GDP to get a more
meaningful number, but this would make government revenue
look relatively higher during recessions and lower during booms.
To get a more stable ratio, we should divide by the economy's estimated potential GDP, which is reported by the Federal Reserve
Bank of St. Louis.[2]

As a share of potential GDP, government receipts have been
much more stable over the past three to four decades (figure 6.2).
While the effect of tax rate changes by the Clinton, Bush, and

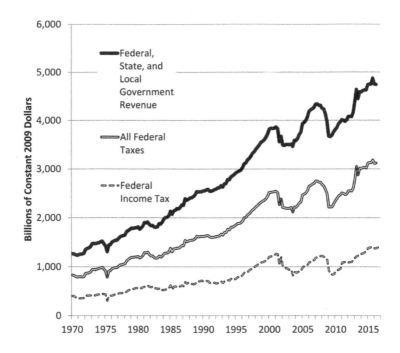

FIGURE 6.1. U.S. Government Revenue, Adjusted for Price Inflation.
Source: Courtesy of the Bureau of Economic Analysis.

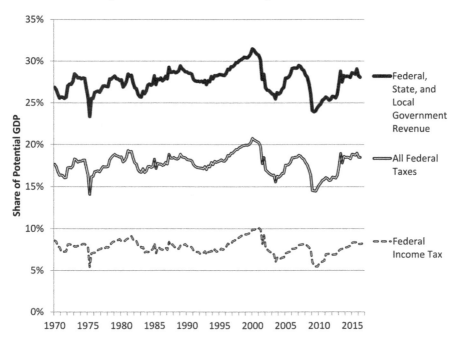

FIGURE 6.2. U.S. Government Revenue, Share of Potential GDP. *Source:*
Courtesy of the St. Louis Federal Reserve Board Economic Research and Bureau
of Economic Analysis.

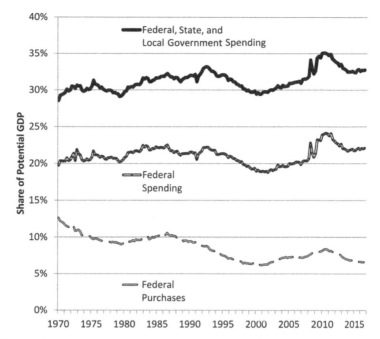

FIGURE 6.3. U.S. Government Spending, Share of Potential GDP. *Source:* Courtesy of the St. Louis Federal Reserve Board Economic Research and Bureau of Economic Analysis.

Obama administrations can be seen in these data, the effect of recessions on tax revenues is much more dramatic. Obviously, people who lose their jobs tend to pay less in taxes.

Of course, taxes are just one side of the government's ledger book, and spending tends to grow during recessions even as taxes are declining. Figure 6.3 shows total government spending over time; we divide this into federal purchases, other federal spending, and state and local government spending. Purchases are defined as spending in which government gets something in return; this includes what government pays to its employees and what government spends to buy goods and services from the private sector, like roads, bridges, tanks, and planes. Figure 6.3 shows that purchases have been a declining share for decades.

The bulk of other federal spending is for what are called transfers, in that money is spent but nothing is provided in exchange. The largest transfer programs are Social Security and Medicare.

Spending in these areas, for what some call entitlements, is growing faster than the economy, helped in large part by an aging population and a decades-long increase in medical costs.

The federal government also transfers a significant amount of money to state and local governments to help pay for things like highways. The remainder of state and local government spending is added to get to total government spending, with adjustments to make sure we are not double-counting money that is passed through from the federal government. The lion's share of state and local spending is for K–12 education, public safety, and similar purchases, but Medicaid is a significant area of state transfer spending that is subsidized by the federal government.

Figure 6.4 compares the federal totals from figures 6.2 and 6.3: the difference is the federal budget deficit. Federal deficits hit their highest levels in peacetime during the 1980s, after President Reagan implemented two tax-cut packages and increased military spending; these deficits were then eliminated by the end of the Clinton administration. Budget deficits grew again under President George W. Bush, for several reasons. First, a slow economy after the 2001 recession reduced tax collections, and in 2001 and 2003 tax cuts were passed that reduced federal revenue by roughly $300 billion per year; some parts of these cuts were phased in over ten years. Second, wars in Iraq and Afghanistan increased debt by roughly $3 trillion, and obligated us to pay future costs for veterans. Tax collections then fell dramatically when the recession started in 2007, and the Economic Stimulus Act President Bush enacted in February 2008 contributed $150 billion more to the deficit. The bank bailouts passed in October 2008 added $700 billion more. President Bush's budget of fiscal year 2009 was thus on track to be the biggest budget deficit since the Second World War, even before President Obama took office.

Immediately after taking office, President Obama pushed through the American Recovery and Reinvestment Act to stimulate the economy and help slow the worsening recession. This made the 2009 deficit even larger. Roughly a third of the increase in the deficit came from tax cuts, which were eventually followed by a cut in payroll taxes. Another third came in the form of support for the states to help them avoid crushing cuts to education,

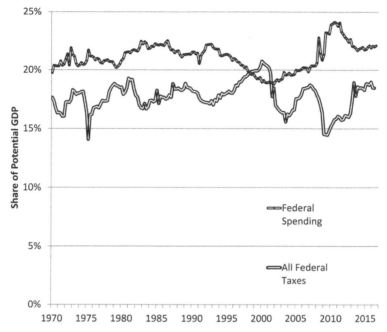

FIGURE 6.4. Federal Taxes and Spending, Share of Potential GDP. *Source:* Courtesy of the St. Louis Federal Reserve Board Economic Research and Bureau of Economic Analysis.

and Nevada in particular benefited from this support. The rest went for investment projects, including some infrastructure projects that were considered "shovel ready," as well as investments in areas such as alternative energy and health information systems.

It was a perfect storm. The states quickly drained their unemployment funds, and borrowed from the federal government. Many people who lost their jobs decided to retire early or go on disability, and many became eligible for Medicare and social services. The last of the Bush tax cuts, delayed until the tenth year, went into automatic effect. And finally, those born during the baby boom, which began nine months after soldiers began returning from the Second World War, began turning sixty-five in 2011 and filing for Social Security. By 2010 federal personal income tax collections had fallen to 6.3 percent of GDP, the lowest share since 1950, and expenditures never came back down to their pre-recession levels.

Though the broad consensus of economists is that government intervention prevented a much worse recession, it was not easy for most voters to understand why the recession never seemed to end. The Democrats lost control of the House of Representatives in the elections of 2010, and the federal budget deficit became the focus of Republicans. Sequestration became code for arbitrary budget cuts, and filibusters in the U.S. Senate almost led the country over the fiscal cliff. In the debates about the federal budget deficit that followed the Great Recession, the focus was always on spending budgets.

Of course, borrowing to cover the deficit adds to the federal debt, and figure 6.5 shows the federal debt as a share of potential GDP since 1950. Because a substantial amount of federal debt is held by the Federal Reserve Bank to back up the money supply, and more is held by federal agencies (especially the Social Security Administration), this figure distinguishes between the gross federal debt and the debt held by the public. During the Second World War the gross federal debt reached almost 120 percent of GDP, but this ratio declined for three decades as the economy grew. In the 1980s it grew again as a result of large budget deficits, before declining in the late 1990s. In the Great Recession, however, the ratio really jumped up. By 2014 the gross federal debt had reached almost 100 percent of potential GDP, and almost 60 percent was held by the public.

It is one of the quirks of the United States Congress that it votes separately on tax policy, spending budgets, and the federal debt limit, and there is no legal legislative requirement that these policies be consistent. Thus, Congress can vote to cut taxes, increase spending, and limit borrowing, even though this would force the U.S. Treasury into an impossible situation. This inconsistency gives Congress leverage in dealing with the president, who is usually loath to allow the U.S. Treasury to default on the nation's debt. Such a default would be unconstitutional, and it would likely send financial markets into a tailspin and raise the costs of federal borrowing for decades.

This chapter includes seven columns written between 2010 and 2012, during the debates about the federal budget deficit.

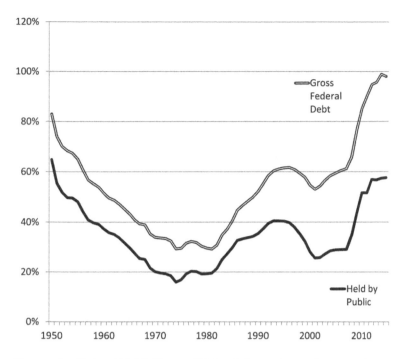

FIGURE 6.5. Federal Debt, Share of Potential GDP. *Source:* Courtesy of the St. Louis Federal Reserve Board Economic Research and the White House's Office of Management and Budget.

They explain concerns over the deficit and try to help readers understand where all the money goes.

1. Does Government Spending Hurt the Economy? (2010)[3]

Most goods and services are more efficiently produced by private firms. However, there are many public goods that the private sector fails to provide well, but are important to both the economy and society. These public goods include roads, ports, bridges, schools, national defense systems, courts, and a social safety net; they also include human resources such as police, firefighters, bank auditors, and cloud seeders. If the benefit to us is greater than the cost, then it makes sense for government to ensure these public goods are available. Government can either buy these goods from the private sector or provide them directly. Even though government agencies might not always be run well by the politicians who manage them, economies that don't deliver these public goods fail to prosper.

Most economists think of the relationship between the size of government and the growth of the economy as an inverted-U. At the extremes, you have Somalia or Haiti without a functional public sector, and the now-deceased Soviet Union that had no functioning private sector. Economic development is most successful somewhere in between. Compared to those of other developed countries, our government is relatively small. While the political left and right squabble over whether the optimal level is more or less than our current amount, others try to look at what the statistical evidence tells us.

When looking at the overall level of government spending, macroeconomists once thought the effect was clearly positive. They theorized that when government spent more, those who provided these goods and services made more money, and they in turn would spend more on goods and services provided by others. Tax cuts provided a similar, if smaller, effect.

Economists today are now more skeptical. Many claim that government spending often crowds out private spending, especially when unemployment rates are low and markets are functioning reasonably well. If government gets its spending money from taxpayers, then private households have less for their own consumption, and so the public goods need to be worth it. If government still spends while cutting taxes, then it has to cover the deficit by borrowing from capital markets, leaving less for the private sector. This increases real interest rates and reduces private investment.

If the deficit is instead financed with lending from the central bank, new money is created, resulting in inflation if the money supply grows faster than the money demanded by the needs of the real economy. If the deficit is financed by borrowing from abroad, then exports fall instead, since every dollar a foreigner lends us is a dollar that he or she does not spend on our goods. That borrowing is why we have a huge trade deficit, and it won't turn around until we start paying back what we owe.

Good policy, then, means taxing ourselves enough to pay for

the public goods that we think benefit us. In the long run, the overall deficit should be no more than enough to finance a small increase in money supply that just meets the demands of a growing economy.

But extraordinary things happen sometimes, and private markets can function badly. Balancing the government's budget in such times can make things much worse. In good times, government should save with budget surpluses, and pay down its debt. In bad times like these, we can then more easily borrow to keep providing those public goods, and keep spending in the private sector to avoid spiraling ever downward.

2. Slowing the Growth of Debt, Both Public and Private (2010)[4]

As an economist who has long been troubled by excessive debt, both public and private, I am relieved to see people becoming aware of the problem debt poses for our future.

Federal government debt was higher than GDP after World War II, but by 1979 this debt had fallen to only 25 percent of GDP because the economy outgrew the debt. Then, in the 1980s, we dropped the ball. The budget deficit rose to almost 5 percent of GDP, and the federal debt had risen back to almost half of GDP by 1993.

Then some deficit reduction efforts, combined with a strong economy, turned it all around. The federal budget was in surplus by 1998. By 2001 the debt had fallen to less than a third of GDP, and Alan Greenspan actually warned Congress against paying it off.

Instead of paying down the debt, or setting some money aside for future Social Security and Medicare obligations, we had several tax cuts and a couple of wars. The federal deficit again became a problem.

This growth in public debt was dwarfed by the growth in private debt. Outstanding mortgage debt was less than half of GDP before 1999, but by 2007 it had risen to 80 percent. Virtually every other type of debt also grew faster than the economy.

Tax cuts, low interest rates, financial misbehavior, and ineffective regulatory oversight enabled Americans to live beyond their means, so we borrowed from foreigners who actually saved. By 2006 foreigners held a majority of our public debt.

Then the chickens came home to roost, and the Great Recession hit. Tax receipts fell off dramatically, while the need for public spending increased. Without the financial bailout and the federal stimulus spending—most of which either went to the states or back to taxpayers—the economy would be in much worse shape than it is.

However, the budget deficit was 5 percent of GDP in 2008 and almost 9 percent in 2009. Public debt is expected to grow to almost 65 percent of GDP in the next decade, unless we do something to change our fiscal structure.

We really had no good choices: public debt was necessary to prevent a full-scale depression. In the short run, it was necessary for us to borrow, but in the long run we need to consume less and invest more, so we can keep both our public debt and our private debt from growing faster than our overall economy.

While there is an element of partisan opportunism in the current attention on the debt, it is reassuring that many Americans are willing to make sacrifices, especially once we emerge from this recession, to save more and pay the taxes necessary to provide the public goods we demand, so we can stop relying on borrowed money.

3. Do Taxes Kill Jobs? (2010)[5]

It is now our biennial silly season, when politicians hoping to get elected often say the strangest things.

One argument making the rounds is that our state economy is in such sad shape because of the tax increases passed by our legislature. My assemblyman, Ty Cobb, who was running for the state senate, said the legislature expanded government with a billion-dollar spending increase funded by job-killing tax hikes. Governor Gibbons called it the worst thing we can do.

Republican primary voters made a decision last week on the argument's leading advocates. Perhaps we can now also dismiss the argument itself.

Did last year's tax increase expand state government? Of course not. Government services in Nevada have been shrinking during this recession, not growing. State tax revenues declined much faster than the rest of our economy, and the tax increase replaced only some of the lost revenue.

More importantly, do taxes stifle economic growth? Many think the answer is obvious. Taxes reduce what the private sector can save or spend, and employers paying higher taxes have less to spend on paying their employees or their suppliers. Taxes also provide a disincentive to do whatever activity is being taxed.

But what about the other half of the equation? If those taxes are being collected to pay for things like education, law enforcement, or highway construction, then jobs are being funded in those sectors. Are those jobs not valuable, too, and are those goods and services not important to the state? There are trade-offs between how taxes affect the taxpayer and what the taxes pay for.

An analysis of the connections between U.S. GDP, Nevada's GSP, and tax policy shows no tendency for the economy to grow faster after tax cuts. In fact, sometimes the opposite relationship is found. President Clinton's tax increase in 1993 was followed by the fastest growth since the 1960s, whereas President Bush's tax cuts in 2001 and 2003 were followed by a slow economy.

In Nevada Governor Guinn's tax increase in 2003 was followed by a short-lived boom. In general, however, tax changes don't appear to have clearly affected growth one way or another. Our two most recent state tax hikes were clearly in response to declining income, not the cause of it.

Why would taxes not hurt growth? Perhaps because tax rates in the United States are low, relative to those in the rest of the developed world. Relative to the rest of the states, state taxes in Nevada are even lower. Our general fund is not much more than 2 percent of our GSP—not a burden, by any definition. At that low level, the trade-offs might weigh more in favor of what the taxes pay for than in favor of what they cost the taxpayer.

Finally, there are big differences between taxes that fund new programs and taxes to prevent cuts to existing programs. When our state government is already small, it is more likely that the services that government provides are the most valuable ones. Funding those services is not really the worst thing we can do.

4. Recessions, Taxes, and the Federal Deficit (2010)[6]

The federal deficit in 2009 hit a postwar record. Many assume that this deficit is the result of out-of-control spending, but is this entirely true?

In the debate over government spending and the deficit, economists usually look at the size of government compared to the economy's GDP. During a recession, government spending usually increases as a share of GDP. Some kinds of spending increase automatically, while other discretionary spending might also increase in an effort to stabilize the economy.

But we forget that this ratio will also rise because GDP is falling, even if government spending is constant. That is, government spending becomes a relatively bigger share of a smaller pie. The key is to first smooth out GDP so it grows at a stable rate, and to see how government spending compares with that. Adjusting for inflation and population growth, we find that real per capita GDP grew by about 2.2 percent per year from 1950 to 2000, so let's use that number to figure out the trend.

Federal spending rose significantly in the 1960s, to 20 percent of trend GDP, and then rose again to 23 percent by 1985. This ratio had fallen gradually to 19 percent by 2000, and remained relatively steady until 2007.

State and local government spending followed a similar pattern, with spending doubling from 5 percent of the economy in 1950 to 10 percent in 1975, remaining more or less steady afterward.

While state and local revenues must match their spending, revenues didn't always keep up with spending on the federal side. Deficits tend to rise during recessions, but before 1970 the federal budget was balanced, on average. Then deficits became acceptable, sometimes even when the economy wasn't in recession.

During the Reagan administration, these deficits reached postwar records due to tax cuts, increases in military spending, and the worst postwar recession up to that time. During the Clinton administration, the federal budget finally returned to surplus, helped by tax increases and economic growth.

After 2000, tax cuts and a recession led to deficits again. Unfortunately, the economy never really caught back up, and by 2007 our economy was 5 percent below where it would have been had it kept growing at the trend rate. In 2008 we hit this awful recession, and by last year our actual GDP was 13 percent below the trend, a serious decline indeed. Less income leads to fewer taxes paid.

In response, the share of state and local spending was cut more than at any time since 1934. The share of federal government expenditures rose, partly to bail out the states to prevent even more cuts. But, most of all, federal taxes fell dramatically. Reduced tax collections were amplified by more tax cuts as the federal government tried to slow the economy's contraction.

How do we restore balance to the budget? In the short term the best thing to do is to restore growth. If the economy recovers, tax collections will rebound, too. Letting the past decade's tax cuts expire might also significantly reduce the deficit.

In the long term, of course, there are other budget-busting trends we will need to manage, like the growth of Medicare spending and rising interest payments on the national debt. These are serious future concerns, but they are not really the cause of current deficits.

5. How Big Is Our Government? (2011)[7]

At the core of the debate over the proper size and function of government in American society is the assumption that our government is big and growing. But is this true?

In absolute terms, of course, the answer is yes. The United States is the world's largest economy, and our government has grown along with it. In military purchases alone, for example, the United States spends about as much as every other nation in the world combined, even though we have only 5 percent of the world's population. Add in population growth and inflation, and it is easy to draw scary pictures.

In relative terms, however, things look different, whether we look at how many people work for the government, how much government spends, what it produces, or even what it purchases.

More than a decade ago, an oft-cited paper in the conservative *Cato Journal* argued that our government had grown too big.[8] But in their very first table, authors Gwartney, Holcombe, and

Lawson showed that total government outlays, relative to GDP, were lower in the United States than in any other OECD country. In 1996 the average ratio for these twenty-three most-developed nations was 48 percent, while the U.S. ratio was less than 35 percent, roughly where it had hovered since the 1970s.

Some countries do have relatively smaller governments. For the most part, these tend to be the poor countries, those with dysfunctional economies due to major deficiencies in the rule of law, protection of property rights, transportation systems, education, and other infrastructure. But in other cases, you still need to be careful to not compare apples with oranges. Hong Kong, for example, does not have a military. In China, statistics show a relatively small government, but state-owned enterprises are not included in the numbers, and China has minimal transfer benefits like social security.

Last year, according to the Bureau of Economic Analysis, total spending by federal, state, and local governments in the United States summed to $5.5 trillion, about 38 percent of our GDP. The federal government alone spent $3.9 trillion, while states spent about $1.5 trillion and local governments spent about $1.3 trillion.[9] Note that these numbers don't add up, because governments transfer monies to each other.

Another way to measure the size of government over time is to consider the number of people with government jobs, though international comparisons are difficult. At the end of 2010, after the decennial census was complete, about 2.8 million civilians worked for our federal government, less than 2 percent of the total labor force.

In addition to these civilians, of course, the federal government has 1.4 million military personnel on active duty, but this proportion is much less than it was during the Cold War. Another 5.2 million civilians worked for states, and 14.5 million for local governments. In total, government employees account for about 15 percent of the U.S. labor force. It has been almost fifty years since this share was any lower. This share is also much less than total expenditures, because most of what government spends goes either to private companies, such as those who pave roads or build tanks, or to private individuals in the form of social benefits.

If you consider only the goods and services government purchases, either from its suppliers or from its employees, then total government accounted for 20.7 percent of GDP in 2010, significantly higher than the 17.4 percent share in 2000 and slightly higher than the 20.1 percent in 2008. National defense expenditures grew from 2.7 percent of GDP to 5.6 percent over the past decade, while other federal purchases grew from 2.1 percent to 2.8 percent. Meanwhile, state and local government purchases grew from 11.6 percent to 12.3 percent of GDP, mostly in spending on K–12 education.

Why did government's share of the economy grow? Partly it is because GDP fell, so government spending now makes up a bigger share of a temporarily smaller pie. Partly it is because, as in most countries affected by the Great Recession, government has tried to soften the blow and make up some of the difference in lost income. We are not alone. In the twenty-seven countries of the European Union, for example, average government outlays rose from 46 percent in 2007 to 51 percent in 2010. Most reasonable predictions expect this ratio of government spending to fall once our economy is really growing again.

Except for the rise in national defense expenditures, the growth in federal government spending is almost entirely due to increased payouts in social benefits, particularly loans to the states to pay for extended unemployment benefits. Meanwhile, state and local governments have been shrinking since 2008 in response to falling tax revenues, dampening any effect from temporary increases in federal spending.

Thus, the debate over the proper size and role of government appears to not account for the fact that the United States has a relatively small government for a developed nation. With the exception of the temporary effects of a deep recession, this share has not shown any significant growth in decades. The evidence that a smaller government would improve our economy is thus limited to a comparison with either an imaginary ideal of what might be, in a much different or much poorer nation, or with a time before most of us were born, when our standard of living was much lower and our economy and society were much less complex. Such comparisons should probably be taken with a grain of salt.

6. Budget Deficits and the Fiscal Cliff (2012)[10]

This week's Republican convention highlighted the growing federal debt. Yet if Congress does nothing, as its recent track record suggests will happen, taxes will increase and government spending will fall starting January 1. This is projected to cut the annual budget deficit in half, to a rate more consistent with economic growth.

How did we get to the edge of this fiscal cliff, as some call it, and is it necessary in order to slow the growth in federal debt?

We have actually been in a similar situation before. After more than a decade of large budget deficits, President Clinton signed the Deficit Reduction Act of 1993 over Republican opposition. That year federal spending totaled 22 percent of our GDP, and federal tax receipts totaled 17 percent. Seven years later, after one of the fastest and longest economic peacetime expansions in U.S. history, federal spending was down to 18 percent of GDP while tax receipts rose to 21 percent, with surpluses projected to continue into the distant future.

In 2001, however, the Bush administration passed a ten-year phase-in of dramatic tax cuts, and then expanded these in 2003 in spite of starting two unfunded wars. By the fiscal year ending in September 2008, federal spending and receipts switched places: spending had risen to 21 percent of GDP, mostly due to increased military spending, while federal receipts had fallen to 18 percent.

Between 2000 and 2008 the average federal income tax paid to the IRS by those earning more than $500,000 per year fell from 28 percent to 23 percent of income. People of more-modest means also received income tax cuts: for example, the average income tax rate for those earning $50,000 per year fell from 11 percent to 9 percent, although those in lower tax brackets still paid a much larger share of their income for payroll taxes and state sales taxes than the wealthy.

The Great Recession of 2008, however, led to a big fall in federal revenues, and big increases in spending. President Bush's Economic Stimulus Act of 2008 added $0.2 trillion to the fiscal year 2008 deficit, while his Emergency Economic Stabilization Act added another $0.7 trillion for bank bailouts to the fiscal year

2009 deficit; the surge in Iraq added even more. Even before the election of 2008, the federal deficit was on target to reach $1.2 trillion. As GDP dropped, spending rose to 25 percent of GDP, and total tax receipts plummeted to 15 percent.

State and local governments also had big falls in revenues, but they didn't have the option of running deficits. The result would be reductions in spending and employment that continue to this day, and threats of much, much bigger cuts. This would significantly and unexpectedly slow the recovery.

President Obama's American Recovery and Reinvestment Act of 2009, which passed over Republican opposition, added $0.2 trillion to the fiscal year 2009 budget deficit, plus $0.4 trillion to fiscal year 2010 and $0.2 trillion more to fiscal year 2011. About a third of this fiscal stimulus went to the states to help them prevent even bigger cuts to education. Another third went for more tax breaks, and the rest went toward increased infrastructure investment and other things.

The biggest jump in spending, however, went to help states pay for their unemployment and Medicaid benefits, while spending on Social Security and Medicare also increased significantly. Furthermore, in 2010 President Obama agreed to a two-year extension of President Bush's tax cuts, and then added a one-year cut to payroll taxes, which was extended another year in 2012.

No matter what anybody claims, this stimulus helped stabilize the economy. The financial crisis made this recession most similar to the Great Depression, but back then the Hoover administration and the Federal Reserve did everything wrong and made a terrible situation worse. This time, fiscal and monetary intervention made it much less awful. However, the increase in federal government purchases was almost entirely negated by cutbacks at the state and local levels, and frankly the president was far more optimistic about the recovery than he should have been.

Federal spending is currently 24 percent of GDP. A quarter of this budget is defense related, while Social Security, Medicare, and other health-care spending together account for 43 percent. All other spending, including interest on the national debt, accounts for only a third of the total. Those who advocate trying to reduce the budget deficit entirely through spending cuts have been intentionally vague about what they would cut, because it is mathematically impossible to accomplish what they propose without either a magic genie or huge cuts to defense, Medicare benefits, and other popular programs.

Meanwhile, total federal tax receipts are now only 16 percent of GDP, and Americans are paying the lowest income tax share to the federal government since the Second World War. The deficit has so far come down only slightly since fiscal year 2009.

Through an accident of timing and an inability to get any legislation passed, several things are set to occur in 2013. First, the Bush tax cuts will finally expire, for all income levels, and the Obama payroll tax cuts will expire with them. Second, the so-called sequestration cuts will go into effect. These spending cuts, which were intended only to scare Congress into an agreement last year, will have an impact on defense and all other discretionary spending, which in turn will have a huge impact on federal money for states. Finally, congressionally mandated limits to Medicare spending will force a reduction in payments to physicians.

These changes are projected to have a significant impact on reducing the deficit. If the deficit is what matters to you most, you might feel pretty good about that.

The problem with cutting deficits so quickly is that it could backfire by pushing our economy back into recession. Just as increasing spending and cutting taxes in a recession helps the economy, decreasing spending and raising taxes hurts it. This is not so much of a problem when the economy is running near peak speed and the private sector is able to take up the slack, but we aren't there quite yet. Consumers and firms have been dealing with their own excessive debt since 2008, and are not quite ready to begin buying again.

If we are wise, we will phase in some of the tax increases and spending cuts over the next couple of years, so as to avoid returning to recession. Congress will almost certainly act by early 2013 to address the fiscal cliff. But our experience back in the 1990s should also show us that we can raise taxes and cut spending to balance the federal budget without necessarily jeopardizing

TABLE 6.1. Federal Budget for Fiscal Year 2011, per Dollar of GDP

FEDERAL EXPENDITURES		FEDERAL REVENUES	
National Defense	5¢	Personal Income Tax	7¢
Social Security	5¢	Payroll Taxes	5¢
Health Programs	5¢	Corporate Income Tax	2¢
Income Security	4¢	Everything Else	1¢
Interest on Federal Debt	2¢	FEDERAL REVENUES	15¢
Support for Veterans	1¢		
Everything Else	2¢	FEDERAL BUDGET DEFICIT	9¢
FEDERAL EXPENDITURES	24¢		

economic growth, at least once the private sector is ready to step up to the plate.

7. Making Cents of the Budget (2012)[11]

The news is full of the so-called fiscal cliff, where, through an accident of timing and procrastination, big cuts to the federal deficit will be automatically implemented on January 1.

It is not as dramatic as it seems. The cliff is more of a downslope, one we can climb back up if we choose. If we get past the new year without a deal, the economy does not go into free fall.

For those who aren't news junkies, it can be hard to make sense of what all these numbers mean. Congress plans the budget for the next decade, and this makes all the billions and trillions seem incredibly large. I suggest thinking about these amounts relative to GDP.

For every dollar of GDP, the federal government spends about a nickel each for national defense and Social Security, and another nickel for Medicare, Medicaid, and health insurance for children. Then we add four cents for income security (a range of programs including the Earned Income Tax Credit), two cents for interest on the federal debt, a penny in support for veterans, and two cents for everything else the federal government does (see table 6.1).

All this adds up to twenty-four cents. About three cents of this total amount goes as grants to state and local governments, mostly for Medicaid, income support, and highways. About nine cents of the total is considered discretionary.

In 2009, at the bottom of the recession, the federal government was spending about twenty-five cents, so it is down a little,
partly because the stimulus has mostly expired. But back in 2000,
when the economy was running at full speed, we weren't in a war,
and the baby boomers weren't retiring yet, the federal government spent only nineteen cents for each dollar of GDP.

Back in 2000, of course, we were running a budget surplus, at
least until President Bush pushed for a large and popular tax cut.
Tax rates fell, especially for capital gains, while spending rose and
deficits returned. Federal revenue is now down to fifteen cents
for each dollar of GDP, nowhere near what we need. On average,
Americans—especially wealthy Americans—now pay a lower
share of their income in federal income taxes than at any time in
the past sixty years.

So the federal debt is now growing by nine cents a year for
each dollar of GDP. Since in normal times our GDP (including inflation) can be expected to grow by 4 to 5 percent, we need to
cut the deficit in half just to keep the national debt at a constant
share of GDP.

In the short run, borrowing sometimes makes sense. In a recession, when people aren't spending and government revenues
are temporarily low, deficits are a natural result. A balanced
budget in a recession sends the economy into a tailspin. Borrowing for investment can also make sense, if the eventual return on
investment is higher than the cost of borrowing. Otherwise, it is
hard to imagine this growth in the national debt being sustainable in the long run.

But the baby boom generation has reached retirement age,
and this means that spending on Social Security and Medicare
is going to rise, and fewer people will be paying in to the system.
With fewer people working, some economists expect real GDP
growth to slow down in the future, even once we are finally past
the nasty aftereffects of the Great Recession.

A year and a half back, Congress passed a set of automatic
spending cuts that they refer to as sequestration. These were intended to be arbitrary and painful cuts to the military budget
(except pay and benefits) and discretionary spending, as a threat
to recalcitrant members of Congress who failed to come to a

bipartisan agreement. These cuts are supposed to kick in on January 1, and they will reduce federal spending by another cent for each dollar of GDP.

Letting the tax cuts expire would add in about two to three cents. President Barack Obama proposes to let the cuts expire for the top 2 percent of income earners, but keep the cuts for everybody else. Unless the Republicans agree, it is likely that the cuts will be allowed to expire for everybody, which changes the question somewhat after January 1.

Back in October, the Republican presidential candidate, Governor Mitt Romney, advocated capping some deductions for the wealthy. The big deductions are for mortgage interest, medical insurance premiums, 401(k) plans, and state and local taxes. Obama includes this idea in his proposal, too; higher rates and lower deductions together would raise one cent in taxes for every dollar of GDP.

President Obama's cuts to the payroll tax are about to expire, too, and that will bring back another cent in revenue. There appears to be no political interest in extending these, even though they affect many more people than income taxes, probably because these cuts affected the projections of the long-term solvency of Social Security and Medicare, since the lost revenue was not replaced.

Taxing capital gains at the same rate as regular income is not seriously under consideration, even though there is no real evidence that the preferential treatment for capital income over labor income has increased savings and investment. This could raise up to one cent per dollar of GDP, but never mind.

Starting with a nine-cent deficit, and subtracting one cent each for spending cuts, income taxes on the wealthy, and payroll taxes for working stiffs, we are down to six cents. What's next?

To reach our sustainable target, the final ingredient is more economic growth, which will increase tax revenues, reduce the need for some types of spending, and increase the sustainable target deficit. Housing prices have finally stopped falling; that was a huge drag on the economy. Firms and consumers have been paying down debt as much as the recession allowed, but spending in the United States appears to be picking up again and the unemployment rate is starting to come down.

However, these three ingredients—reduced spending, increased taxes, and more growth—are likely to mix badly. Discretionary spending cuts, especially arbitrary ones, are projected to have a negative impact on state budgets, where times have been hard for years. Sudden increases in taxes are also not likely to be popular.

Europe's recent efforts at government austerity have helped push that region back into recession, making their debt problems worse, not better. Economists expect that austerity would have a similar effect on the U.S. economy. Reducing the deficit too quickly could backfire.

In the long run, the argument that lower tax rates (especially the very low rate on capital gains) are needed for economic growth just does not hold water. The federal government needs to collect enough taxes to cover what it spends, and in normal times spending should come down before taxes are allowed to. We should never again create a debt crisis for political purposes.

But in the short run, at least during a recession, higher taxes reduce overall private spending, especially for those with lower incomes. Reduced government spending reduces private spending too, and together this means less income and fewer jobs.

Skiing down such a precarious fiscal slope, it is hard to keep our balance. We must hope we won't go too far downhill before Congress reconsiders.

Notes

1. L. B. Johnson, "Commencement Address in New London at the United States Coast Guard Academy," June 3, 1964, http://www.presidency.ucsb.edu /ws/?pid=26290

2. Federal Reserve Bank of St. Louis, FRED Economic Data, "Nominal Potential Gross Domestic Product," https://fred.stlouisfed.org/series /NGDPPOT

3. Originally published as E. Parker, "Does Government Spending Help or Hurt the Economy?," *Reno Gazette Journal*, January 27, 2010.

4. Originally published as E. Parker, "Slowing the Growth of the National Debt, Both Public and Private," *Reno Gazette Journal*, April 21, 2010.

5. Originally published as E. Parker, "Do Taxes Kill Jobs? Let's Look at the Facts," *Nevada Appeal*, June 20, 2010.

6. Originally published as E. Parker, "Recessions, Taxes and the Growing Federal Deficit," *Nevada Appeal,* July 11, 2010.

7. Originally published as E. Parker, "How Big Is Our Government, Really?," *Nevada Appeal,* October 23, 2011.

8. J. Gwartney, R. Holcombe, and R. Lawson, "The Scope of Government and the Wealth of Nations," *Cato Journal* 18, no. 2 (1998): 163–90.

9. Bureau of Economic Analysis, U.S. Department of Commerce, https://bea.gov

10. Originally published as E. Parker, "Budget Deficits at the Edge of the Fiscal Cliff," *Nevada Appeal,* September 2, 2012.

11. Originally published as E. Parker, "Making Sense of the Fiscal Cliff," *Las Vegas Sun,* December 9, 2012. This was also published as "Skiing Down the Fiscal Slope," *Nevada Appeal,* December 9, 2012.

CHAPTER 7

Returning to Normalcy

I been down so long, seem like up to me.

— FURRY LEWIS[1]

Introduction

All good things must end, but so too do most bad things. The effects of the Great Recession lingered for many years, but eventually things started to improve. By 2013 Nevada was showing signs of recovery, and housing prices were finally beginning to rise. By 2015 the state's population was once again growing faster than the national average, confidence was returning, and the state's unemployment rate was no longer the highest in the nation.

Almost 100 years ago President Harding campaigned on the promise of returning to normalcy. After the trauma of the First World War he said, "America's present need is not heroics, but healing; not nostrums, but normalcy; not revolution, but restoration; not agitation, but adjustment; not surgery, but serenity; not the dramatic, but the dispassionate; not experiment, but equipoise; not submergence in internationality, but sustainment in triumphant nationality."[2] It is a sobering thought that the return to normalcy was followed in less than a decade by the Great Depression, and then the Second World War a decade after that.

This chapter includes a vignette from Kate about creating a line of credit, and another on how we first met, along with her efforts to find a solution to the state's budget crisis. The first column in this chapter was written at the start of the 2013 legislative session, in the middle of Governor Sandoval's first term. This is followed by a column on the housing recovery, which I argued was the essential condition for the economy to turn around. The last three columns were written after the 2014 election, and focused on the continuing problems that the state budget presents. I also include several figures showing the most recent data for higher education spending, housing prices, median household income, taxable sales, gaming wins, and state general fund budget revenues.

1. Nevada Needs a New Economic Mindset (2013)[3]

Governor Brian Sandoval delivered his annual State of the State speech a little more than a week ago, and set out his budget proposal for the next biennium. A little more than a week from now the legislature will begin to consider whether that budget is a realistic statement of where we are and an appropriate vision of where we need to go.

How stands the state of the state? It's not rock-bottomed and copper-sheathed, as Daniel Webster might have wanted, but it has improved from the dark days when all economic indicators pointed down.

There are signs that Nevada's economy is improving. The key is housing, where real inflation-adjusted average prices have risen by more than 10 percent over the past nine months, compared to a two-thirds drop over the six years prior. Personal income has kept up with inflation over the past three years, after dropping dramatically between 2007 and 2009. And Nevada's population is once more growing faster than the nation's, which is odd considering that our unemployment rate remains the highest of any state.

Sandoval pointed out that there are about 30,000 new jobs in Nevada compared to two years ago. We lost almost 180,000 jobs in the three years from 2007 to 2010, which canceled out all the job gains since 2002.

Where are these new jobs? In spite of efforts by the governor to attract new business, they are in the same old sectors. Almost two thirds of these new jobs are in the so-called leisure sector, mostly meaning hotels, restaurants, and casinos, and almost a third are in retail trade, warehousing, and transportation. Some are in the gold mines of northeast Nevada.

Unfortunately, the rest of our state's economy continued to lose jobs over the past two years. While 70,000 construction jobs were lost in the first three years of the Great Recession, in the past two years another 6,000 were lost. Manufacturing lost another

1,000 jobs, while falling property tax revenues led to the loss of another 3,000 jobs in city and county governments. Everything else has been flat over the past two years, with 2012 a little better than 2011.

What of the efforts to attract new business? In spite of a few highly touted examples, we have very little to show for it so far. We give tax rebates and other special favors without demanding anything in return, without really accounting for the giveaways or holding the beneficiaries to their promises. As a result, we have yet to see many new jobs created by the state's efforts to bring businesses to Nevada, although we can hope there will eventually be a payoff.

In a flat economy, perhaps it should come as no surprise that the governor's budget proposal is also flat. A general fund budget of $6.5 billion over two years sounds like a lot of money, but it works out to less than 2.5 percent of our GSP. The budget's proposed growth over the present biennium is less than the inflation rate plus population growth, so in real per capita terms the budget is still falling.

The governor includes a few little gifts here and there, and his tone is optimistic and grand, but a close look at the budget allocations says we are doing everything on the cheap. Compared to the other forty-nine states, this is still the smallest state government budget in the country, relative to GSP. We are even hiring teachers on the cheap, expanding the Teach For America program for low-income schools instead of hiring more professional teachers who will be here for the long term.

Compared to the past five years, flat is good. Like other faculties, faculty at my university are relieved not to be going through another near-death experience. Over the past five years, as figure 7.1 shows, state appropriations for UNR have been cut by 30 percent, even though prices have risen by 9 percent and enrollments have grown by 18 percent. Students have paid for about half of these cuts with higher tuition and fees. But both Sandoval and his predecessor, Governor Jim Gibbons, proposed much larger decreases in higher education funding, so we are thankful it wasn't worse, and thankful even more cuts are now off the table.

Sandoval has proposed restoring some funding to the Guinn

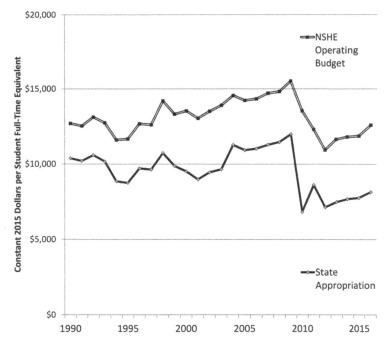

FIGURE 7.1. Nevada System of Higher Education Operating Budget and State Funding per Student FTE, Adjusted for Inflation. *Source:* Courtesy of the Nevada System of Higher Education annual budgets.

Millennium Scholarship program—not to adjust for tuition increases, but enough to keep the program through the end of his term. He proposes cutting state employee furloughs in half, though these should be eliminated entirely, perhaps through a trigger if revenues continue to exceed Economic Forum forecasts. Although Sandoval has not suggested restoring the pay cuts state employees took two years ago, he has proposed restoring some merit or step increases after another year. And he supports the new higher education budget formula, which will reallocate a larger share of a fixed higher education pie to Clark County while giving colleges and universities more control over their own student tuition.

Still, it is hard not to be disappointed that this budget makes few real changes. Many studies collect dust on the legislative shelf, telling us we need to restructure our state revenues to fit our economy. Nevada's casinos might have stabilized, but they are not likely to be a source of growth in the future, and we still depend on the gaming tax for a quarter of state revenue. Sales and use taxes—which mostly exclude services, even though services account for the larger part of our economy—bring in another third of revenue.

Mining taxes, meanwhile, provide only 3 percent of state general fund revenue, and represent a total of about 1 percent of gold production in Nevada. Though many argue that mining ought to pay more in taxes for extracting our state's natural resources, comparable perhaps to what oilmen in Texas pay, the governor's budget actually projects declining mining taxes.

A good tax system draws revenue from a broad spectrum of sources, from a diversified base that allows low rates. We could easily adopt tax structures from other states without reinventing the wheel, at low rates that keep us competitive. This budget does not do that.

Instead of a low-tax state, Nevada is in many ways a no-tax state. Nevada is one of only seven states without a personal income tax, and one of only five states without a corporate income tax. The governor now proposes cutting the low modified business tax, while at the same time draining the rainy-day fund, an odd proposal since our economy is no longer in free fall.

Even including our modified business tax and other miscellaneous taxes, the Tax Foundation rates Nevada as the state with the third-most-business-friendly tax climate. So why do we attract so few businesses? If you ask the corporations, it's because we lack the infrastructure and the education system they require.

The Great Recession has taught us that we can no longer rely on Nevada's old economy to pull us toward a bright future. What we need from our governor and legislators is a new vision that will take us where we want to go, to a prosperous future in which our taxation, education system, health care, recreation opportunities, and public infrastructure not only draw big firms here, but also dissuade our entrepreneurs and our best and brightest students from leaving the state for a better education and better business opportunities elsewhere. A new economy requires a new mindset.

That mindset was not in evidence in the State of the State address. Although the speech was well delivered, it essentially postpones taking the kind of action needed to take us beyond a flat economy and a flat future, in which we remain as vulnerable as ever to the next recession that might come along.

>> Treasurer's Vignette: Beginning with No

I think of capital as different from money. Money purchases goods and services. Money purchases labor in the form of your paycheck. Capital, on the other hand generates wealth. Most of us know instinctively that our paychecks do not generate wealth. Paychecks let us eke out a living. The problem, as I see it is that the state government, like many of its residents, is living paycheck to paycheck, and I want to do something about it.

What to do comes to me in the form of a series of "no" answers. Each "no" serves as a door taking me closer to my goal.

My first "no" comes in 2010 from a very successful businessman whom I meet for coffee at a Starbucks in Reno. I like this guy, and it is easy for me to talk to him. He supported me early with the maximum donation when I first declared for the treasurer position, and that signaled to others that I was a horse to back. I remain convinced that he paved my path to victory in that one act. I like him because he has stayed married to his wife for so long, and I like him because I am always impressed with people who can remember names. It is a skill I wish I had.

Over coffee, he tells me just how bad it is for a businessman in Nevada. I have been hearing this same message over and over. There is no capital moving through Nevada—none for his businesses, none to start a business, none to expand a business, none to build out an idea. No capital! We wade through the ins and outs of trying to run a business, expand a business, hire, build, sell, and market. We discuss what it means when capital doesn't flow.

While he is talking, my mind is running through options. I think about how I invest the state's money in businesses that are incorporated in Delaware. Why, I think, can't I invest in businesses that are incorporated in Nevada? If they meet the same criteria, what's the problem? Other state treasurers can do this, so why can't we?

Afterward, I call my staff. I tell them to use one of the bill drafts I am allowed for making these investments, so we can bring capital to Nevada. "What are you talking about?" they ask. "Make it broad," I say. "I am talking about an idea, and I will flesh it out later. Just get it in." The deadline for bill drafts has passed, they tell me. "Get a waiver!" I shout. And so we begin.

My second "no" comes from white-haired financiers who live in Lake Tahoe. My staff and I convene a group of experts to guide us on what to do and what to avoid. These men, and they are all men, live right here in Nevada. They made their fortunes in Silicon Valley or on Wall Street. They built an empire and then built homes in Lake Tahoe. They assemble in my office and we pull in extra chairs.

We tell them we want to create the state's first private equity fund to invest in businesses here in Nevada and to leverage that capital to bring in even more investment to Nevada. I tell them other states have done this, with both successes and failures. Then we fold our hands and wait for the advice of our sages. For the next two hours they tell us "no." We are fools. It has been tried before. "For twenty years!" they say. They furrow their brows and tell us the law is against us. They lean forward in their seats and tell us Nevada does not have "deal flow." They sigh and wistfully explain that while I am nice and well intentioned, it really can't be done.

After I thank them for their time, I tell them three things: One, I say, they begin with "no." Two, I begin with "yes." And three, they underestimate me. They are nonplussed.

My third "no" comes from my fellow Democrats. The state senate majority leader is most helpful and sets up a meeting with his caucus so that I have the opportunity to explain what I am proposing and answer any of their questions. We will invest in businesses in Nevada and the earnings from those investments will go to education, I tell them. When I tell them I have lined up Republican support, they balk. Why would we support a Republican bill? I explain that I thought the bill would be easier to pass with support from both sides of the aisle. One senator asks, "Well, who is the Democrat, then?" My heart sinks.

"Me," I say. "I am the Democrat." Another member of the caucus leans forward as if to pat my knee and says, "Look, you're a very nice lady, but let's be honest: You have no idea what you're doing. You really don't know anything about money." I choose not to remind him that I very successfully manage billions of dollars for the state.

My fourth "no" comes from the Legislative Counsel Bureau, when they tell me my bill does not pass legal muster. Worse, they tell me I will not even get a hearing on the bill unless I can get a judicial opinion that I can do this, and it is already late March.

I go home and write a brief to file with the court. I also drop my computer on the kitchen floor.

My fifth "no" comes shortly after that, while standing in the Apple store with my broken computer. I get a call from somebody who works for the attorney general, and he tells me he doesn't think my legal argument holds water. The conversation is not pretty. At some point, I realize that the Apple store has gone silent, that I have pounded my fist on a table holding some very expensive electronics, and that a man is standing in front of me asking if I need help. He looks at me like I am surely deranged. They fix my computer and hurry me out of there.

Finally, the tide begins to turn, and I begin to hear "yes" more often. The doors open. My brief is filed. The judge issues his opinion, and he sides with my argument. The hearing is held. Our bill passes on the last day of session, with forty seconds left until sine die.

My chief treasurer comes into my office the next morning. "Now what?" he asks.

"Now," I say, "our work begins."

2. Nevada's Housing Recovery, with Brian Bonnenfant (2013)[4]

Is Nevada's housing market really recovering? For eleven straight months, home prices in Las Vegas have been rising, and the rest of the state appears to be following. If so, then this is a positive indicator for Nevada, as well as for the entire country.

Nevada accounts for less than 1 percent of the nation's economy, but we accounted for a much larger proportion of the financial crisis, which created the Great Recession. The housing bubble began on the coasts, especially in the behemoth to our west. Nevada benefitted as homeowners, retirees, and investors began looking for cheaper alternatives. Construction became one of our state's major industries, propelling growth and interstate migration even as our famous gaming industry was waning. Assisted by easy credit and speculative behavior, home prices rose by 120 percent from 2000 to 2006, a 90 percent increase relative to inflation.

When the bubble popped in 2006, housing prices plummeted more in Nevada than in any other state, though some suburban pockets elsewhere had similar experiences. In California, as in the country as a whole, the average decline in the housing market brought prices more or less back in line with where they had been in 2000, adjusting for inflation. In Nevada, however, the correction was much more severe. As figure 7.2 shows, home prices dropped by two thirds relative to inflation, and in 2013 still remained 30 percent below where they were for several decades before the bubble. From a historical perspective, homes became a real bargain.

More than half of Nevada's total job losses in the Great Recession came in the construction sector, and the fact that this sector was twice the size of the national average almost entirely explains why Nevada's unemployment rate became the highest in the nation—until, finally, last month.

With the highest unemployment rate, the largest drop in personal income, the highest percentage of newly occupied homes, and the biggest fall in housing prices, it is no surprise that two thirds of homeowners had negative equity by 2011—the highest in the nation, of course—and that Nevada had the highest foreclosure rates, roughly five thousand per month at their peak. Many homeowners found it very difficult to sell their homes and impossible to refinance them, so many walked away out of choice or necessity. One in seven homes was left vacant, although a low level of new home construction continued for the small number of buyers who preferred their houses unused.

Banks got a little hurried and careless in processing all these foreclosures, and in 2011 the state legislature responded to abuses

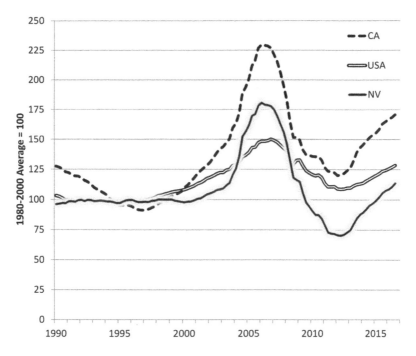

FIGURE 7.2. Updated Housing Price Indices, Adjusted for Inflation.
Source: Author's calculations based on the Federal Housing Finance Agency and the Bureau of Labor Statistics, U.S. Department of Labor.

by passing Assembly Bill No. 284, amending state law to prevent robo-signing and fraudulent foreclosures. On the surface this could have been innocuous, since the law required a signed affidavit from a bank official, but in practice it led to a dramatic 57 percent drop in the number of foreclosures. More Nevada homeowners then remained in their homes—some estimate 50,000 or more— even after they stopped making their mortgage payments, instead of sending their keys in "jingle mail" to their bank.

On the one hand, keeping more people in their homes—even those not paying their mortgages—led to fewer empty houses in neighborhoods where such vacancies affected the home values of the neighbors who kept paying their own mortgages. On the other hand, it reduced the supply of cheap homes, constricting the real estate market, and it might have created an artificial mini bubble in the local market.

In 2010 many properties were available on the courthouse steps at cheap prices for buyers with cash, and foreclosures accounted for half of all home sales. By early 2012, however, there were often bidding wars for the few properties coming to market, and prices began to turn around. Some credited the number of un-foreclosed properties with the rise in retail sales, especially for automobile purchases, while personal income barely kept up with inflation and population growth. Based on available data, however, it is not likely that these unpaid mortgages exceeded 1 percent of Nevada's personal income in total, whereas taxable sales in Nevada rose by 6 percent in 2012 over the prior calendar year.

There appears to be much more going on than can be explained by Assembly Bill No. 284, or by the construction defect law known as Chapter 40, a decade-old law from which some law firms profited at the expense of construction firms.[5] Foreclosures decreased in 2012 nationwide, helped along by the Mortgage Settlement Agreement between forty-nine state attorneys general and the five biggest mortgage servicers.

The national market is showing the same signs of market recovery that we see in Nevada. Vacancy rates are beginning to drop, and the Census Bureau calculates that homeownership rates have dropped from 69 percent to 66 percent, roughly where they were in 1997, before the bubble began.

The inventory of homes on the U.S. market has dropped from a twelve-month to a four-month supply, the lowest levels since 1994. Builder confidence fell this month for a very unusual reason: there is too much demand for new houses, relative to the available land, labor, and building supplies. Housing starts are beginning to recover from their record lows, and the number of construction workers building homes nationally has actually risen, albeit only a little, for two years in a row. According to Fannie Mae, a majority of Americans now think home prices will continue rising.[6] This confidence is essential.

Nevada is lagging behind the national market in the short supply of housing, not leading it. Construction employment has continued to fall, even though state population has continued to grow despite pessimistic expectations. The share of homes underwater has fallen from two thirds to one half, still the highest in the nation but a big improvement.

So far, most of the real estate activity has been in the lower price ranges. In Washoe County fully two out of three homes sold over the past two years was below $200,000, the portion of the market in which foreclosure rates have been higher. In Las Vegas foreclosures now account for fewer than 10 percent of sales. Homeowners who might have put their homes on the market have been waiting for prices to start rising, and many buyers have been nervous about buying a home at a price that they fear might continue to fall. It has been hard to compete with the sale of distressed properties. But all this is starting to change, and the share of homes sold at the upper end is starting to rise. Once we actually see firm data on this change, we will be able to breathe easier.

There are still a substantial number of mortgages more than ninety days past due, especially in Nevada, and once these hit the market there might be a drag on price increases. The number of bank-owned properties is down considerably over the past year, though the number of mortgages in the preliminary stages of foreclosure is up. But these effects are likely to be dwarfed by both pent-up demand and pent-up supply, as the market finally starts returning to normal and home prices are still far below long-run values. If so, we can expect a little upward pressure on mortgage interest rates to begin, and we can expect to finally see the end of the deleveraging process, which has led to this long, long recession.

» Treasurer's Vignette: I May be Wrong, but I Have No Doubts

How did I meet Elliott? A rather personal question, don't you think? Which, of course, deserves a politician's answer. Elliott says we first met at the Washoe County Democratic Convention in 2006, when I was first running for office.

I remember speaking in Las Vegas in the morning and landing late in Reno. There were sheets of rain. I practiced my speech in the car, caught my shoe on the curb, and stood at the back of the room looking at the audience. Was there a man in a cap talking to me? Elliott says that was him, but I don't know. Walking up the aisle as they call my name, climbing the steps, repeating my speech to myself. Ready? And then the county chair says, "You can say hello, then get off. We're running late and everybody wants to go home."

How did I meet Elliott? Honestly, I can't remember.

But later, as the financial crisis unfolded, I needed information and so I talked to everybody. I had my chief of staff connect with former governor Guinn. I assembled a round table that we called the Bond Rating Advisory Team, made up of financial officers from utility companies and casinos and retailers and real estate associations. Somebody actually gave us mugs labeled "The BRAT Pack."

I was told there was an economist at UNR who knew something about recessions, money, and international finance, so I called his office and asked to meet for coffee before work.

This information gathering was a key reason I was able to hold on to our credit rating for as long as I did. Of course, during the legislative session the problem wasn't a lack of information, but what to do with it. Everybody had a different opinion on that, including me.

We had a budget hole of what? $1.2 million? On top of that, we were borrowing money from the Federal Reserve just to pay out unemployment. The credit agencies hated my line of credit. "When is your legislature going to solve its budget problems?" they asked me. "It needs to address the state's revenue problem. There can be no more sweeping accounts and praying for manna from heaven."

"The legislature is required by law to balance the budget," we replied, as if it were as simple as dropping off shirts at the cleaners.

My coffees with Elliott suddenly turned from me asking him about financial markets and the national economy to him arguing desperately that the university could not absorb even more cuts, not without real long-term damage being done. Was there a plan? He wanted to know.

I recognized his desperation. A rural senior citizen's group had phoned me earlier: "We're being told we won't even have enough money to buy glasses for people."

Letters had arrived from all across the state; people would describe when they'd moved to Nevada, how they'd raised their children, and how much their utility bill was. Folks would call because they had been dropped from some social program and couldn't afford their prescription medicine.

I went to one of my favorite capital reporters with these letters. "Write something," I demanded.

He turned to a table, grabbed a five-inch folder stuffed to the gills, and replied, "Add it to the pile."

Later, he came to my office, and simply said, "Don't do it."

"Don't do what?" I asked.

"Whatever plan you have, don't do it."

"Who said I have a plan?"

"Oh, you have a plan," he said. "But the legislators need to do their job. So, don't do it. Don't save them. Let them do their job."

"Are we off the record?" I asked.

"I assumed it was a standing order with you."

"It's too early to raise taxes. We should put an increase in place and then give the business community a year to adjust until it kicks in and I can close the gap during that time. Why is that so bad?"

"Because you're too clever by half, that's why." He then added, "Because the legislature will take your idea and do something else with it. Even now, they want to take your line of credit and make it permanent."

"That's bullshit," I interrupted, "and I am not going to let that happen. It was a bridge to get them to session."

"And they took it and ran with it. That's the problem. So, I'm telling you, don't do it." He thought for a moment. "How much does your plan make, anyway?"

"Are we off the record?"

He sighed. "As previously agreed."

"Not enough. I can come up with $300 million–350 million, that's all. But I assume the gap will come down to about that."

He said again, "Don't do it. I have been around longer than you and I'm telling you, don't do it."

"If it works, we can put a revenue plan in place and give everyone time to adjust," I replied. "I know I'm right."

"You're not right, that's the problem. You're just smart. Smart and stupid."

We exchanged a friendly insult or two, but his last words on his way out the door were, "Don't do it."

So I decided not to reveal my plan to close the gap, not unless the legislature mades a request. Elliott guessed that I had something in my back pocket, but I didn't reveal it to him either. I tried to work behind the scenes with one legislator on a tax plan that would be deferred for a year, but neither of us had any say on the matter and so it went nowhere. I was never asked for my input on the budget.

When I made my run for Congress, I stated publicly that I didn't think we should raise taxes. I was skewered by my fellow Democrats. It was so bad that I went to lunch with a different reporter and he spent the entire meal telling me it would be okay to tell him if I was once registered as a Republican. No matter how many times I told him emphatically that he was wrong, he just replied, "Oh, come on, you can tell me."

At the same time, Republicans were running an ad suggesting that the president and I had the same speech writer. I've never had a speech writer. They also electronically modified my voice to make it sound higher than it already is.

Elliott grabbed another coffee with me and told me that he understood what I meant. "And what did I mean?" I asked, rolling my eyes and waiting for another conclusory lecture.

"You meant, 'Don't raise taxes *now*.'"

"Of course that's what I meant. Wasn't that obvious?"

"No," he said. "You didn't use the right words. Politicians use code words."

Soon after, my favorite capital reporter wandered into my office without knocking or checking if I had a meeting. "I know when you have meetings," he said, when I protested.

"What, then?" I demanded.

"Put your chin down when you speak and speak slower."

"Will that make everybody love me?"

"Everybody does love you. It will lower your voice."

"Everybody hates me, and they think I am a Republican."

"That'll pass. Take a breath; you're doing just fine. Work on speaking slower."

"They think I am a lousy politician."

"You are a lousy politician; that's why everybody loves you."

More friendly insults were exchanged, and then I tell him, "Get out, I have a meeting."

"You don't have a meeting," he retorted, but he left me to my little pity party.

In the end, the Democrats took a pass on a revenue plan. As inadequate as our state budget was, it would take a Republican governor and a Republican legislature in another session to raise taxes.

Go figure.

3. The State of the State Economy (2014)[7]

The year 2014 is ending, and it is good that Nevada is finally growing again. Now we need to prepare for what type of economy our state will grow into.

Payroll employment has grown by 27,000 jobs over the past twelve months, a 2.3-percent growth rate that puts us in the top quarter of states for the first time since the Great Recession began. Since we hit bottom in 2011, a year after the rest of the nation, we have recovered 110,000 of the 186,000 jobs we lost.

GSP grew by 2.4 percent last year—less than the national average, but still enough to keep pace with population growth and price inflation. Growth in 2014 is expected to be even better. Our unemployment rate is 6.9 percent, no longer even among the top five in the nation. A welcome relief!

Even our population is growing twice as fast as the difference between births and deaths. People are moving here again. The fact that population growth is only a third of the prerecession rate is also good news, because we should be able to sustain this pace and meet the education and infrastructure needs such growth demands.

These are not the heady days before housing prices peaked in 2006. The economy fell off a cliff in 2008. We are still climbing out of the abyss, and we surely don't want to slide back down.

Nevada was a casino economy back then. When our monopoly on gaming began to slip, we placed our trust in construction. Californians moved here for relatively cheaper homes, and people from other states moved here to build those homes or provide other services. Our income per capita was 10 percent above the national average, though our cost of living was also above average, and our population growth rate was the fastest in the nation.

When the ride ended, Nevada lost almost 100,000 construction jobs, more than half of the total jobs lost, and our unemployment rate became the nation's highest. Median housing prices fell by more than half, foreclosures were the highest in the nation, and two thirds of homeowners owned property worth less than the mortgage.

A major driver of our economic recovery is the recovery in home prices. This recovery has a big impact on the confidence and the net wealth of homeowners, which leads to increases in retail sales. It also helped that the national economy began to recover first, and national employment levels finally caught back up to the January 2008 peak this past spring. At our current pace, Nevada will reach that mark in three more years.

Slow and steady GDP growth since 2009 makes the U.S. economy a model, as the European Union has been struggling through a second and now potentially a third recession. Japan has gone back into recession, and while China continues to grow rapidly, its rate is slowing.

For Nevada's economy, it is out with the old to make way for the new, and employment growth this past year has not been in the usual sectors. Almost two thirds of that growth was in the health-care sector and in professional and business services, while there is also growth in financial services, manufacturing, and retail sector employment. After an initial recovery, employment growth in the leisure and hospitality sector has been flat. Construction is only beginning to see some positive growth.

Our recovery is still slow because we aren't able to return to what worked for us before. We are beginning a needed diversification that we have discussed for many years. A number of interesting projects that might help are under way. Tesla is beginning the construction of its giga-factory east of Sparks, and Nevada was one of six sites selected nationally for unmanned aircraft research.

It is hard to overstate how much the average Nevadan needs this growth. On average, our residents suffered a far bigger drop in income than those in any other state, as figure 7.3 shows, and

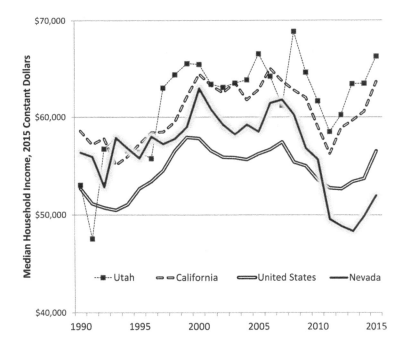

FIGURE 7.3. Real Median Household Income. *Source:* Courtesy of the United States Census Bureau.

those at the lower end suffered the most. While income per capita was 16 percent lower in 2013 than in 2008, our median household income fell by 22 percent. Nevada had more people entering poverty from 2007 to 2013 than any other state. So far, none of these measures has shown signs of improvement.

Job growth helps, but many in our current workforce must now adjust to a changing economy. Nevadans are hard-working people, but that is not enough. For this diversifying economy to succeed, new business sectors must expand and grow, and the public and private sectors must partner up to empower Nevadans to become tomorrow's workforce.

As our state legislators come into the next legislative session, they need to put their priority on engaging employers, educators, unions, nonprofits, and our new entrepreneurs in order to improve workforce training and education. If we want all Nevadans to share in the opportunity of a diverse and robust economy, then now is the time to create that future.

4. The State of the State Budget (2015)[8]

Almost eight years after the start of the Great Recession, our economy is growing again, and yet the Economic Forum tells us we are in another budget hole. As Yogi Berra supposedly said, it's like déjà vu all over again.

State revenues are below projections, we've eaten into our required 5 percent reserve, and all $28 million in the rainy-day fund will now be drained. The budget office has desperately scoured all of its accounts, and has proposed sweeping them of money to get us through the fiscal year. Moreover, we appear to be short of money to pay for education at our currently budgeted rates.

Meanwhile, we are one of the last states in the union with state employees still required to take unpaid furloughs, yet we have the fewest state employees, relative to population, of any state in the union.

At 2.4 percent of GSP over the past three years, or roughly $1,170 per resident per year, our state general fund is among the smallest in the nation. If we add in state spending financed by federal funds, other state funds, and bonds, the total rises to 6.5 percent of GSP, the lowest of any state. Our budget remains significantly below the cap written into Nevada Revised Statutes (NRS) 353.213 by the legislature in the late 1970s, a cap that indexes the budget of that time for population growth and price inflation without adjustment for the changing needs of the state.

Including our cities and counties, we are dead last in our share of public education employees, including school teachers and professors, and we spend the least per resident on public education.

Ever since Governor Robert List (1979–82) shifted the state from property taxes to sales taxes, every governor has had to cope with a budget crisis. Figure 7.4 shows the tax base for both the sales tax and the gaming tax. Three quarters of Nevada's state government revenue now comes from one kind of sales tax or another, including the tax on gaming win. Very few states have a higher share. By contrast, we are one of only seven states with no individual income tax, and one of only six states without a corporate income tax—and three of those six have an alternative tax on business income.

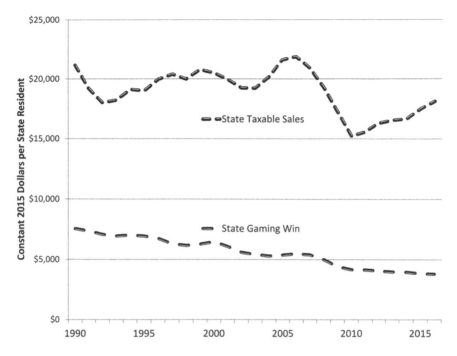

Figure 7.4. Nevada's Current Tax Base, Adjusted for Population and Inflation. *Source:* Author's calculations based on the Nevada Gaming Commission and the State of Nevada's Department of Taxation.

The economy is diversifying, but this will not solve our boom-bust budget without legislative focus. While we are striving for a Tesla-driven, Switch-powered, solar-paneled economy, our state's revenue structure is still riding a swaybacked mare more than thirty years old.

In reviewing our budget, Governor Sandoval and the newly elected legislature might consider the following:

First, the gaming sector's past success means that gaming has now spread nationwide and overseas. Thus, a good question to ask is whether revenues related to this sector should remain a mainstay of our state budget, since our cash cow no longer provides as much milk.

Second, property taxes are capped, and while this primarily has an impact on city and county governments, this leaves the state on the hook for school funding obligations when local governments come up short. Capping property taxes for primary residences is a blessing for Nevada's homeowners, because many are still faced with declining wages and increasing health-care costs, but the legislature should look into whether some major corporations are using the peculiarities of the property tax formula to pay less than the legislature intended.

Third, inequality is baked in. Our tax structure means that working-class families in Nevada pay a much larger share than the rich. It is estimated that a Nevada family earning $40,000 per year pays around 9 percent of its income in state and local taxes, while a family making $800,000 pays only around 2 percent. In Utah, another fiscally conservative state, the top 1 percent of income earners would pay around 5 percent of their income, a rate still below the national average.

Fourth, the budget is still Internet-challenged. States that rely on sales taxes have watched their revenues slip away even as sales grow, because many of those sales take place on the Internet. In spite of recent negotiations to capture some of these sales, brick-and-mortar stores and the customers who support them still bear most of the tax burden. Similarly, our economy has become more reliant on the sales of services, most of which are not taxed.

Nevada is coming of age. This gives our governor and legislators the opportunity to review the tax structure to make sure it fits the economy we are creating, not the economy we once had. As we diversify, we want to maintain our competitiveness with our neighbors. It is generally better to have a lower tax rate on a wider base, and ensure our rates are not higher than other states around us.

There is a story often told about Governor Guinn. During the 2003 legislative session, Nevadans from around the state had gathered in front of the legislative and capitol buildings to protest the lack of money for roads and schools and the need for high-paying jobs. As the story goes, the governor's chief of staff walked in on him looking out the window on the protestors below. "Those are my people," the governor said. "Those are my people."

These are our people. Let us hope our elected officials remember that Nevada's budget should serve them.

5. How Big Is Nevada's New Biennial Budget? (2015) [9]

Nevada's legislature will soon make its final decision on Governor Sandoval's $7.4-billion general fund budget. Our legislators have voted for most of what they want to spend. By the time you read this, we should know whether they are willing to vote for the taxes to pay for it.

Almost 40 percent of the proposed general fund is targeted toward K–12 education, since the state splits the cost with local governments and is the guarantor of any shortfalls. Roughly 30 percent of the general fund will go for social services, and 15 percent will help support higher education. The remaining 15 percent or so will pay for everything else, including public safety, prisons, infrastructure, elected officials, and the staff of state agencies. The general fund does not include federal money supporting Medicaid and the highway fund that uses the gas tax to pay for road construction.

Only two other states have smaller general funds as a share of GSP, and state general funds nationwide average over 4 percent of GSP. If it passes, Nevada's new general fund will rise to an estimated 2.5 percent of GSP—not enough to affect our ranking as forty-eighth among states, and significantly lower than it was ten, twenty-five, or even thirty-five years ago.

Ten years ago, for example, Governor Kenny Guinn approved a budget of $5.8 billion for the 2005–7 biennium. In real per capita terms—that is, adjusting for population growth and inflation over the past decade—that budget would be $8.8 billion now.

Eight years ago, Governor Jim Gibbons approved a budget of $7.4 billion. In real per capita terms, his budget would be $9.8 billion today. Some of that budget was unspent, however, because the Great Recession intervened.

Still, Governor Sandoval's general fund budget is $1 billion more than the one he signed two years ago, and only half of that comes from inflation and population growth. To pay for the remaining real per capita increase, he has proposed new taxes on business that he estimates will provide $0.5 billion to the biennial budget.

There are bookshelves full of studies telling us we need to broaden our tax base. Our state's current tax system relies primarily on sales and use taxes, which have been falling as a share of our economy due to untaxed Internet sales and the rising share of untaxed services, and on the gaming tax, which has been declining as gaming has spread internationally. An insurance premium tax and Governor Guinn's modified business tax also provide some funds, though not enough to make up for the decline in the first two.

With a few exceptions, state and local governments tend to rely on taxes that are regressive in practice. In Nevada, upper-income households are estimated to pay half the effective rate paid by lower-income households. Most states try to offset this a bit with state income taxes, but not Nevada.

Nevada is also one of only a few states without a business profits tax, and those few other states have other business taxes. The governor's current tax plan restructures his earlier proposal for a business license tax (BLT), and like any good sandwich it puts the meat between two slices of bread.

First, it aims to increase the modified business tax, including the sunset taxes that were due to expire. For most industries, the modified business tax rate will increase from 1.170 percent to 1.475 percent of payroll. The exemption would also fall, so more of our small firms would have to pay it.

Second, the proposal aims to increase the $200 annual business license fee to $500 for corporations and $300 for other businesses. Roughly 330,000 firms currently pay this fee, and the state would seek better compliance from those who don't. This tax increase hits smaller businesses more, but the increased cost could be offset somewhat if the state could do a better job of working with the cities and counties to make registering a business much less time-consuming and inconvenient. As it is, small business owners have to go from office to office, taking time away from actually running their firms.

But the bacon in the sandwich is a new "commerce" tax on gross receipts that would apply only to bigger firms with more than $3.5 million in revenue. Up to half this tax would count as a credit toward the modified business tax, easing the burden on labor-intensive firms. The rates would still vary by industry, so some firms might play games with how they define their businesses to get the lower rates. But the rates would still be much less than 1 percent of gross receipts, so the impact of these differences might not be significant.

While some of any business tax is passed on to customers, the rest will still be paid by those who own these firms, so these new taxes will redistribute the burden somewhat. However, even including the existing modified business tax, these business revenues will still be low relative to those in most other states, and will still be dwarfed by sales and gaming taxes.

No tax is perfect. Our goal should be for any tax to be as efficient as possible, so that it can be as lean as possible.

But we must also look at the value of what those tax revenues are spent on. These taxes should mostly be spent on trying to improve our dismal K–12 rankings. There can and should be lively discussion of some of the governor's proposals for how to improve our children's education; we can still agree on the desired ends, however, because an improved education system is essential to the new Nevada we need to create.

Economists generally agree that taxes are less inefficient if you apply low rates to many things rather than high rates to a few things. A tax base should be diversified and stable so that revenues don't decline too much during recessions or lead to excessive spending during booms. Taxes should be fair and easy to collect, they should grow with the economy, and they should be spent carefully on things that offer long-run benefits for the state and its people.

Even with these new taxes, as figure 7.5 shows, Nevada will still be a very-low-tax state, and the general fund will still be one of the smallest in the nation. But if we want to start improving the education of most Nevadans, there are few alternatives left.

≫ Treasurer's Vignette: The Ripples of Hope

As the state's treasurer I was once invited to attend the Ripple of Hope Gala at the Robert F. Kennedy Human Rights organization in New York City. Former vice president Al Gore got up to introduce the awards and brought the audience back to the "Ripples of

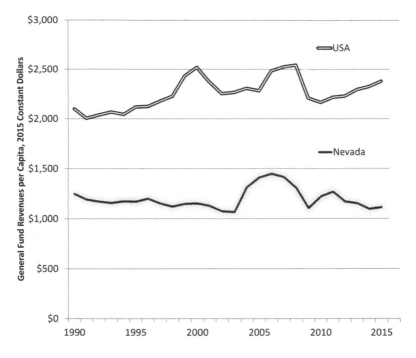

Figure 7.5. Real State General Fund Revenues per Capita, Nevada vs. U.S. Average. *Source:* Courtesy of the Nevada Legislature and the National Association of State Budget Officers Web Site.

Hope" speech Bobby Kennedy gave in South Africa in 1966. After hearing Gore's introduction, I went back and read the speech. I was struck by its beauty, but also that here we were, forty-five to fifty years later, still grappling with the same issues. Kennedy spoke about four obstacles to change.

The first obstacle is futility—the idea that no one person can change anything, so why bother? My experience has been the opposite, and that we do things one by one by one. When I was in the Peace Corps, I would help one person and the world would change for them. It is never futile, not in this time when a tweet, a door knock, or an e-mail can reach someone who hasn't been reached before.

The second obstacle is expediency—the idea that our hopes, our beliefs must bend to necessity. For example, we might resign ourselves to the belief that we cannot fund education because of the budget crisis. We cannot take care of our environment because we need the energy. Yet in order for this country to continue to be the greatest country in the world, we must adhere to those standards that have set us apart as a nation.

Every country has rich people and poor people. What has always set us apart is a thriving, robust, and educated middle class. We must support and nourish this which is at the very core of our success. With our environment, we need only remember songs from childhood to know what we have cherished in this country: "amber waves of grain...from sea to shining sea." We live in a beautiful country of natural abundance with mountains, valleys, rivers, and lakes. We cannot leave our ideals on the side of the road. Our beliefs must go hand in hand with our needs.

The third obstacle is timidity—our fear of the disapproval of our friends, our neighbors, or our colleagues. Perhaps because I worked for the Department of Justice as an antitrust lawyer, I have long admired President Teddy Roosevelt, the biggest trustbuster of them all. Roosevelt once said that a man's character is defined not by whether he wins or loses, but by whether he enters the arena. There are some very loud voices these days, but when I consider the legacy we shall leave our children, I realize we must give voice to truth. Do not be timid. Speak your beliefs. I know that, for my daughters, I must.

The final obstacle is comfort—for those who have it, the opportunities of education and the ease with which their ambitions can be provided for. We are a great nation, the wealthiest in the world. Yet we shall not be judged by what we have been given, but by what we do and what we do not do. Be willing to disturb your life, and make a difference for the better in someone else's life. Some of you might believe that the goals we seek seem just out of reach, but today, here, let us reach together. Let us move this country forward so that our children—your children and mine—will accept our heritage with open arms. How else can we make a difference, if we don't try?

Martin Luther King Jr. reminded us of the words of the abolitionist Theodore Parker, when he said that the arc of the moral universe is long, but it bends toward justice. How is it possible that we are still grappling with these same fears five decades later? The arc is long indeed.

Notes

1. Furry Lewis, "I Will Turn Your Money Green," *Furry Lewis*, Folkways Records, Memphis, TN, 1928/1960.

2. See "Warren G. Harding: Readjustment," originally delivered May 24, 1920, http://www.americanrhetoric.com/speeches/warrengharding readjustment.htm

3. Originally published as E. Parker, "Nevada Needs a New Economic Mindset," *Nevada Appeal,* January 27, 2013.

4. Originally published as B. Bonnenfant and E. Parker, "Is Nevada's Housing Market Really Recovering?," *Washington Watch,* March 2013.

5. "Chapter 40—Actions and Proceedings in Particular Cases Concerning Property," Nevada Revised Statutes, https://www.leg.state.nv.us/nrs/NRS -040.html. "Actions Resulting from Constructional Defect" encompasses NRS 40.600 to 40.695.

6. "Federal National Mortgage Association (Fannie Mae), National Housing Survey Monthly Indicators: Americans Expect Home Prices and Mortgage Rates to Increase; Attitudes about Economy and Household Finances Remain Flat," http://www.fanniemae.com/portal/research-insights/surveys/monthly -february2013.html

7. Originally published as K. Marshall and E. Parker, "State Economy Is Improving, but It's Time to Look to the Future," *Las Vegas Sun* and the *Nevada Appeal,* Sunday, December 28, 2014.

8. Originally published as K. Marshall and E. Parker, "The State of the State Budget," *Las Vegas Sun* and the *Nevada Appeal,* Sunday, January 11, 2015.

9. Originally published as E. Parker, "How Big Is Nevada's New Biennial Budget?," *Las Vegas Sun* and the *Nevada Appeal,* Sunday, May 31, 2015.

CHAPTER 8

Nevada Matters

*As we advance in life it becomes more and more difficult, but in fighting
the difficulties the innermost strength of the heart is developed.*
— Vincent Van Gogh[1]

Introduction

After eight years as Nevada state treasurer, Kate was term-limited
out. Because she wanted to keep serving the people of Nevada,
she decided to run for secretary of state. The campaign went well,
and she raised enough money, mostly from small donations. She
performed well in the debates, and made no mistakes. But the national climate in 2014 was bad for Democrats, with concerns over
ISIS and Ebola driving many to the polls; in Nevada, the Democrats
did not have a serious candidate running for governor, nor was a
U.S. Senate seat being contested. Instead, there was only the Education Initiative, also known as the Margins Tax, which Republicans opposed and most Democrats refused to support. Like the
sequestration process discussed in an earlier chapter, the initiative was really only meant to spur legislative action, and was not
written with the intent of actually becoming law. Not surprisingly,
thousands of Nevada Democrats who would normally vote stayed
home in the 2014 election, especially in Clark County. Republicans took every statewide office, and also took control of both the
state assembly and the state senate.

A week later, Kate gave an impromptu speech about what
really matters, and why we keep fighting. Nevada matters, she
said, and she went one by one through the issues that matter to
Nevadans. This speech so moved many people in the room that
we decided afterward to make this the theme for a series of columns we would coauthor. These columns were then published
simultaneously in both the *Nevada Appeal* in the north, where

we hoped legislators would read them, and in the *Las Vegas Sun*. These columns, nine of which are included in this chapter, hit on many of the themes covered in previous chapters, and expanded into a few new areas where we thought changes were needed.

1. Public Education Matters (2015)[2]

With an economy based largely on casinos and construction, the old Nevada had less need of an educated population than most other states. Workers with or without high school diplomas could make good money here building homes, serving drinks, or parking cars, at least while they were still young and healthy. Many students who wanted a good college education left the state, and the state could afford to be a tax haven for shell corporations, millionaires, and retirees.

As Governor Sandoval's recent State of the State speech reminds us, that old Nevada is disappearing. Today, on many measures, we do not look like an attractive state for people who want a good education for their children. While we might prefer to ignore the challenges of education, the governor and many other elected leaders have said this challenge cannot go unanswered. We are at the threshold of a new Nevada, and that Nevada requires a high-skilled, well-educated workforce to build its future.

Governor Sandoval called for increased state revenues to help educate our residents, and recommended a significant increase in state support for K–12. For higher education, the governor recommends enough of an increase in state support to cover inflation, population growth, and the end of mandatory state employee furloughs. How badly does our education system need this funding?

Nevada's high school graduation rate is the very lowest of any state in the nation. Average ACT and SAT scores generally place us at number forty or worse, as do proficiency levels on fourth- and eighth-grade reading and math tests. Starting salaries for teachers in Nevada are only slightly below the national average, but our spending per pupil puts us near number forty-five because we have a very high pupil-to-teacher ratio.

In higher education, our universities are recovering from severe cuts in state support and beginning to hire again, but only because students now bear more of the cost. We are number forty-nine in the share of residents who enter college, and number forty-four in the share of residents with a college education. That latter statistic is better than in some states in the Deep South or Appalachia, but only because some of the people who have moved here have college degrees. While we have one of the highest community college retention rates, we are ranked number forty-nine in the share of our population that goes to a community college. And so forth.

Providing the opportunity for public education is part of the social contract that maintains our democracy, but public education is a challenge to provide. When parents are less educated, it has an effect on the next generation. Parents who never valued education have more difficulty convincing their children to value it; even if they have learned the error of their ways, they have a tougher time helping their kids succeed. Meanwhile, we have a relatively large immigrant population and a significant number of transient residents, which makes it so much more difficult for teachers. Indeed, more than half of our students now qualify for a free lunch. A new Nevada must cultivate a culture that supports and strives for a good education system.

You can't solve problems as deep as we have simply by throwing money at them, but neither can you solve the problems without money. Reforms have been resisted in the past because they were seen as smokescreens for implementing pay cuts and increasing class loads. Hostility to public education led many teachers to feel defensive and disrespected, as critics used the examples of a tiny minority to paint the rest with a broad brush.

With new money on the table, it might be easier to bargain for reforms. We should begin not only by setting up a committee of business leaders, as the governor has done, but by asking teachers. Many have good ideas for how to improve the system, and many know where the waste is and which teachers have burned out. Listening to our teachers and offering them real help is a good place to start when constructing reforms.

Some of the governor's proposed reforms have merit, and some raise questions that have yet to be answered. Full-day kindergarten has been authorized for a decade but has not been fully funded, even though most studies conclude that it gets students off to a better start than half-day kindergarten. Appointing school boards, if done correctly, could improve the expertise of school board members and reduce the number of board members who see it as just a springboard for higher office. The creation of smaller school districts might lead to more-attentive management, but it is also likely to increase administrative costs per pupil and has led in many places, to richer areas having better-funded schools while poorer areas spiral downward. Most critical, perhaps, is changing the formula to one that considers the needs of our different student populations.

The governor, with his proposal to add money to the table, recognizes that if we want to improve our education system we will need to adequately fund it. Still, his proposal is likely to receive stiff opposition from some who long for the old Nevada. Perhaps they might consider the stories of Horatio Alger, in which every child who went from rags to riches combined hard work with opportunity. An adequately funded education system still requires our children to work hard, and the path to school can still be uphill both ways, but in order for children to be successful they must have the opportunity that only a good education provides.

The governor's proposal is a start. If it passes the legislature, our funding for public education will still be significantly below the national average, though perhaps no longer at the very bottom. If we use it well, we can improve the quality of our state education and prepare the workforce that our new Nevada needs.

2. Falling Wages for Nevada's Team (2015)[3]

Baseball is a lot like life, they say: the only thing that's fair is a hit between first and third.

Certainly, salaries are as unequal on the field as they are among the fans. Top professional baseball players earn an average of twenty times more than typical players, yet studies show that few of these stars do much more than the average player to help their teams win. Fans get annoyed, for good reason, when their high-paid prima donna hits into an easy double play.

The same is true for Nevada's middle class in the game of life. It used to be a basic principle of economic fairness that wages should be determined by how much is produced with a person's labor, but today it just ain't so, Joe.

Until the 1970s average real wages grew at the rate of labor productivity. From the 1970s through 2000, labor productivity grew by 1.9 percent per year, while real wages rose at only half that rate. Since 2000, however, labor productivity has grown slightly faster (2.1 percent per year), while the growth rate of wages declined even more (0.6 percent per year). Cumulatively, real wages are now 40 percent lower than what labor productivity would predict, and the American middle class no longer leads the world.

This stagnation of wages looks even worse if we consider the median worker, since rising wages at the high end have pulled up the average, just as one overpaid star can distort a team's average payroll, or one billionaire in the room can make everybody there a millionaire on average. Nationwide, real median wages have not improved in decades.

The median household in Nevada earned about $27,000 per year in 1987, according to the U.S. Census, and spent approximately 19 percent of that income on rent. Measured in today's dollars, the purchasing power of that income is about $53,000.

In 2013 that same median Nevada household earned only $45,000 per year, in spite of being more productive and somewhat better educated than in 1987, and spent 23 percent of it on rent.

Until 2007 median incomes were 5 to 10 percent higher in Nevada than in the rest of the United States, but today they are more than 10 percent below the rest of the nation. In Nevada, our team is working harder and earning less.

Incomes have also become increasingly unequal. The Economic Policy Institute reports that the average real income of Nevada's top 1 percent more than doubled from 1979 to 2012. Meanwhile, real incomes for everybody else fell by an average of 40 percent; Nevada is one of only four states in which real incomes declined both before and after the Great Recession. It is now the third most unequal state in the country: Nevada's top 1 percent used to earn ten times the average income of the rest of us, but it now earns forty-four times as much.

Americans like to believe that the highest-paid players earn more because of better skills or harder work. More often it's just plain luck, such as when a player has an unusually good season just before he becomes a free agent. In other cases, as Coach Barry Switzer once remarked, "Some people are born on third base and go through life thinking they hit a triple."[4]

In baseball and in life, there are several reasons for the growing pay gap. In both, big organizations that play winner-take-all games tend to pay erratic superstars many times more than they pay players who reliably hit singles. For Team Nevada, technology has changed the value of certain skills, and the pace of education hasn't been able to keep up. The erosion of the bargaining power of the middle class vis-à-vis "the owners" has also been a key factor, and this loss of bargaining power has been driven by the fact that the share of workers represented by unions has fallen.

Tax policy has also played a significant role. From the Second World War until 1964, as American society became more equal and worker productivity soared, federal income taxes on the top 1 percent remained at very high rates. President Johnson reduced this top rate significantly, especially for earned labor income.

President Reagan cut rates further, and President Bush cut them even more. Federal income taxes became much less progressive, inheritance taxes fell while payroll taxes rose, and capital income was taxed at lower rates than labor income. State and local taxes became increasingly regressive, and middle-class families in states like Nevada now typically pay twice the tax rate of families with much higher incomes.

At what point do we call foul? Part of the social contract in the United States is that we all should have the opportunity to improve ourselves, and hard work should pay off. Those who benefit from the system the most should give back, and opportunities should be extended to those at the lower end who are willing to work hard.

Part of the legislature's job is to ensure that we maintain that social contract for all Nevadans. Nevada is going to get ahead only if all of our players are on the same team, and if regular folks have an incentive to keep hitting singles. An increasingly global economy should motivate Nevada's policy-makers to strengthen workforce development and build a stronger higher education system that will prepare Nevadans to meet technological and global changes head on. Instead, our legislature underinvests in training and undermines the ability of workers to get better wages, as if "the owners" were the only ones that mattered.

Baseball shows us that success comes from hard work and sacrifice, but also from having opportunities. The members of Nevada's middle class step up to bat every day for the financial security of their families and their future. It is fair to ask our legislators to do everything they can for the home team.

3. Retirement Security Matters (2015)[5]

As our state legislature considers reforms to the state's pension system, some observers advocate effectively dismantling it. Is this really a good idea?

First, some facts. The Public Employee Retirement System is the pension system for more than 150 different public employers in the state. Our state government and its employees account for less than 10 percent of its future liabilities. Unlike some of these other public employers, the state requires its employees to pay half of the calculated cost of their retirement.

According to the Public Employee Retirement System, in 2012 the average state employee in Nevada retired at age sixty-four and earned a monthly benefit of $2,603. Since the AARP reports that nationally the average retiree's total monthly income was $2,645 in 2012, it is hard to argue that this is excessive.

During an individual's career in the private sector, the average employee contributes a total of 8.2 percent of income to his or her retirement plan, while the average employer contributes approximately 8.9 percent, which includes the employer's participation in Social Security.

State employees currently pay 13.25 percent of their income into retirement, which the state matches instead of participating in Social Security (which would require a match of 6.2 percent). The governor proposes increasing this contribution to 14.5 percent each, which would raise the state's cost by a little under $10 million, or less than 0.2 percent of his proposed $7.3 billion budget.

We often read of some CEO who diverted money from employee pensions and mismanaged his company, but who still left the company with millions of dollars in his pocket. It would be unfair to say this abuse is typical. In the public sector, we hear of a small share of public retirees who get far more than their fair share of these pension funds. This, too, is not typical.

As with any program, good management requires diligent oversight to identify such abuses and eradicate them. For example, we should make sure that overtime isn't included in a retiree's base pay when we calculate his or her benefits. We can close these loopholes without having to tear the whole system apart.

It is tempting, but incorrect, to equate other compensation problems with the Public Employee Retirement System. Some city and county governments have also promised more benefits, such as subsidized health care for retirees, which those governments can no longer afford on their current revenues; in Nevada, these local governments also typically pay much higher wages than the state.

However, there is one big difference between public and private pensions, especially in Nevada. Around 75 percent of our public-sector employees, but only about 33 percent of our private-sector employees, participate in a retirement plan.

Our real problem is that a large majority of Nevadans—and of Americans in general—are not saving enough for retirement.

Back when Social Security was first enacted, most men who reached thirty could expect to live until sixty-eight. Women could expect to live a couple years longer, but those in poorer income groups usually lived about a decade less. Pensions for those over sixty-five were thus not expensive, since most people would not need them for long, and for the poor they were often a bad bet.

Social Security made old age less precarious, and in the 1960s Medicare helped make it less unhealthy. The longevity gap for women grew, yet the gap between the richest and the poorest fell by half. While public-sector pensions became common in the 1920s, private-sector pensions to supplement Social Security became common in the 1940s. The poverty rate for the elderly plummeted, but because people lived longer the need for retirement savings grew and the cost of pensions rose.

From the 1950s to the 1970s Americans saved around 10 percent of their personal incomes. This rate began to fall after 1982, and hit bottom at a 2 percent savings rate in 2005. This drop was partly driven by the rising cost of health care during that period and by stagnating incomes for the middle class, which made it harder to save. Homeownership rates are now roughly where they were in 1980, so the drop was not driven by people saving in other ways.

Over the past two decades, because people have been living longer and saving less, the private sector has begun to dismantle its pension system, especially for those employees with lower incomes. Plans have shifted toward employee choice, but tax-deferred savings primarily benefit those in higher tax brackets.

Retirement plans have also shifted from defined benefits that put the risk on the employer, but also tempt them to underfund the system, to defined contribution plans, like that used by NSHE. These latter plans shift the risk to the employee, and in general earn lower rates of return and pay higher fees. They are, however, more portable, and they more clearly connect the benefit to the contribution.

The real question is, How do we ensure that all our workers, both those in the small public sector and in the much larger private sector, save enough to avoid an impoverished retirement?

There are lessons to be learned from other states. While Illinois has one of the most troubled public pension systems in the nation, the result of years of underfunding and overpromising, it has recently become the first state to create an automatic retirement savings program for the private sector.

The Illinois Secure Choice Savings Program will require all private employers with at least twenty-five employees and no qualified retirement plan to offer access to an auto-IRA; failure for employers to do so will result in a fine. A 3 percent payroll deduction goes automatically to retirement savings invested in a target-date fund, and employers don't have to match their employees' contributions. Employees can opt out, but research has shown that most won't and that their retirement savings will rise.

We should study these lessons and seek to adopt best practices. We should be wary of those who argue that public employees and their employers should save less, and become more like those in the private sector. We should focus instead on how to help more of the middle class obtain retirement security.

4. Higher Education Matters (2015)[6]

Ever since the Morrill Act of 1862, Nevada's public higher education system has been a balancing act between what is good for our students and what is good for our state.

Milt Glick, the late president of UNR, used to say that the university not only helped its students to make a good living, it also helped them to create a good life.[7] We provide our students with vocational skills that help them get better jobs, but we balance vocational education with the liberal arts and sciences to help them become better citizens and better understand our world.

Good students should have the opportunity for a first-rate education, but educational quality has to be balanced against access. Higher education needs to be affordable to support the creation of a strong middle class. We began with good intentions: state law even forbids charging tuition to in-state students. Over time, the legislature and the board of regents have gotten around this law by charging registration fees instead.

Governor Guinn's Millennium Scholarship program tried to balance these two targets: First, he sought to provide opportunity for those students whose families could not afford to send them to college, but who were willing to work hard at their studies. Second, he wanted to encourage families who were sending our best and brightest out of state to keep them here. A kid who leaves Las Vegas to study in Reno is more likely to remain a Nevadan than a kid who goes to college out of state.

A college education can be expensive, though it varies. Nationwide, annual tuition and fees for a full-time undergraduate averages $9,140 in public four-year colleges, or $22,960 if the undergraduate is from out of state. Room and board can easily add another $10,000 per year. Private colleges usually charge much more, though some private colleges are better able to afford financial aid for students.

How much does our state support public higher education? Last year NSHE was allocated a total of $488 million from the state's general fund, 62 percent of its total state-supported operating budget.

If you include all of NSHE, the state spent $7,550 per student FTE. Before the Great Recession, the state spent $10,100 per student, so this support has fallen by 25 percent. Excluding the parts of NSHE that don't educate undergraduates (such as the Desert Research Institute and the professional schools), the state spent an average of $5,800 per student FTE, slightly more for the universities and the small rural colleges and a bit less for the state college and the urban community colleges.

While the sticker price at UNR or UNLV is $6,255, not counting textbooks, lab fees, and room and board, costs at our other institutions are much lower. On average, full-time students within NSHE actually pay $3,970. While this is still a bargain, it has doubled since before the Great Recession.

Nevada still has one of the smallest higher education systems in the nation. That state is ranked forty-ninth in the number of degree-granting institutions of any kind per state resident. As a share of its labor force, Nevada has the lowest number of employees working in public higher education, even though it also has among the fewest private colleges.

We don't do a good job providing educational opportunities for our kids. Most of our neighbors send substantially more kids to college. In student FTE per state resident, Arizona educates 2.5 times as many college students, Utah 1.7 times, California and New Mexico 1.6 times, Oregon 1.3 times, and Idaho 1.2 times. Only Alaska has a smaller share of residents who attend a degree-granting institution than Nevada.

Too few Nevadans go to college, and too few college students who leave the state ever come back. To keep our best students here, we need to provide them with universities they are proud to attend, but doing this raises the cost because it requires that our universities balance teaching with research. Universities create knowledge as well as pass it on, and universities with good reputations for producing quality research attract both better faculty and better students. Some of that research will attract other types of external funding, and some will pay dividends in the forms of new patents and technologies.

But we must also balance the needs of our best and brightest with the needs of those who need a good education to improve their lot in life. Nevada needs both groups, if Nevada is to create a new economy. We need welders as well as engineers. We need associate degrees and certificates, not just bachelor degrees. We need a vibrant community college system—not just as preparation for the universities, but also for vocational education.

In the old Nevada, driven by casinos and construction, we did not need an educated workforce. However, the Great Recession taught us that the states with better-educated workers recovered faster, while Nevada remained in the economic doldrums much longer. In the new Nevada we have to do a better job creating a skilled workforce, not just hoping that skilled workers will move here from elsewhere.

The current debates in Carson City deservedly focus on K–12 education, because we need to walk before we can run. We need to do a much better job getting more of our kids a decent education and a high school diploma, and doing this will also make us more attractive to educated people who want to move here without giving up on a decent education for their kids. But we should not forget about higher education, to keep our best and brightest here and to create a stronger middle class by giving opportunities to young people who will work hard, despite lacking in money. They need Nevada and Nevada needs them.

5. Financial Security Matters (2015)[8]

No state suffered as much from the Great Recession as Nevada. No state saw a bigger drop in median incomes or a bigger share of its residents descend into poverty. No state saw higher foreclosure rates or a greater proportion of its mortgages go under water. At the depth of the recession, no state suffered more bankruptcies per capita. While some of this might have been due to factors beyond our control, there is no denying that poor financial decisions contributed to the crisis we experienced.

Knowing how to manage finances and get access to the resources we need to better our financial prospects—whether education, a job, or a retirement plan—leads to improved financial security. The more we improve our financial security through better-informed decision-making, the stronger and more resilient Nevada will be. This in turn will better position us to meet the demands of a global marketplace and strengthen the rungs of our economic ladder.

Approximately a quarter of Nevadans are under-banked, which means that they either have no bank account or no access to affordable credit. Often, they must rely on alternative high-cost financial services, like payday loans, to pay for basic needs, money they have great difficulty repaying. Two thirds of Nevada's adults have subprime credit, and the average credit card debt of an adult Nevadan now exceeds $9,000.

Over half of Nevada's households lack enough savings to cover ninety days of expenses should there be a job loss, medical emergency, or other financial setback. Fewer than 40 percent of Nevada's workers participate in an employer-based retirement plan, and more than a third of our residents indicate that they have no retirement savings at all.

Thus, while Nevada's economy has begun to improve and people are feeling more confident about the future, our personal finances have a long way to go to provide the financial security necessary to connect Nevadans to the economic prosperity we hope is in store.

What can we do to build a bridge from the financial strains of the Great Recession to the financial security we hope will come with economic expansion? How can we strengthen individuals and families to help them attain and preserve assets, become more financially stable, and achieve long-term financial security?

It might be helpful to think of our financial future as resting on four pillars: financial education, earning a decent living, saving and asset-building, and consumer protection. As we build these pillars, each of them works with and strengthens the others.

First, financial education matters. The legislature is currently reviewing a bill, Senate Bill 220, to expand financial education in our schools. Current instruction is woefully inadequate for students facing the financial complexities of modern life, and leaves them unprepared to deal with tomorrow's financial challenges. More than ever before, young adults need to know not simply how to find and keep a job, but also how to budget, how to save, and how to use banks, loans, and credit cards responsibly.

But the problem is not limited to students. More than 40 percent of adults give themselves a grade of C, D, or F on their personal knowledge of finances. In some states, like Texas and New Mexico, there has been a movement to create financial coaching networks, where organizations and employers can train their members and employees to reach their financial goals. Nevada might consider doing the same.

Second, earning a decent living matters, and workforce development is a key ingredient. Nevada must match the needs of its workforce with the demands of its employers and those employers it wants to attract. It helps to have portable credentials, and these should go beyond the diplomas, degrees, and certificates offered by our schools into the workplace, where most develop their skills. If we, as Nevadans, are going to get the most out of our economic expansion, we need to be constantly orienting our education and workforce services with metrics that look at education and employment outcomes to support the needs of both employers and employees

Third, saving and asset-building matter. We need policies that encourage more of us to save, whether for our kids' college or for our own retirement. We should encourage more Nevadans to become homeowners, but only owners of homes they can afford. We should be wary of asset limits for government assistance that discourage the poor from trying to save. We should encourage more of Nevada's employers to offer retirement programs to their employees and, at a minimum, we should demand such retirement programs be offered by every firm we woo to Nevada with tax breaks.

Finally, consumer protection matters. Consumer fraud is becoming more and more of an everyday problem for Americans, taking mulitiple forms ranging from identity theft to financial exploitation of our elders. Our state government is often too far behind the crooks to catch up with them. Nevadans also face increased challenges in the area of mortgage fraud and in the growth of fraud targeted at Spanish-speaking consumers. An example of a consumer protection measure is Assembly Bill 318, a bipartisan bill before the legislature. It extends the Military Lending Act to our veterans here in Nevada. The Military Lending Act was passed by the U.S. Congress at the request of the U.S. Department of Defense to cap interest rates charged at active duty military to 36 percent per year. It's an important start.

What more can we do to put our financial house in order? The legislature might consider passing Senate Bill 381, which would establish a task force to review Nevada's financial security. The task force would identify best practices from around the country and report back to the legislature with recommendations on how the public, private, and nonprofit sectors can work together to strengthen Nevada.

Nevadans need to be better prepared for the next financial crisis when it rolls around.

6. Good Government Matters (2015)[9]

The humorist P. J. O'Rourke once said, "Democrats are...the party that says government can make you richer, smarter, taller and get the chickweed out of your lawn. Republicans are the party that says government doesn't work, and then they get elected and prove it."[10] How can we find a middle ground between overpromising and underperforming?

Americans have a history of distrusting government that dates back to at least the American Revolution. But we also know that government is necessary, and countries without well-functioning governments are terrible places to live.

Competitive private markets are good at many things, and the profit motive provides a clear reward structure. But private markets don't consider the many ways that one person's actions can affect another, and some markets are not very competitive, leading to higher prices and lower quality of goods and services. We distrust big corporations and big money just as much as we distrust big government, and our state government can be a small but effective counterbalance.

We complain about government being ineffective, and it certainly can be. But sometimes this is because we give government responsibility for fixing problems that the private sector left undone or really screwed up, and then we assume that government created the problems in the first place.

We complain about government bureaucracy, but the legislators we elect write detailed rules to prevent abuse of power, and agency managers are afraid of being embarrassed by scandal. Government employees learn they must follow the rules carefully to avoid taking risks for which there are no rewards. Government often spends $1,000 to prevent $100 from being misused.

We complain about government employees having protected jobs, but this system was created for a reason. The federal civil service was created after the Civil War to prevent political parties from treating government jobs as the spoils of war. We wanted to professionalize government service, and to reduce nepotism, partisanship, and favoritism. Elected politicians can make terrible managers, but sometimes the rules that insulate government employees from the politicians can also insulate some of those civil servants from being held accountable for their performance.

Though Americans spend less on government than citizens in most other developed countries spend, we still complain about the cost. Some of the complaints are simply due to the nature of the services government provides, but many of them are due to the way our legislature structures incentives.

Our legislators refuse to allocate funds for long-term investment in infrastructure, and then act shocked to discover that agencies are using outdated technologies and that facilities are in disrepair.

To stabilize the budget, we need to save during good times in order to mitigate spending cuts and tax hikes in bad times. Yet we sweep unspent funds from government agencies at the end of the year, and cut their budgets if the agencies haven't spent the funds allocated to them. This provides no incentive for agencies to cooperate in reducing costs, and we are then surprised when they waste money buying things they don't need in order to preserve their budgets.

We want our government to be effective and our resources to be allocated efficiently, but to be successful our leaders cannot continually frame their proposals as an attack on public employees and on government itself.

Nevada can certainly do better than this.

People don't spend other people's money as frugally as they spend their own; this is also true for government agencies and large private companies. Regular audits are important to make sure public money is well spent.

However, nobody has a monopoly on good ideas; if you want to know what really needs fixing, you need the cooperation of those who actually do the work. If you are just using audits and other means of investigation to embarrass public employees or justify deep budget cuts, you will have trouble really knowing what needs fixing. If you make it clear that audits will be used to reallocate existing resources from what doesn't work to what does, then you will have lots of help.

We need to bring together all stakeholders, and we should engage the private sector as well as the public-sector employees who work in the area of concern. We need to create a government culture that is customer service–oriented, but we can't do that if reform is seen as an excuse for a purge.

We need to pay public servants a good wage, and then set high standards for integrity and accountability. We should also offer to pay our teachers well, in return for standards of performance that can weed out the small share of poor teachers who give the rest a bad name and that can place the focus on improved, measurable outcomes for our children.

Longer-term decision-making is important. The two-year election cycle creates very poor incentives for elected politicians, particularly when they have only a few months to do their work. We need legislators to take more responsibility for the future. We need a different way of accounting for spending on infrastructure, perhaps like the private sector does, so that money spent to get a future return is not treated like money wasted. Top priorities such as education require long-term strategic planning and the ability to rely on a revenue stream to reach long-term goals. One-shot projects create good sound bites, but not necessarily good long-term outcomes.

Finally, we should look for lessons from other states, and stop trying to reinvent the wheel. Other states have likely dealt with issues similar to what we are struggling with, such as tax policy or water rights, and we should start any discussion by looking at their experiences. Where the experiences of other states provide little guidance, we should experiment with a range of pilot programs to determine what works best, and take the time necessary to do the job right.

7. Campaign Finance Reform Still Matters (2015)[11]

The U.S. Supreme Court recently upheld a Florida law that prohibits judges from personally soliciting campaign funds. Integrity is critical, Justice Roberts wrote, because the public must have confidence in a judge's ability to administer justice without fear or favor.

Unfortunately, the Court has not been willing to extend this sound logic to politicians.

The U.S. Constitution guarantees the right of citizens to lobby their government, and the right to free speech. Yet today it appears that we have taken these noble ideas and created a system that goes far beyond the founders' intent, where elected officials have to spend more time asking for money than asking for votes, and more time on their campaigns than on governing.

Justice Roberts cited the *Federalist Papers* to support his decision, but in those same papers James Madison argues that it violates the principles of a republican government to favor "the elevation of the few on the ruins of the many."[12]

Most political candidates must raise money to be viable. They need to pay for travel, campaign staff, a get-out-the-vote effort, and enough advertising to have voters recognize their names and reputations. Advertising is expensive, TV stations take advantage of the increased demand, and the campaign season gets longer and longer.

In addition to the hundreds of millions that candidates raise, so-called independent expenditures have soared. More than $550 million was spent on last year's midterm election by groups not directly controlled by the candidates or the parties, twice the amount spent on the prior five midterm elections put together. Super PACs have become commonplace. More than $1 billion in outside money was spent on the election of 2012, three times as much as was spent on the 2008 election, even after adjusting for population growth and inflation, and over twenty-five times as much as was spent on the 1992 election.

This doesn't count the more than $3 billion that is spent each year funding professional lobbyists to influence legislation.

Candidates say one thing before prospective voters and often give a different message to their financial backers. For example, a U.S. senator who takes a public stance against gay marriage recently reversed himself in front of wealthy donors who thought otherwise, and most Americans don't even think this is newsworthy.

A recent study found that when a small, but wealthy, minority disagrees with the majority of voters on government policy, the views of the wealthy win out. It's no wonder that "we the people" are losing faith in the system.

Recent polling found that 96 percent of registered voters think it is critically important to reduce the influence of money in politics, but 91 percent think nothing can be done about it. Thus, when one asks voters to identify the critical issues that their elected officials should address, campaign finance reform falls well behind other issues. Yet a member of Congress who must spend hours each day dialing for dollars doesn't have much time to spend on the issues the voters say they care about.

Houston, we have a problem.

More dollars are swaying fewer voters, or being used for attack ads to discourage voters from turning out. In 2012 only 55 percent of the nation's voting-age population voted in the presidential election, one of the lowest rates among the developed and democratic nations of the world. Only 64 percent of eligible Americans even registered to vote. In the midterm 2014 election only 36 percent of the eligible population voted, the lowest rate since the Second World War.

Nevada's turnout was even worse. Only 31 percent of Nevada's 1.8 million potential voters participated in last year's election. A candidate could have been supported by only 16 percent of the electorate and still won the election, a fact that some think explains a lot about our current state legislature.

The Supreme Court helped create this mess in 1976 with *Buckley v. Valeo.* Campaign communication costs money, so the Court reasoned that restrictions on campaign expenditures would limit the ability to express one's views. The Court connected money with speech, but failed to consider that, under this logic, those without money would have their voices drowned out.

What can we do about it? Could we provide tax incentives for small donations to political campaigns and causes? A law recently passed in Tallahassee, Florida, provides up to a $25 tax rebate for campaign contributions. This law could begin to dilute the impact of big donors.

Could we restore some version of the fairness doctrine to broadcasters using the public airwaves, to give time to both sides of an issue? It might dampen the enthusiasm of some if they knew that for every million they spent on the airwaves they would be providing their opponent equal time.

Could we stop with the gifts, already? Arkansas voters recently passed a ballot initiative prohibiting constitutional officers and legislators from accepting any and all gifts from lobbyists. Most voters don't get free tickets to NASCAR races, and most voters consider a meal at a fancy restaurant to be more appropriate for Mother's Day than for doing the state's business.

Can we require transparency, by requiring all groups to identify their biggest donors, perhaps those who contribute over 1 percent of the total money raised? Can we eliminate the tax exemption for political organizations that disguise themselves as nonprofit social welfare organizations?

Could we induce more people to vote, perhaps by providing tax incentives for those who vote? Would getting more people to vote incentivize candidates to care more about their voters than about their donors?

The point is not to limit speech or prevent people from donating to political issues they feel strongly about. The point is to reduce the oversized influence of the very wealthy on government policy, at the expense of the interests of the middle class. As James Madison wrote, "Who are to be the electors of the federal representatives? Not the rich, more than the poor; not the learned, more than the ignorant; not the haughty heirs of distinguished names, more than the humble sons of obscurity and unpropitious fortune. The electors are to be the great body of the people of the United States."[13]

8. The Problem of Poverty (2015)[14]

"There will never cease to be poor in the land," the Old Testament says, asking us to "open wide your hand to your brother, to the needy and to the poor."[15] Most religions recognize the need to care for the poor, and the difficulty of making poverty disappear. Most governments, at least those in developed economies, make a significant effort to try.

How significant is poverty in our land?

The federal government uses the Orshansky measure to define the poor as those earning a cash income less than three times the cost of a frugal, but nutritionally adequate diet, without adjusting for any benefits received. The threshold is about $1,000 per month for an individual, or about $2,000 for a family of four. For comparison, the gross pay of a full-time minimum wage worker is about $1,300 per month.

The Census Bureau estimates that 45 million people, or 14.5 percent of Americans, fall below this threshold, while another 15 million are the near-poor with incomes below 125 percent of the threshold. Poverty ranges by state, from Utah (8.3 percent) to Mississippi (22.5 percent). Poverty rates are highest in Appalachia and in the Old South.

Nevada used to have a poverty rate not much higher than Utah's. Since 2007, however, Nevada has seen a larger share of population enter poverty than any other state. Our current poverty rate of 17.4 percent threatens to make us, once again, into the Mississippi of the West.

Poverty is not just a problem for minorities. Though the proportions of Hispanics and African Americans in poverty are higher, non-Hispanic whites account for half of those in poverty.

High school dropouts and female-headed households with no husband present have a very high poverty rate, as do those under age eighteen. More than half a million Americans—roughly 1 percent of the poor—are homeless.

The best antipoverty program is a job, but employment is easier said than done. In fact, a quarter of those in poverty are employed, as are most of the near-poor.

Public-sector jobs, be they in the military or the civil service, used to be one way out of poverty, but these jobs have been declining for years. Moreover, private-sector jobs have moved away from the neighborhoods the poor can afford, and in cities without good public transportation this shift makes finding work difficult for those who can't afford a car.

President Johnson once said that education was the only valid passport out of poverty. Similar to the percentage in other states, only 58 percent of low-income students in Nevada graduate from high school, compared to 70 percent of students who aren't poor. We usually spend less per student in poor neighborhoods, even though the needs are greater.

The poor are also much less likely to graduate from college. A recent study found that 77 percent of students from high-income families graduate by age twenty-four, up from 35 percent since 1970. By contrast, only 9 percent of low-income students graduate, up slightly from 6 percent.

For a person without education or skills, the available jobs don't always offer a clear path to a better life. Had the minimum wage kept up with inflation since 1968, it would now be almost $11 per hour, almost enough for a single breadwinner to keep a small family out of poverty. Even the average Nevadan is struggling. Adjusting for inflation, the income of the median household has fallen by 27 percent in Nevada since 2000, compared to a fall of 9 percent nationwide.

The poor often pay higher rent for what they get, much more than the mortgage they would pay for owning their property, because they can't get affordable credit. Most of the poor are under-banked, and pay higher fees and interest rates for financial transactions. It is no wonder that many of the poor feel trapped by their circumstances, with no good future to look forward to.

How much do we open our hands to the poor?

Americans spend about 2 percent of GDP on charitable donations. Half of this goes to churches and schools, but the largest charities tend to be those focused on helping the poor.

Taxpayers currently spend about $600 billion, about 3.5 percent of GDP, to help the poor through a variety of government programs. This is roughly the same as the amount we currently spend on national defense.

Half of this spending is for Medicaid, which pays medical expenses for 31 million children, 11 million parents, and 14 million disabled or elderly Americans, many of whom need long-term care. Medicaid costs roughly $450 per person per month.

The second biggest program is the Earned Income Tax Credit, which goes to 27 million of the working poor or near-poor. This credit averages about $190 per month per recipient. The cost in lost tax revenue is about the same or less as other popular breaks, such as the child tax credit, the mortgage interest tax deduction, or special tax provisions targeted toward specific corporations (also known as corporate welfare).

SNAP (Supplemental Nutrition Assistance Program, formerly the Food Stamps Program) is the third biggest program, and costs about $170 per month for each of the 46 million people in it. Spending on SNAP doubled during the Great Recession, though it is starting to come back down now. Next, Supplemental Security Income provides an average of $760 per month to almost 6 million elderly and disabled Americans. Then we have a scattering of uncoordinated small programs, such as housing assistance and Pell Grants for college.

If we gave the poor just enough cash to raise their incomes to the poverty line, it has been estimated that it would cost taxpayers about $180 billion per year. Excluding Medicaid, however, the federal government spends roughly $300 billion on poverty programs, enough to raise the incomes of both the poor and the near-poor to 125 percent of the poverty threshold. Still, poverty rates remain stubbornly high in the United States, especially compared to most other developed market economies.

Why is fighting poverty so expensive, and how could we do it better? We will address these questions next week.

9. Fighting Poverty Matters (2015)[16]

Fifty years ago, President Johnson announced a War on Poverty, and it was a war most Americans hoped we might eventually win. Today, however, poverty remains an intractable and expensive social problem.

The Census Bureau reports the poverty rate back to 1959, but economists have estimated it back even further. The drop from Roosevelt to Nixon was remarkable: the poverty rate was

65 percent in 1935, 33 percent in 1948, 22 percent in 1959, and 11 percent in 1973. Many people even thought that the rate would fall to zero by the 1980s.

For the past forty years, however, the poverty rate has varied from 11 percent in good times to 15 percent in bad times.

Of course, the official rate has flaws, including the fact that it does not account for the impact of government benefits. Recent studies show that poverty rates would have risen significantly since 1967 without government programs.

Americans can be a generous people, if we know that our money is being well spent. However, fighting poverty is expensive, and the problem remains. The amount we spend is estimated to be significantly more than the poverty gap, or the amount it would cost to bring every poor American up to the poverty line with a cash payment.

Why does it cost so much? Why not just give the poor cash and be done with it?

If we give benefits only to those with few assets and little income, we discourage people from building up assets to escape poverty, we encourage them to hide their income, and we add costly bureaucracy to try to prevent the wrong people from receiving benefits.

If we draw a bright line above which people no longer qualify, we discourage work. Earning more money might raise you barely out of poverty, but it also might push you over a cliff when all your benefits are taken away. Ironically, you could be worse off as a result of trying to better yourself. Basic economic theory suggests that cash payments to bring everybody up to the poverty threshold would severely diminish the incentives of the working poor, and the cost could easily double if many minimum wage workers dropped out of the workforce.

To reduce this disincentive to work, some poverty programs slowly phase out benefits as recipient incomes rise, and continue to pay out even if they rise above the poverty line. Thus, the near-poor thus still receive some benefits, although fewer than those with lower incomes. As a result, using just the poverty gap will lead us to significantly underestimate the cost of raising people out of poverty.

Of course, we might also be uncomfortable with giving cash

payments to the poor. Some tend to see all poverty as a moral failing, a result of choice, not circumstance. That view measures morality by dollars earned, a patently absurd idea, and it falsely equates the working poor with others such as the mentally ill or drug addicted.

Before the Great Recession, the census estimated that fewer than a quarter of those below the poverty line remained there for more than three years. For most of the poor, poverty was a temporary condition of six months or less. Almost half of those who escaped poverty eventually achieved incomes of 150 percent or more of the poverty line.

Poverty is also expensive because programs for dealing with it are scattered around different agencies with little coordination. Each has its own system of record keeping, its own standards, and its own administrators. Consolidating and streamlining these variables would make sense.

Negotiating this system can be a nightmare, particularly for people who already feel powerless and are uncomfortable with bureaucracy. Many poor thus fall through the cracks, while others learn to take advantage of the system's many flaws.

Can we break the poverty cycle, by expanding what works and dropping what fails?

We need to create powerful incentives for the poor to work, but we also need better incentives for the poor to be hired. We need an economy that creates jobs for the poor and provides opportunities for the poor to gain the skills they need to obtain employment.

We need to incentivize private employers to take a risk on those without a well-established record of productive work, but in a way that does not easily invite fraud. We also need to change the "cliff" incentive, so that those who work are better off as a result, not worse off.

For example, should unemployment benefits beyond the first few months require work on public projects? We know that Job Corps programs successfully improve earnings, and they also reduce incarceration rates. Could we create programs to hire young people in blighted neighborhoods to improve their communities? Could such programs include a financial skills component?

For example, Reno has the successful MyPath Savings program, an innovative savings program that uses a teen's first paychecks to teach healthy financial habits and skills.

We also need to recognize those things that tend to ensnare Nevadans in poverty, such as income volatility, or a lack of access to financial tools, or adequate health care.

We need to make it easier for the poor to get the education and skills they need to get jobs that pay a decent wage. Investing in education will take a long time to pay off, but it is a critical part of a solution. While Governor Sandoval's programs might or might not work as hoped, they do at least recognize the need for this investment.

What have other states done that might work for Nevada? In order to help people out of poverty, South Carolina has tried to create more skilled middle-class jobs by offering a tax credit to companies that offer apprenticeships, in the building trades as well as in nursing, pharmacy, and information technology. By 2014 South Carolina had enrolled 670 companies and had created 11,000 apprentices.

We should not let the difficulty of the problem dissuade us from the merits of trying new approaches. Conservatives and liberals might disagree on the means of fighting poverty, but they should always agree on the ends.

In the book of Matthew, Jesus said, "Truly, I say to you, as you did it to one of the least of these my brothers, you did it to me."[17] There are few problems more challenging than fighting poverty, but we cannot give up.

» Kate's Vignette: The Fell Clutch of Circumstance

During Holy Week of 2016 I was diagnosed with breast cancer. The doctor who read the mammogram could not bring himself to talk with me. "Call for a biopsy," he said, and carefully backed out of the room. I decided that the time of year was a sign to count my blessings, and so I did, every evening, holding my pen tightly and numbering the list for posterity. Truth be told, there were many.

There were medical blessings that I leaned on. The oncologists in my town met and discussed the care of every cancer patient, ensuring that my treatment was the right care for me. Surgeons, radiologists, pathologists, nurse navigators, physical therapists, and others coordinated their roles to make the process smoother and more efficient. Much of the time they called me to make sure that I was able to get to my appointments and move on to surgery as quickly as possible.

There were financial blessings. Even though I was no longer the state treasurer, Elliott and I had married in 2014 and so I was covered under his insurance. Every procedure, from genetic testing to mastectomy to reconstruction to lymphedema therapy, was covered under the new law. We hit our maximum annual dollar limit in thirty days. When I broke into a panic that we would go broke or be denied coverage, Elliott assured me that such actions were things of the past.

There were personal blessings. My daughter would creep into my bedroom, sometime after midnight, and hug me very lightly so as not to wake me. I have three sisters. If you want to know my faults, they could tell you, and they would be thorough. But in my night, black as the pit from pole to pole, they told me they loved me and wanted me close.

There were a number of scary moments, and early on I told Elliott how he should divide up my few possessions between my daughters. After a couple of months, however, the news got better. The cancer was slow growing, and had not spread beyond the first lymph node. Radiation and chemotherapy would not be necessary after surgery.

After the oncologist told us I would lead a very long life, Elliott leaned against the elevator door and giggled like a schoolboy. My friends, who had so often been too busy, kept knocking on my door. After surgery, I was reminded how well they could cook.

It must be something about being raised in this country that we think we are masters of our own fates, but it is not the whole truth. We think maybe we can just square our shoulders and stand against the wind, and we complain when others falter. But, to be honest, I know I winced and shut the door, and I cried. If my head appears indeed unbowed, it is because in this great land of ours, when I reached out my hand, I found I was not alone.

Notes

1. I. Stone and J. Stone, *Dear Theo: The Autobiography of Vincent Van Gogh* (New York: Plume, 1995).

2. Originally published as K. Marshall and E. Parker, "Public Education for the New Nevada," *Las Vegas Sun* and the *Nevada Appeal,* Sunday, January 25, 2015.

3. Originally published as K. Marshall and E. Parker, "Falling Wages for Nevada's Team," *Las Vegas Sun* and the *Nevada Appeal,* Sunday, February 22, 2015.

4. T. Shatel, "The Unknown Barry Switzer: Poverty, Tragedy Built Oklahoma Coach into a Winner," *Chicago Tribune,* December 14, 1986.

5. Originally published as K. Marshall and E. Parker, "Retirement Security Is an Issue for All Nevadans," *Las Vegas Sun* and the *Nevada Appeal,* Sunday, March 15, 2015.

6. Originally published as K. Marshall and E. Parker, "Balancing Nevada's Need for Higher Education," *Las Vegas Sun* and the *Nevada Appeal,* Sunday, March 29, 2015.

7. This is probably not original, and seems to be a commonly repeated phrase. For a recent example, see http://cop.hlcommission.org/Student -Success/obanion16.html

8. Originally published as K. Marshall and E. Parker, "Improving Financial Security for All Nevadans," *Las Vegas Sun* and the *Nevada Appeal,* Sunday, April 12, 2015.

9. Originally published as K. Marshall and E. Parker, "Understanding the Limitations—and Benefits—of Government," *Las Vegas Sun* and the *Nevada Appeal,* Sunday, May 3, 2015.

10. P.J. O'Rourke, *Parliament of Whores* (New York: Atlantic Monthly Press, 1991), 19.

11. Originally published as K. Marshall and E. Parker, "Campaign Finance Reform Matters: Here's Why," *Las Vegas Sun* and the *Nevada Appeal,* Sunday, May 17, 2015.

12. J. Madison, *Federalist Papers,* no. 57, February 19, 1788, http://avalon.law .yale.edu/18th_century/fed57.asp.

13. Ibid.

14. Originally published as K. Marshall and E. Parker, "The Problem of Poverty," *Las Vegas Sun* and the *Nevada Appeal,* Sunday, June 21, 2015.

15. Deuteronomy 15:11, English Standard Version.

16. Originally published as K. Marshall and E. Parker, "Fighting Poverty," *Las Vegas Sun* and the *Nevada Appeal,* Sunday, June 28, 2015.

17. Matthew 25:40, English Standard Version.

CHAPTER 9

The Canopy of Hope

by Kate Marshall

The land was ours before we were the land's
...
Something we were withholding made us weak
Until we found out that it was ourselves
We were withholding from our land of living,
And forthwith found salvation in surrender.
Such as we were we gave ourselves outright
...
To the land vaguely realizing westward,
But still unstoried, artless, unenhanced,
Such as she was, such as she will become.
        — ROBERT FROST, "THE GIFT OUTRIGHT"[1]

The statistics of the financial crisis in Nevada were stark, as the earlier chapters of this book have described: we faced the highest unemployment rate, the greatest reduction in income and housing prices, the highest foreclosure rates, the largest percentage of our population reduced to poverty, and so forth. These statistics, however, cannot convey the true pain of families across Nevada. As I traveled around the state, again and again I came in contact with stark reminders of the grim reality of families that were squeezed beyond endurance, and that could not be captured by the facts and figures that Elliott's columns tried to make comprehensible.

At one Title I elementary school, I asked the principal why the classrooms I visited had children sharing desks and chairs, and she replied that her classes were overflowing because of the high number of waivers they had in their district.[2] I raised an eyebrow. While not unusual for schools in wealthier neighborhoods, waivers are surprising in low-income schools. The principal touched my elbow, and told me sadly that so many families had lost their homes they had to move in with other family members and so needed waivers.

When we set up the foreclosure workshops, we learned to include other agencies to help with the increased emotional stresses and strains on families losing their homes. And even as Nevada began to move slowly toward recovery, real estate agents would tell me that houses under $200,000 would sell and those over $1 million would sell, but everything in between was dead. It was clear that even in recovery our economy favored some, but left many behind.

The American dream fans out over this country and its people like a tablecloth spread before the wind, like a canopy of hope. The true effect of the financial crisis is that both the dream and the reality of that canopy have shrunk. Our task now—indeed, our obligation—is to set to work broadening its reach yet again. There is no better place to start that process than at the beginning, with the mandate of our forefathers, "We hold these truths to be self-evident, that all men are created equal, that they are endowed by their Creator with certain unalienable Rights, that among these are Life, Liberty and the pursuit of Happiness."[3] When we speak of our rights, we usually focus on individual, social, or religious rights. Martin Luther King Jr., however, stressed that hope cannot be offered only to one's soul: it must also take a material form. Before we can delve into the loftier ideals of liberty and the pursuit of happiness, we must seek out more-mundane solutions regarding the basic economic truths of life.

Many families today are faced with an ever-shifting economic landscape, and the path to an affordable life appears ever more constrained. This dimming of economic opportunity affects Americans of all colors, creeds, and lifestyles, nowhere more than in Nevada. Although enlarging the economic path for Americans is both realistic and achievable, it requires more than just one family's hard work. Our best opportunities for success will not be found in a single solution or come from a single agent, whether it be it a government program or a private-sector push. Today's challenges are more complex, and do not easily yield to one-shot solutions or easy fixes. True hope will come from harnessing the commitment of both public and private stakeholders across sectors to mutually reinforce each other's actions.

To create an economy where hardworking Nevadans can get ahead requires this state to re-create itself and address our major structural challenges. We must tackle at least four problems. First, we need to invest in the creation of new productive resources, both human and physical, and we need to better nurture the resources we already have. Second, we need to combat rising inequality, particularly by focusing on the needs of those working families aspiring to the middle class. Third, we need policies that ensure continued job growth. Fourth, we must build a resilient state economy and make sure our state government can take advantage of future economic opportunities.

As Elliott described in the first chapter, Nevada's past has too often relied on gimmicks for growth. An economy that relies on the next boom is always dealing with the last bust. People and fortune seekers have rushed across our borders for silver and gold, for divorce and diversion, and even to make a quick buck during our housing boom. In a globalized world we must leave such gimmicks behind and build a more mature economic framework.

Education is a critical part of the answer: higher education was on the chopping block during the Great Recession, but we have also underinvested in K–12 education. Developed economies tend to get most of their growth from rising productivity through human capital, and states that had invested more in education were quicker to bounce back from the downturn. A mature economy can rely on its skilled workforce. For Nevada to increase the value of its human capital, we must address both the dream and the opportunity for a quality education to place our workforce in the most attractive position possible. As Elliott would prefer to say, we need to address both the demand and the supply.

When my eldest daughter was six, we were zoned for a Title I elementary school. As she entered first grade, her dad and I dutifully attended Parent Night. The principal spoke of the children surviving the year, not of the opportunities it offered. A couple months into second grade, I asked her teacher why no field trips were planned. She responded with a voice filled with despair, speaking of the value of a trip to a farm (we still have one in town) or the kids' museum. Unfortunately expectation about test results and a student transiency rate near 80 percent meant that she had to focus on testing, testing, and more testing.

A trip to a farm or a museum is not the solution, of course, but we must include in the education of our children a continuing conversation about what opportunities are possible. As state treasurer, I created the Nevada College Kick Start Program, seeding $50 into a college savings account for every kindergartner in Nevada and providing matching funds to the contributions of low-income parents. Of course, this was not meant to fully fund a child's college costs, but it was meant to communicate to both the child and the parents the importance of having a post–high school plan, to remind them of a future of possibilities, and to extend a helping hand for getting things started. If we want our children to take those small steps that will turn into giant leaps for Nevada, we need to offer them big enough shoes for the job.

To make the opportunity of a post–high school plan realistic for more Nevadans, we need to make education an ongoing priority in our government budgets. In recent years, unfortunately, it has become fashionable for some of our political leaders to seek political gain by choosing an enemy and then, like a picador on horseback, drawing blood from that imagined enemy to earn cheers from the crowd. It makes for great politics, but drags the whole state down in the process. Our education policy cannot be framed as teachers versus students, or north versus south. By creating these false divisions, we tear each other down when we should be lifting each other up.

Education funding clearly helps us all. It's not that we cannot afford to provide a good education and stellar universities in this state—it's that we cannot afford not to. We need to support and motivate our teachers and professors to provide the best instruction possible, and we need to hold them accountable when they don't. We must also recognize that our teachers and professors cannot do it alone, not without the support of parents and the community, and that they in turn need support. Thus, funding education must be coupled with addressing some of the underlying issues of poverty. These require cross-sector solutions. To address educational opportunities, we must also make sure there are job opportunities.

Instead of making long-term investments in education, Nevada's economic development policy has trended toward providing substantial tax breaks to lure companies here, followed by exuberant press releases touting future jobs and investment. But comparing our incentives to what other states have done, and looking at the preliminary results of our policies, it seems that we still believe in gimmicks and the next big boom.

Nevada has provided billions of dollars in tax incentives and credits to get companies to locate here, but the jobs and investment dollars always appear to come in much lower than the companies initially promised. For example, in one instance, a promise of 700 permanent positions and $1 billion in investment became a paltry 272 workers and $374 million in investment. In contrast, South Carolina tied tax credits directly to the number of apprenticeships companies offered in the building trades, nursing, pharmaceuticals, and information technology industries, and created 11,000 jobs in 670 different companies. The state government used its tax leverage to support its own workforce. There is a big difference between providing top-down incentives and telling everyone it will rain, and structuring tax incentives to build a positive business climate that also provides a positive economic climate for the middle class. Our most productive resource should be our human capital, and any tax policy or subsidy should be directly tied to investing in and promoting our own citizenry.

How do you pay for it? This is the great Gordian Knot for the American people and its leaders. As President Johnson's quote in chapter 6 made clear, Americans are not fond of being taxed, with or without representation, and this is especially true in Nevada. Part of the answer is about priorities. What would the budget look like if lost revenues from STAR (Sales Tax Revenue) bonds and tax credits had been allocated to education instead? Any revenues needed to provide a better education for our people must be accompanied by improved transparency and accountability. Another priority should be that our revenue structure not benefit the few over the many and that it be directly linked to economic opportunities and supporting an affordable life for our citizens.

As Elliott tried to make clear, especially in the column he co-authored with Senator Bill Raggio, since deceased, we make a mistake by debating the size of government or the level of taxes, as if there was some optimal number. Financing is a tool, not the goal. Government budgets are inherently different from corporate budgets. Government's need to spend goes up at the very moment that its revenues go down. To get beyond the boom-and-bust nature of our financial structure, we must increase our rainy-day fund, rather than raid it in both good times and bad. We must build in some austerity during the good times so that we have the reserves to spend what is necessary during the bad times.

During the financial crisis, Nevada could have significantly benefited from infrastructure projects that improved our freeways, rebuilt our sewerage and water systems, added electrical distribution capacity to our grid and positioned us to attract companies that needed all three. Instead, many companies looked at Nevada but declined to invest because we lacked the infrastructure they required and the educational quality thy wanted. Since the crisis, local and state officials can be heard lamenting our lack of infrastructure, in these areas and more, but our budgets were never constructed to invest in long-term resiliency. The idea of funding major work projects that join the public and private sectors and utilize our skilled workforce is attractive, but we have not constructed a budget that gives us the ability to issue and pay for the debt funding it would require.

The Great Recession exposed Nevada as a state that too often takes shortcuts. We have looked for tourists to pay for taxes and fuel our booms, and our leaders often behave as if they doubt the value of investing in our own future. Perhaps, in writing this conclusion, I make it appear as if investing in our own people and creating a more mature, resilient economy is easy. It is not. But if we are going to collect and spend public money, we should do it to build on our strength and aspirations, and widen the canopy of hope in its material form so that the American dream is realistic and accessible by hard-working families. Today, our youth worry that their future is no longer bright. Success in America has always come from reaching, not retreating. Nevada must take the opportunity to re-create itself. In doing so, we shall decide the tagline for our future.

Notes

1. These are excerpts from "The Gift Outright," Robert Frost's poem that he recited at John F. Kennedy's Inauguration in 1961. See https://www. jfklibrary.org/Research/Research-Aids/Ready-Reference/JFK-Fast-Facts /Frost-Gift-Outright.aspx

2. This refers to Title I of the Elementary and Secondary Education Act, which provides financial assistance to schools with a high percentage of children from low-income families.

3. The second paragraph of the Declaration of Independence, of course.

About the Authors

ELLIOTT PARKER is professor of economics at the University of Nevada, Reno (UNR), where he has made a home since 1992. He earned his doctorate at the University of Washington, and has taught comparative and international economics, and the principles of microeconomics, to many thousands of Nevada students. He has served as coeditor of the *China Economic Review,* president of the Northern Nevada International Center, chair of the faculty senate, chair of the Department of Economics, and director of the university Core Curriculum. He is currently associate dean for undergraduate programs and administration in the College of Business, and a member of the Advisory Council for the Kenny Guinn Center for Policy Priorities. He has two children, Reuben and Maya, from a prior marriage, and he married Kate Marshall in 2014.

KATE MARSHALL (NÉE SOLTERO) is the former state treasurer of Nevada. She was elected in 2006 and reelected in 2010, and served from January 2007 to January 2015. Kate grew up in the San Francisco Bay Area in a working-class neighborhood, and worked her way through high school, college, and law school. She joined the Peace Corps and later served with distinction in the Department of Justice. Kate then became Nevada's senior deputy attorney general under Attorney General Frankie Sue Del Papa. As treasurer, she has been credited with improving and implementing programs that have saved millions in taxpayer dollars, reducing spending by making government more efficient, and identifying innovative methods for increasing economic development for Nevada. In addition, she has created one of the nation's first statewide college savings program, the Nevada College Kick Start Program, at no expense to the taxpayer. Kate's record has always been about helping Nevada families with pocketbook issues. She has two children, Anna and Molly, from a prior marriage and she married Elliott Parker in 2014.

Index